THE

IMPREGNABLE ROCK OF HOLY SCRIPTURE

THE

IMPREGNABLE ROCK OF HOLY SCRIPTURE

BY

THE RT. HON. W. E. GLADSTONE, M. P.

REVISED AND ENLARGED EDITION

PHILADELPHIA
JOHN D. WATTLES & CO.
1898

Hawarden Castle
Nov. 5. 1890

My dear Sir

I have revised the series
of Articles published by you
in America, and have introduced into them some further
illustrations of the subject
in the shape of particular arguments.

So far as criticism upon them
has yet proceeded, I have not
found it necessary to withdraw
or weaken the statements they

contain. I have however written a prefatory Note on some observations in a Jewish publication with respect to the Massorah.

I am sensible that these Essays are far below the rank and the demands of their subject; yet I would hope that they constitute a contribution, however feeble, to the great stove of rational argument for belief.

I remain, my dear Sir,

Faithfully yours

W. E. Gladstone

A. C. Trumbull

My dear Sir

I commend herewith to your care the second Edition of the "Impregnable Rock of Holy Scripture", in which I have endeavoured to make that little work somewhat less unworthy of the purpose for which it is intended.

I remain my dear Sir

faithfully yours

WEGladstone

Hawarden June 11. 1892

H. Clay Trumbull

Philadelphia

PREFACE

TO THE SECOND EDITION.

The primary purpose of this little work is to point out that recent controversies stand related rather to the literary form than to the substance of the divine revelation conveyed to us in the Old Testament; and to insist upon some of the arguments which tend to prove that in the main the old belief as to that substance is plainly the right belief. It is attested by the laws of literary probability, rising into moral certainty. It is also attested in a special manner by the unparalleled phenomenon of the Jewish race, such as it has been and is down to the present day; and by the flood of reflected light which streams back upon it out of the entire history of Christendom.

This distinction between the substance and the

literary form supplies the basis of the remarkable and powerful essay which Dean Milman prefixed in 1863 to the second edition of his " History of the Jews." He tells us that " he has been able to follow out all the marvellous discoveries of science, and all those hardly less marvellous, if less certain, conclusions of historical, ethnological, linguistic criticism, in the serene confidence that they are utterly irrelevant to the truth of Christianity, and to the truth of the Old Testament, as far as concerns its distinct and perpetual authority, and its indubitable meaning." [1]

He cites a passage of great breadth and lucidity from Paley, which *inter alia* delivers a challenge not yet, as I believe, answered from any hostile camp.

" Undoubtedly our Saviour assumes the divine origin of the Mosaic institution; and, independently of his authority, I conceive it to be very difficult to assign any other cause for the commencement or existence of that institution : especially for the singular circumstance of the Jews adhering to the

[1] Page vi.

Unity, when every other people slid into polytheism; for their being men in religion, children in everything else; behind other nations in the arts of peace and war, superior to the most improved in their sentiments and doctrines relating to the Deity."

They could not even attract the notice, during long ages, of the more famous races: "Lo, the people shall dwell alone, and shall not be reckoned among the nations" (Num. 23 : 9).

Paley then proceeds to show that these strong statements of principle entail no servile literalism:

"Undoubtedly also our Saviour recognizes the prophetic character of many of their ancient writers. So far, therefore, we are bound as Christians to go. But to make Christianity answerable with its life for the circumstantial truth of each separate passage of the Old Testament, the genuineness of every book, the information, fidelity, and judgment of every writer in it, is to bring, I will not say great, but unnecessary difficulties into the whole system." [1]

1 Paley's "Evidences," Part III., Chap. III.

In direct confutation of those who conceive that down to the present generation theology has permitted of no dispute or doubt as to any of the minutiæ of the sacred volume, Dean Milman observes that in his early days—that is to say, when the century began—Paley's " Evidences " (from which the foregoing citation is taken) furnished a text-book for important seats of learning and of religious education.

After citing the opinion of Ewald, that the whole Pentateuch was pre-Exilic, the Dean[1] declares this assertion not to be adequate to the entire breadth of the case.

" I am persuaded that the written law, even Deuteronomy, was of far earlier date : indeed existed, if not in the absolutely perfect form as it now exists, yet as the recognized, well-known, statute law of the people."

The integrity and authority, then, of the Old Testament in its substance, need not and do not suffer from the recognition of a latitude, even if

[1] " Hist. Jews, ' I. 43, note.

it be a wide latitude, as to its literary form. But
that which perplexes and may even alarm a sober-
minded reader is, that we have suffered controversy
on the form perhaps almost to hide the substance
from our view, certainly to lower and enfeeble the
living sense, which the body of believers has always
entertained, of its authority, its majesty, its stringency, ay of the terrors of the law for those who
will not accept its blessings. It really too often
seems as if, when we are arguing about the authenticity of Genesis or Exodus, we had no weightier
task in hand than if we were discussing the Epistles
of Phalaris, or the letters of Ganganelli, or the
authorship of Junius. And yet there they stand,
these great facts and doctrines, in all the primitive
severity of their outline, unshaken and august.
There we find, now as heretofore, the doctrines of
creation, of life, of human life, of the introduction
of sin into the world, of the havoc which it wrought,
of the simultaneous promise of redemption, of the
selection of a special race for special purposes, and
of the gradual preparation of the nations until the

fulness of time had come. I have here said nothing of that exhibition of preternatural power, which is supplied by prophecy and by wonder. These I forbear to dwell on, not so much because they cannot add to the marvel of Creation, as because they seem to make a presupposition or postulate of religious faith, while facts of the class of those above recited, and of those before quoted from Paley, rest in general upon grounds of known fact, or of evidence cognizable by all.

More particularly I own does it appear as if there had now spread among many of the teachers of religion an apprehension of fully unfolding and strongly enforcing on their hearers of to-day the doctrine of sin, and of its moral and judicial consequences, such as it is taught in the Jewish and the Christian Scriptures. But this I have no doubt is due in part to an enemy very far more powerful than what is called the higher criticism, namely, the world and its increasing power over our minds and lives.

Finally: It is good without doubt to place our

views of the venerable Torah in harmony with
sound research and with the best understood conditions of historical experience and of Providential
action; but it is anything rather than good, if, in
our debates about the setting, we become blind to
the lustre of the jewel it enshrines.

In the present issue of this work, the text has
been revised throughout, and the argument has
been enlarged by additions at various points.

In "The Creation Story" I have more largely
and explicitly declined to take my stand upon the
plea that it is concerned only or mainly with physical adjustments. I have endeavored to set forth
more fully the immense importance of the announce-
ment concerning Creation with which the sacred
volume opens; and I have supplied for popular
purposes an account of the contents of the great
chapter, which must, I fear, fall far short of scientific precision. I have also prefixed to this essay
a remarkable statement from Häckel's "History
of Creation."

In "Mosaic Legislation" I have inserted some

remarks on the Prophets and their mission; and at the close I have endeavored to exhibit the singularly marked evidences of Providential action in the final catastrophe of the Temple and of Jerusalem.

And lastly, I have added to the volume a note on the Swine Miracle of the Synoptic Gospels, which appeared to be called for by a criticism of Professor Huxley's on a portion of the text of the first edition.

Since these chapters were sent to press, I have read the work [1] of Dr. Warring on " Genesis I. and Modern Science." This acute and comprehensive criticism appears to proceed from a gentleman of recognized scientific attainments. But not less remarkable than his talent or his knowledge is his courageous tone. He is no "reconciler;" for Genesis and science according to him are already at one by what they respectively testify. He thinks it has been the halting and shifting state of science

[1] "Genesis I. and Modern Science." New York: Hunt and Eaton. 1892.

in former days which has helped to prevent a due appreciation of the inestimable treasures contained in this great chapter. Instead of taking refuge in half-hearted pleas of poetry and vision, he is struck especially by the " intense literalism "[1] of the Mosaic account.

Dr. Warring needs no sponsorship from me, and I am far from supposing that he has supplied the last word on this great subject, or that every word of his treatise can be perfect. But the closeness and fulness of his minute examination is extremely valuable, were it only for this, that it affords to opponents all that they can desire in amplitude and definiteness of opportunity for criticism or for confutation, and that it helps to put out of countenance and drive off the field what I have termed the half-hearted method of defense.

In his contentions there are some few that offer an aspect of novelty; as, for example, his most interesting exposition[2] of the function of the heavenly

---

[1] " Genesis I. and Modern Science," p. 189.

[2] Pages 114, *seqq.*

bodies (vs. 14-18), and his restricting the verses on plant and animal life to "present genera," or that "culmination of plant-life," and those highly developed organisms, which he refers to the latter part of the tertiary period.[1]

No doubt there may be some differences of interpretation even among those who unite in maintaining the authenticity of the record. But I cannot help remarking that even these differences, subsisting in a scientific period, illustrate the wonderful efficacy with which the Mosaic narrative did its practical work among the Hebrews, to whom, together with the other Scriptures, it was intrusted. That practical aim was not the work of expounding the nebular theory, or the deposition of the rocks. It was the moral and spiritual work of inculcating the grand doctrine of Creation, of exhibiting as the operations of God the grand physical conditions of our life, and thereby of opening to the chosen race that great Book of Nature which other races of higher intellectual gifts failed to open

[1] " Genesis I. and Modern Science," pp. 106, 183.

for any moral purpose, but which has so long been recognized, and is now to be acknowledged more than ever, as one of the principal vehicles for conveying a knowledge of the Most High to his rational creatures.

LONDON,
May, 1892.

CONTENTS.

The first is, that there is a very large section of the
community, whose opportunities of judgment have
been materially smaller than his own.   The second
is, that though he is greatly wanting in the valuable
qualifications which grow out of special study in
this field, he has, for more than forty years (believing that change of labor is to a great extent the
healthiest form of recreation), devoted the larger
part of all such time as he could properly withdraw
from political duties to another, and in several
respects a similar, field of specialism.   I mean
hereby the earnest study of prehistoric antiquity
and of its documents in regard to the Greek race;
whose destinies have been, after those of the Hebrews, the most wonderful in themselves, and the
most fertile of results for us, among all the races of
mankind.   As between this field, which has for its
central point the study of Homer, and that of the
early Scriptures, which may, in the mass, be roughly
called contemporary with the Homeric period, much
light is, and with the progress of research more can
hardly fail to be, given and received.   Moreover, I

CONTENTS.

I.

FIRST VIEW OF THE IMPREGNABLE ROCK OF HOLY SCRIPTURE.

It is a serious question how far one ignorant, like myself, of Hebrew, and having no regular practice in the study and explanation of the text of the Old Testament, is entitled to attempt representations concerning it, which must present more or less the character of advice, to any portion of his fellow-men. It is clear that he can draw no sufficient warrant for such a course from the mere warmth of his desire to arrest a prevailing mischief, or from his fear lest any portion of the British public should lose or relax unawares their hold upon the book which Christendom regards as an inestimable treasure, and thereby bring upon themselves, as well as others, an inexpressible calamity. But, on the other hand, he has some better pleas to urge.

The first is, that there is a very large section of the community, whose opportunities of judgment have been materially smaller than his own.   The second is, that though he is greatly wanting in the valuable qualifications which grow out of special study in this field, he has, for more than forty years (believing that change of labor is to a great extent the healthiest form of recreation), devoted the larger part of all such time as he could properly withdraw from political duties to another, and in several respects a similar, field of specialism.   I mean hereby the earnest study of prehistoric antiquity and of its documents in regard to the Greek race; whose destinies have been, after those of the Hebrews, the most wonderful in themselves, and the most fertile of results for us, among all the races of mankind.   As between this field, which has for its central point the study of Homer, and that of the early Scriptures, which may, in the mass, be roughly called contemporary with the Homeric period, much light is, and with the progress of research more can hardly fail to be, given and received.   Moreover, I have there had the opportunity of perceiving how, among specialists as with other men, there may be fashions of the time and school, which Lord Bacon called idols of the market-place, and currents of prejudice running below the surface. These, it is obvious, may detract somewhat from the authority which each inquirer might justly claim in his own field, and from his title to impose his own conclusions upon mankind. As a judicious artist likes to know the opinion even of one not an expert on his picture, and sometimes derives benefit from it, so in all studies lights may be thrown inwards from without. Such a process is likely to be particularly needful in cases where the special branch deals with a subject-matter that both takes deep root in our nature, and is the source of profoundly interesting controversies for mankind at large. Yet I do not feel sure that these considerations would have led me to make the present attempt, were they not capped with another of great importance.

It appears to me that we may grant, for argument's sake, to the negative or destructive special-

ist in the field of the ancient Scriptures all which
as a specialist he can by possibility be entitled to
ask, respecting the age, text, and authorship of the
books; and yet may hold firmly—as firmly as of
old—to the ideas justly conveyed by the title I
have adopted for these papers, and may invite our
fellow-men to stand along with us on "the impregnable rock of Holy Scripture."

These words sound like a challenge. And they
are a challenge to some extent, but not in the sense
that might be supposed. They are a challenge to
accept the Scriptures on the moral and spiritual
and historical ground of their character in themselves, and of the work which they, and the agencies associated with them, have done in the world
for some thousands of years, and are doing still.
We may, without touching the domain of the critics,
contend for them as corresponding by their contents to the idea of a divine revelation to man.
We are entitled to attempt to show that they afford
that kind of proof of such a revelation which is
analogous to the known divine operations in other

spheres; which binds us as to conduct; and which in other matters, from the simple fact that we are rational beings, we recognize as entitled so to bind us.

And again. I hold that the other documents of historic and prehistoric religions are precious in various ways. But we may legitimately ask whether the Scriptures do not differ in such a manner and degree from those other documents, as to leave to them only the office of witnesses and buttresses to Holy Scripture, rather than sharers in it, although in their degree they may be this also.

But all these assertions lie within the moral and spiritual precinct. No one of them begs any literary question of Old Testament criticism. They leave absolutely open every issue that has been or can be raised respecting the origin, date, authorship and text of the sacred books, which for the present purpose we do not require even to call sacred. Indeed, it may be that this destructive criticism, if entirely made good, would, in the view of an inquiry really searching, comprehensive, and

philosophical, leave as its result not less but greater
reason for admiring the hidden modes by which
the great Artificer works out his designs.   For,
in proportion as the means are feeble, perplexed,
and to all appearance confused, is the marvel of the
results that are made to stand before our eyes.
And the upshot may come to be that, on this very
ground, we may have to cry out, with the Psalmist
absorbed in worshiping admiration, "Oh that men
would therefore praise the Lord for his goodness,
and declare the wonders that he doeth for the children of men!" (Psa. 107 : 8.)   For "how unsearch-
able are his judgments, and his ways past finding
out!" (Rom. 11 : 33.)   For the memories of men,
and the art of writing, and the care of the copyist,
and the tablet and the rolls of parchment, are
but the secondary or mechanical means by which
the Word has been carried down to us along the
river of the ages; and the natural and inherent
weakness of these means is in reality a special
tribute to the grandeur and vastness of the end,
and of Him that wrought it out.

So, then, these high-sounding words have been placed in the foreground of the present observations, because they convey in a positive and definite manner the conclusions which the observations themselves aim at sustaining, at least in outline, on general grounds of reason, and at enforcing as a commanding rule of thought and life. They lead upwards and onwards to the idea that the Scriptures are well called Holy Scriptures; and that, though assailed by camp, by battery, and by mine, they are nevertheless a house builded upon a rock, and that rock impregnable; that the weapon of offense, which shall impair their efficiency for aiding in the redemption of mankind, has not yet been forged; that the Sacred Canon, which it took (perhaps) two thousand years from the accumulations of Moses down to the acceptance of the Apocalypse to construct, is like to wear out the storms and the sunshine of the world, and all the wayward aberrations of humanity, not merely for a term as long, but until time shall be no more.

And yet, upon the very threshold, I embrace, in what I think a substantial sense, one of the great canons of modern criticism, which teaches us that the Scriptures are to be treated like any other book in the trial of their title. The volume, which is put into our hands when young under that venerated name, is, like any other volume, made with paper, types, and ink, and has been put together as a material object by human hands. The many and diversified utterances it contains proceeded from the mouth or pen of men; and the question, whether and in what degree, through supernatural guidance, they were, for this purpose, more than men, is to be determined, like other disputable questions, by the evidence. The books have been transmitted to us from their formation onwards in perishable materials, and from remote dates. They were so transmitted, until four hundred years ago, by the agency of copyists, as in the case of other literary productions, and presumably with a like liability to casual error, nay, even to fraudulent handling. That in some sense the Holy Scriptures contain something of a human, or uncertain, element is clear, as to the New Testament, from diversities of reading, from slight conflicts in the narrative, and from an insignificant number of controverted cases as to the authenticity of the text. We have also the Latin Vulgate partially competing with the Greek original, on the ground that it has been more or less based on manuscripts older than any we now possess. As regards the Old Testament, we find the established Hebrew Text to be mostly founded on manuscripts of a date not earlier than (I believe) the tenth century[1] of our era. It is, moreover, at variance in many points with the Greek version, commonly termed the Septuagint; which is considered to date, if not wholly, yet as to very important portions of the work, from the third century before the advent of our Saviour; the framers of which had before them copies older by more than a thousand years; and which appears

---

[1] I understand that, in the case of the Pentateuch, the British Museum has a manuscript which is certainly not later than of the eighth century, and which is in the closest correspondence with the present text.

to have received a certain amount of recognition from our Lord and the Apostles in the citations which they make from it. Thus the accuracy of the text, the age and authorship of the books, open up a vast field of purely literary controversy; and such a question as whether the closing verses of St. Mark's Gospel[1] have the authority of Scripture must be determined by literary evidence, as much as the genuineness of the pretended preface to the Æneid, or of a particular stanza which appears in an ode of Catullus.[2]

Towards summing up these observations, I will remind the reader that those who believe in a divine revelation, as pervading or as contained in the Scriptures, and especially those who accept the full doctrine of literalism as to the vehicle of that inspiraion, have to lay their account with the following (among other) considerations, which it is hard for

---

[1] I have never seen a confutation of the reasonings of Dean Burgon in his treatise on this subject. He supports the text as it stands. The marginal note in the Revised Version is surely unsatisfactory, for it does not tell the whole case, but only a part, and that on one side, about the manuscripts.   [2] Carm. LII. 13–16.

them to repudiate as inadmissible. There may possibly have been—

1. Imperfect comprehension of that which was divinely communicated.

2. Imperfect expression of what had once been comprehended.

3. Lapse of memory in oral transmission.

4. Errors of copyists in written transmission.

5. Changes with the lapse of time in the sense of words.

6. Variations arising from renderings into different tongues, especially as between the Hebrew text and the Septuagint.

7. The inspired writers of the New Testament varied in the text they used for citations from the Old Testament, and did not regard either the Hebrew or the Greek as of exclusive authority.

8. There are three variant chronologies of the Old Testament, according to (1) the Hebrew, (2) the Septuagint, and (3) the Samaritan Pentateuch, respectively. It would apparently be unwarrantable to claim for any one of them, as against the

others, the absolute sanction of a divine revelation; while an historical argument of some importance may be deducible, on the other hand, from the fact that their variations lie within certain limits.

No doubt there will be those who will resent any association between the idea of a divine revelation and the possibility of even the smallest intrusion of error into its vehicle. This idea, however, is by no means altogether a novelty. It is manifestly included as a likelihood, if not a certainty, in the fact of continuous transmission by human means, without continuous miracle to guarantee it. But further, ought they not to bear in mind that we are bound by the rule of reason to look for the same method of procedure in this great matter of a written provision of divine knowledge for our needs, as in the other parts of the manifold dispensation under which Providence has placed us? Now, that method or principle is one of sufficiency, not of perfection; of sufficiency for the attainment of practical ends, not of conformity to ideal standards; and the question what constitutes that sufficiency

is a matter on which we have no more authority to
pass judgment in relation to the Scriptures, than in
relation to any other part of the divine dispensations; on all of which the Almighty appears to have
reserved this matter to himself. Bishop Butler, I
think, would wisely tell us that we are not the
judges, and that we are quite unfit to be the judges,
of what may be the proper amount and the just
conditions of any of the aids to be afforded us in
passing through the discipline of life. I will only
remark that this default of ideal perfection, this use
of twilight instead of a noonday blaze, may be
adapted to our weakness, and may be among the
appointed means of exercising, and by exercise of
strengthening, our faith. But what properly belongs
to the present occasion is to point out that if probability, and not demonstration, marks the divine
guidance of our paths in life as a whole, we are not
entitled to require a different rule in the present
case. When the Almighty, in his mercy, makes
a special addition by revelation to what he has
already given to us of knowledge in Nature and in

Providence, we cannot justly ask that this special gift should be unlike his other gifts, and should have all its lines and limits drawn out with mathematical precision.

I have then admitted, I hope in terms of sufficient fulness, that my aim in no way embraces a controversy with the moderate, or even with the extreme, developments of textual criticism.   Dr. Driver, the Regius Professor of Hebrew at Oxford,[1] personally, as well as officially, a champion of the doctrine that there is a divine revelation, has recently shown, with great clearness and ability, that the basis of such criticism is sound and undeniable, whatever be its liability to aberration either in method or in details.   It compares consistencies and inconsistencies of text, not simply as would be done by an ordinary reader, but with all the lights of collateral knowledge.   It pronounces on the meaning of terms with the authority derived from thorough acquaintance with a given tongue, or with language at large.   It investigates and applies those

---

[1] Contemporary Review, February, 1890, pp. 215–231.

laws of growth, which operate upon language as they operate in regard to a physical organism.

It has long been known, for example, that portions of the historical books of the Old Testament, such as the Books of Chronicles, were of a date very far later than most of the events which they record, and it is widely believed that a portion of the prophecies included in the Book of Isaiah were later than his time.[1] It is now pressed upon us that, according to the prevailing judgment of the learned, the form in which the older books of the Old Testament have come down to us does not correspond as a rule with their titles, and is due to later though still, as is largely held, to remote periods; and that the law presented to us in the Pentateuch is not an enactment of a single date, but has been enlarged by a process of growth, and by gradual accretions. To us who are without original means of judgment these are, at first hear-

[1] I am not aware, however, what is the reply to the arguments (for example) of Mr. Urwick, who contends for the unity of authorship. ("The Servant of Jehovah," Edinburgh: Clark. 1877.)

ing, without doubt, disturbing announcements.
Yet common sense requires us to say, let them
be fought out by the competent, but let not us
who are incompetent interfere. I utterly, then,
eschew for myself the responsibility of conflict
with these properly critical conclusions.

But this acquiescence is subject to the following
remarks. First, the acceptance of the conclusions
of the critics has reference to the present literary form of the works, and leaves entirely open
every question relating to the substance. Any one
who reads the books of the Pentateuch, from the
second to the fifth, must observe how little they
present the appearance of consecutive, coherent,
and digested record. But their several portions
must be considered on the evidence applicable to
them respectively. And the main facts of the history they contain have received strong confirmation from Egyptian and Eastern research. With
regard to the Book of Genesis, the admission which
has been made implies nothing adverse to the truth
of the traditions it embodies, nothing adverse to

their antiquity, nothing which excludes or dis-
credits, as to the older among them, the idea of
their having originally formed part of a primitive
revelation, simultaneous or successive. The forms
of expression may have changed, yet the substance
may remain with an altered literary dress; as some
scholars have thought (not, I believe, rightly) that
the diction and modeling of the Homeric Poems
is comparatively modern, and yet the matter they
embody may belong to a remote antiquity. It is
also conceivable that the diction of Chaucer, for
example, might be altered so as to conform to the
usage of the nineteenth century, and to leave little
apparent resemblance to the original, and yet that
the whole substance of Chaucer might remain.

Further, our assent to the conclusions of the
critics ought to be strictly limited to a provisional
and revocable assent; and this on practical grounds
of stringent obligation. For, firstly, these conclusions appear to be in a great measure floating and
uncertain, to be the subject of manifold controversy. Secondly, they seem to shift and vary with

2

rapidity in the minds of those who hold them. Considering the terms in which he announced, on the title-page, his reproduction of the work of Bleek, in 1878,[1] Wellhausen may fairly be held to accept, in the main, the genuineness of those Davidic Psalms which are contained in the First Book of the Psalter. But I understand that this position has of late years been abandoned, and that, standing, as he appears to do, at the head of the negative

[1] "Einleitung in das Alte Testament," Haupttheil I., C. Die Psalmen. [The edition published and adopted by Wellhausen, to which I refer, is dated ,1878; but the book had been published in 1860.] So recently as in the fifth edition (Berlin, 1886), the Bleek-Wellhausen work assigns much weight to the Davidic titles; gives to David nearly fifty Psalms; and holds that there is no Psalm later than Nehemiah—few so late. (Sections 220–222, pages 457–464, of the "Einleitung.") In the edition of 1878 (note, p. 506), he seems to raise the question whether all the Psalms are post-Exilic, but without deciding it; and this note was subsequently dropped. In March, 1866, Ewald wrote thus his final opinion on the Psalms: "Nothing can be more untrue and perverse than the opinion that there are generally, in the Psalter, Maccabean songs. And now even the greatest part of the Psalter is derived from that source! indeed, songs from the last century before Christ, and of the utterly degenerate Hasmonæan king Jannæos!" ("Commentary on the Psalms," Johnson's Translation, Preface, p. iv.) He thinks the recent innovators as perverse as the "Hengstenbergs and Puseys." (*Ibid.*, p. 7.)

critics, he now brings down the general body of the Psalms to a date very greatly below that of the Babylonic Exile. It is certainly unreasonable to hold a critic to his conclusions without exception. But, on the other hand, it may be asked whether, in order to warrant confidence, they ought not to exhibit some element of stability. The opening of new sources of information may justify all changes fairly referable to such sources; and in minor matters the finer touches of the destructive, as well as the constructive, artist, may be needed to complete his work. But if reasonable grounds for change do not determine its bounds, there must be limits, on the other hand, to the duty of deference and submission on the part of the outer and uninstructed world, with respect to these literary conclusions. It seems doubtful how far they present to us that aggregate continuity and steadiness in the matter of progression, which the whole world recognizes in the case of the physical sciences; and the most liberal estimate can hardly carry them farther than this, that we should keep an open mind till the cycle of change has been run through, and till time has been given for the detection of flaws, and for the hearing of those whose researches may have led them to different results.

In the present instance we have an example, which may not be without force, in support of this warning. Mr. Margoliouth, the Laudian Professor of Arabic at Oxford, and a gentleman of early academical distinctions altogether extraordinary, has published his Inaugural Lecture,[1] in which he states his belief that, from materials and by means which he lucidly explains, it will be found possible to reconstruct the Semitic original, hitherto un-known, ot the Book of Ecclesiasticus. It was written, as he states, by Ben Sira, not in the Hebrew of the Prophets, but in the later Hebrew of the Rabbis (p. 6). I understand that there are three great stages, or states, of the Hebrew tongue : the Ancient, the Middle, and the New ; and that of these the earlier or classical Scriptures belong to

[1] "On the place of 'Ecclesiasticus' in Semitic Literature." Clarendon Press, 1890.

the first, and the Book of Nehemiah (for example) to the second.   The third is the Rabbinical stage. The passage from one to another of these stages is held, under the laws which determine the movement of that language, to require a very long time. Professor Margoliouth finds that Ben Sira wrote in Rabbinical Hebrew, and the earlier we find Rabbinical Hebrew in use, the farther we drive into antiquity the dates of books written in Middle and in Ancient Hebrew.   Suppose, by way of illustration, that Professor Margoliouth shows Rabbinical Hebrew to have come into use two hundred years earlier than had been supposed, the effect is to throw backwards by two hundred years the latest date to which a book in Middle or in Ancient Hebrew could be assigned.   No wonder, then, that Professor Margoliouth observes (p. 22)—

" Some students are engaged in bringing down the date of every chapter in the Bible so late as to leave no room for prophecy and revelation."

But he goes on to add that if, by the task which he has undertaken, and by those who may follow

and improve upon him, this Book shall be properly restored,

" Others will endeavor to find out how early the
professedly post-Exilian books can be put back, so
as to account for the divergence between their
awkward Middle Hebrew and the rich and elo-
quent New Hebrew of Ben Sira.   However this
may be, hypotheses, which place any portion of
the classical or Old Hebrew Scriptures between
the Middle Hebrew of Nehemiah and the New
Hebrew of Ben Sira, will surely require some
reconsideration, or at least have to be harmonized
in some way with the history of the language, before they can be unconditionally accepted."

Hence the spectator from without, perceiving
that there is war, waged on critical grounds, in the
critical camp itself, may surmise that what has been
wittily called the order of disorder is more or less
menaced in its central seat; and he may be the
more hardened in his determination not to rush
prematurely to final conclusions on the serious,
though not as I suppose vital, question respecting

the age and authenticity of the early books of the Old Testament in their present literary form.

There is such a thing as mistaking the indifferent for the essential, and as a slavish adherence to traditions insufficiently examined. But the liabilities of human nature to error do not all lie on one side. It may on the contrary be stated with some confidence that, when error in a certain direction, after a long and quiet sway, is effectively called to account, it is generally apt, and in some cases certain, to be followed by a reign of prejudices, or biassed judgments, more or less extended, and in a contrary direction. There is such a thing as a warping of the mind in favor of disintegration. Often does a critic bring to the book he examines the conclusion which he believes that he has drawn from it. Often, when he has not thus imported it, yet the first view, in remote perspective, of the proposition to which he leans will induce him to rush at the most formidable fences that lie straight ahead of him, instead of taking his chances of arriving at it by the common road of reason. And

often, even when he has attained his conclusion
without prejudice, he will after adopting defend it
against objectors, not with argument only, but
with all the pride and pain of wounded self-love.
And every one of these dangers is commonly
enhanced in something like the same proportion
in which the particular subject-matter embraces
the highest interests of mankind.

What I would specially press upon those to
whom I write is, that they should look broadly
and largely at the subject of Holy Scripture,
especially of the Scriptures of the older dispensation, which are, so to speak, farther from the eye.
They should never allow themselves to be drawn
away from that broad and free contemplation into
discussions which, though in their own place legitimate, nay, needful, yet are secondary, and therefore, when substituted for the primary, become
worse than frivolous.   I do not ask this from them
as philosophers or as Christians, but as men of
sense.   I ask them to look at the subject as they
would look at the British Constitution, or at the

poetry of Shakespeare. Under our existing laws, any one branch of the British Legislature can stop the proceedings of the whole. Again, the House of Commons can reduce to beggary the whole army, navy, and civil service of the country. Neither law nor usage makes any provision for meeting the case, and this although there would ensue from it nothing less than a frustration of the purposes for which men join together in society. We might be pressed by glowing representations of these apparent absurdities. Still there are probably not ten men in the country whose estimate of the Constitution they live under would be affected by these supererogatory objections. And if we are in any measure to grasp the office, dignity, and authority of the Scriptures, we must not suppose we are dealing adequately with that lofty subject by exhausting thought and time in examining whether Moses either edited or wrote the Pentateuch just as it stands, or what was the book of the law found in the temple in the time of Josiah, or whether it is possible or likely that any changes of addition

or omission may have crept into the text. If the
most greedily destructive among all the theories
of the modern critics (rather seriously at variance
with one another) were established as true, it would
not avail to impair the great facts of the history of
man with respect to the Jews, and to the nations
of the world; nor to disguise the light which those
facts throw upon the pages of the sacred volume;
nor to abate the commanding force with which,
bathed, so to speak, in the flood of that light, the
Bible invites, attracts, and commands the adhesion
of mankind.   Even the moral problems, which may
be raised as to particular portions of the volume,
and which may not in all cases have found any
absolute and certain solution, are surely lost in the
comprehensive contemplation of its general strain,
its immeasurable loftiness of aim, and the vastness
of the results which it, and its immediate accom-
paniments in institution and event, have wrought
for our predecessors in the journey of life, for ourselves, and for the most forward, dominant, and
responsible portions of our race.   But these moral

problems, which really form the most important part of the case, have not been dug out of the ground by the recent criticism. They have at all times been present to the mind of the serious reader. Whatever difficulty they present to us is not a new, but an old difficulty.

In a passage which rises to the very highest level of British eloquence, Dr. Liddon,[1] exhausting all the resources of our language, has described, so far as man may describe it, the ineffable and unapproachable position held by the sacred volume. It is too long to quote, too special to appropriate; and to make extracts would only mangle it. The commanding eminence of the great preacher of our metropolitan Cathedral will fasten the public attention on the subject, and will powerfully serve to show that the Scriptures, in their substantial tissue, rise far above the region of criticism, which gives no sign of being about to do anything permanent

---

[1] Sermon preached at St. Paul's on the Second Sunday in Advent, December, 1889, pp. 28–31. [Since this was written, death has extinguished in Dr. Liddon a light of the English Church, singularly bright and pure.]

or effectual to lower their moral and spiritual grandeur, or to disguise or intercept their gigantic work.

I turn to a cognate topic. The impression prevails that, in this and other countries, the operative classes, as they are termed, have at the great centers of population, here and elsewhere, largely lost their hold upon the Christian creed. There may be exaggeration in this belief; but, all things taken together, there is evidently more or less (let us hope less) of foundation for it. It does not mean, at least among us, that they have lost respect for the Christian religion, or for its ministers; or that they desire their children to be brought up otherwise than in the knowledge and practice of it; or that they themselves have snapped the last ties which, on the cardinal occasions of existence, associate them with its ordinances; or that they have renounced or modified the moral standards of conduct, which its conspicuous victory after an obstinate contest of many centuries, and its long possession of the social field, have established for the benefit of mankind. It may mean no more, but also no less, than this : that their positive, distinct, and conscious acceptance of the articles of the Creed, and their sense of the dignity and value of the sacred record, are blunted, or in some cases even effaced.[1]

In passing, I may be permitted to offer a remark. If assent be more or less largely withheld by the less well-to-do segment of society, it is still, notwithstanding the skeptical movement of the day, very generally yielded in this country by the leisured and better provided classes in most, though not all, of their branches. I simply state this as fact, without drawing, in this case, any inference from it.

There seems thus to be, within certain limits, an

---

[1] As I write in the general interests of belief, and on no narrower ground, it is with deep regret that I extract the following statement from the excellent compilation of Messrs. Macmillan, termed the Statesman's Year-Book, for 1890. In France, account is taken at the census of religious belief, and in 1881, for the first time, a column was provided for those who declined to make any declaration of belief. The number of persons returned under this head is no less than 7,684,906.

approach to a reversal of the respective attitudes which prevailed in the infancy of our religion. Then the "poor" were the principal objects of the personal ministry of Christ our Lord, and it was their glory to be the readiest receivers of the gospel.[1] They were then "the poor of this world, rich in faith, and heirs of the kingdom which he hath promised to them that love him." [2]   They had fewer obstacles, especially within themselves, to prevent their accepting the new religion.   It was less hard for them to become "as little children."   They had, to all appearance, more palpable interests in the promise of the life to come, as compared with the possession of the life that now is.   The seeming change in their comparative facility of access to the Saviour, as respects belief, is one to afford much matter for meditation.   The present purpose is to deal, in slight outline at least, with one of its causes. For one such cause certainly is the wide, though more or less vague, disparagement of the Holy

[1] Graetz, "History of the Jews," Vol. II., Chap. VI. (1891).
[2] James 2 : 5.

Scriptures recently observable in the surface currents of prevalent opinion, as regards their title to supply, in a supreme degree, food for the religious thought of man, and authoritative guidance for his life.

Amongst the suppositions, I believe erroneous, which tend to produce this disparagement, are the following:

1. That the conclusions of science as to natural objects have shaken or destroyed the assertions of the early Scriptures with respect to the origin and history of the world, and of man, its principal inhabitant.

2. That their contents are in many cases offensive to the moral sense, and unworthy of an enlightened age.

3. That our race made its appearance in the world in a condition but one degree above that of the brute creation, and only by slow and painful but continual progress has brought itself up to the present level of its existence.

4. That men have accomplished this by the

exercise of their natural powers; and have never received the special teaching and authoritative guidance, which is signified under the name of divine revelation.

5. That the more considerable among the different races and nations of the world have devised, and have established from time to time, their respective religions; and have also in many cases accepted the promulgation of sacred books, which are to be considered as essentially of the same character with the Bible.

6. That the books of the Bible, in many most important instances, and especially those books of the Old Testament which purport to be the earliest, so far from being contemporary with the events which they record, or with the authors to whom they are ascribed, are comparatively recent compilations from uncertain sources, and are therefore without authority.

Most of the foregoing remarks relate to the last of these assumptions; and I shall proceed in due course to observe upon others among them.

There are propositions wider still, but wholly foreign to the present purpose; such as that God is essentially unknowable, that we have no reasonable evidence of a life beyond the grave, and that rational certainty is confined to material objects and to the testimony of the senses. Passing by these propositions, I confine myself wholly to what preceded them; and I shall endeavor, from some points of view, to present an opposing view of the spiritual field. Moreover, as each of these is the subject of a literature of its own which may be termed scientific, I here premise that what I have to say will, though I hope rational and true, be not systematic or complete, but popular and partial only. It will have for its immediate aim to show that there are grave reasons for questioning every really destructive proposition that has been advanced, and for withholding our assent from them until these reasons (and, as I conceive, many others) shall be confuted and set aside.

I shall, however, as being in duty bound to follow the truth so far as I can discern it, have to make many confessions in the course of my argument. These confessions will be to the prejudice, not, as I trust, of Christian belief or of the sacred volume, but only of us, who as its students have failed gravely, and at many points, in the duty of a temperate and cautious treatment of it   Just as, unhappily, we have also failed, and often more grossly failed, in every other duty.   But, as the lines and laws of duty at large remain unobscured, notwithstanding the imperfections everywhere diffused among those bound to follow it, so we may trust that sufficient light yet remains for us, if duly followed, whereby to establish the authority and sufficiency of Holy Scripture for its high moral and spiritual purposes.   For the present, I have endeavored to point out that the operations of criticism properly so called, affecting as they do the literary form of the books, leave the questions of substance, namely, those of history, miracle, and revelation, substantially where they found them. I shall, in some of the succeeding chapters, strive to show, at least by specimens, that science and research have done much to sustain the historical credit of the books of the Old Testament: that in doing this they have added strength to the argument which contends that in them we find a divine revelation: and that the evidence, rationally viewed, both of contents and of results, binds us to stand where our forefathers have stood, upon the impregnable rock of Holy Scripture.

II.

THE CREATION STORY.

"The rising birth
Of Nature from the unapparent deep."
Paradise Lost, B. **VII.**

As respects the general character of the narrative which I have called the Creation Story, I begin by reminding the reader that it has awakened the warm admiration of many who refuse to allow to it a divine origin.

Häckel, in his "History of Creation," excludes entirely the idea of revelation. He also says (I think incorrectly) that the Mosaic narrative erroneously asserts the earth to be the central point of the whole universe; and again, that man was the final aim of the creation of the earth. But upon the narrative he bestows a high eulogium. "Two great and fundamental ideas, common also to the non-miraculous theory of development, meet us in

36

this Mosaic hypothesis of creation, with surprising clearness and simplicity: the idea of separation or *differentiation*, and the idea of progressive development or *perfecting*. Although Moses looks upon the results of the great laws of organic development (which we shall later point out as the necessary conclusions of the doctrine of Descent) as the direct actions of a Constructing Creator, yet in his theory there lies hidden the ruling idea of a progressive development of the originally simple matter. We can therefore bestow our just and sincere admiration on the Jewish lawgiver's grand insight into Nature, and his simple and natural hypothesis of creation, without discovering in it a so-called "divine revelation."[1] The negative unequivocally conveyed in the last words of this remarkable passage embodies the very question which I now seek to try upon the evidence before us.

In recent controversies on the trustworthiness of the Scripture record, much has been thought to

[1] From the translation of Häckel's " History of Creation," London, 1876, Chap. II. p. 33. So Professor F. P. Lesley, in the Forum (New York) for October, 1890, at p. 211, eulogizes the pre-Abrahamic

turn on the Creation Story; and the special and separate importance thus attached to it has given it a separate and prominent position in the public view. This constitutes in itself a reason for addressing ourselves at once to the consideration of it, apart from any more general investigation touching either the older Scriptures at large, or any of the books which collectively compose them.

But there are broader and deeper reasons for this separate consideration. It is suggested, first, by the form which has been given to the relation itself. The narrative, given with wonderful succinctness in the first chapter of the Book of Genesis and in the first three verses of the second chapter, stands distinct, in essential points, from all that follows in the Scriptures. It is a solitary and striking example of the detailed exposition of physical facts. For such an example we must suppose a purpose; and we have to inquire what that purpose was. Next, it seems as it were to trespass on the

story (at the same time pushing negation unto its highest extravagance) as "a product of the genius of the last and most splendid age of the nation, just before its dispersion on the face of the earth."

ground of science, and, independently of investigation and of evidence, to assert a rival, nay, a paramount authority. And further, forming no part, unless towards its close, of the history of man, and nowhere touching directly on human action, it severs itself from the rest of the sacred volume, and at first sight appears rather as a preface to the history than as a part of it.

And yet there are signs, in subsequent portions of the volume, that this Tale of the Creation was regarded by the Hebrews as both authoritative and important. For it gave form and shape to portions of their literature in the central department of its devotions. Nay, traces of it may, perhaps, be found in the Book of Job (Job 38), where the Almighty challenges the patriarch on the primordial works of creation. More clearly in Psalm 104, where we have light, the firmament, the waters and their severance and confinement within bounds; a succession the same as in Genesis. Then follow mixedly the animal and vegetable creations, and man as the climax crowns the series in verse 23.

So in Psalm 148 we have first (1-6) the heavens, the heavenly bodies, and the atmosphere; then, again mixedly, the earth and the agents affecting it, with the animate population (7-10), and lastly man.   If there be some variations in the order of the details, still the idea of consecutive develop- ment, or evolution, which struck so forcibly the intelligence of Häckel, is clearly impressed upon the whole.   At a later date, and only (so far as is known) in the Greek tongue, we find a more nearly exact resemblance in the Song of the Three Chil- dren.   The heavenly bodies and phenomena occupy the first division ot the Song; then the earth is invoked to bless the Lord, with its mountains, vegetation, and waters; then the animate popula- tion of water, air, and land follows in the order pursued by the first chapter of Genesis; while, as in Genesis, there is no separate mention of the great kingdom of the Reptiles. Then follow the children of men; and these fill the closing portion of the Song. The most noteworthy differences (which, however, are quite secondary) seem to be that there is no mention of the first beginnings of vegetation, and no supplemental notice, as in Genesis 1: 24-30, of any reptiles.

But also the sun, moon, and stars, which are categorically placed later in Genesis than vegetation, precede in the Song any notice of the earth. Let not this difference be hastily called a discrepancy. Each mode is to be explained by considering the character and purpose of the composition. In Genesis, it is a narrative of the action; in the Song, it is a panorama of the spectacle. Genesis, as a rule, refers each of the great factors of the visible world to its due order of origin in time; the Song enumerates the particulars as they are presented to the eye in a picture, where the transcendent eminence of the heavenly bodies as they are, and especially of the sun, gives to this group a proper priority. Each co-ordination would have been improper in the other place, but is proper in its own.

But a yet more remarkable proof of the influence exercised by this great chapter is found in the fact that it conveyed to the Hebrews the idea of Creation pure and simple.

But this Creation Story may have an importance for us even greater than it had for the Hebrews; nay, greater than it could have in any of those ages when all men believed, perhaps even too freely, in special modes of communication from the Deity to man, and had not a stock of courage or of audacity sufficient to question the possibility of a divine revelation. For we have now to bear in mind that the Book of Genesis generally contains a portion of human history, and that all human history is a record of human experience. It is not so with the introductory recital; for the contents of it lie outside of, and anterior to, the very earliest human experience. How came, then, this recital into the possession of a portion of mankind?

It is conceivable that a theory of Creation, and of the ordering of the world, might be bodied forth in poetry, or might, under given circumstances, be, as now, based on the researches of natural science.

But, in the first place, this recital cannot be due

to the mere imagination of a poet. It is in a high degree, considering its brevity, methodical and elaborate. And there is nothing either equaling or within many degrees approaching it, which can be set down to the account of poetry in other spheres of primitive antiquity, whatever their poetical opulence may have been. Further, the early Hebrews do not appear to have cultivated or developed any poetical faculty at all, until we come down to that which was exhibited in strictly religious work, such as the devotions of the Psalms, and (principally) the discourses and addresses of the Prophets.

As they were not, in a general sense, poetical, so neither were they in any sense scientific. By tradition, and by positive records, we know pretty well what kinds of knowledge were pursued in very early ages. They were most strictly practical. Take, for example, astronomy among the Chaldees, or medicine among the Egyptians. The necessities of life then, as now, pressed upon man. We may say with much confidence that in remote antiquity there existed no science like geology, aiming to give a history of the earth. So, again, there was no cosmogony, professing to convey a history of the *kosmos*, as it was then understood; which would have included, together with the earth, the sun, moon, planets, and atmosphere.

When, at a later date, speculation on physical origins began, it was rather on the primary idea than on any systematic arrangement or succession. With the Ionic, which was the earliest school of philosophy, the human intelligence was mainly busied in contending for one or other of the known material elements, as entitled to the honors of the primordial cause. Nor had even the Greeks or Romans formulated any scheme in any degree approaching that of Genesis for order and method, so late as the time when they became acquainted with the Hebrew Scriptures, through their translation into Greek. The opening statement of Ovid in the " Metamorphoses " is remarkable;[1] but at the

[1] Ov. "Met." I., 1–31. It is noteworthy that in the verses which follow (32–88), where the poet adheres less closely to the lines of Genesis, he also travels farther from scientific results.

time when he wrote, the Book of Genesis had long been accessible to educated persons in what was then the chief literary language of the Romans. There is not, then, the smallest ground for treating the Mosaic cosmogony, whether in the way of original or copy, as the offspring of scientific inquiry.

Again, to speak of it as guesswork would be irrational. There were no materials for guessing. There was no purpose to be served by guessing. For a record of the formation of the world we find no purpose in connection with the ordinary necessities or conveniences of life. Not to mention that, down to this day, there exists no cosmogony which can be strictly called scientific, though there are theories both ingenious and beautiful, which apparently are coming to be more and more accepted; these, however, being of an origin decidedly late even in the history of modern physics.

But, further, as the Tale of Creation is not poetry nor is it science, so neither, according to its own aspect or profession, is it theory at all. The method here pursued is that of historical recital. The person, who composes or transmits it, seems to believe, and to intend others to believe, that he is dealing with matters of fact. But these matters of fact were, from the nature of the case, altogether inaccessible to inquiry, and impossible to obtain by our ordinary mental faculties of perception or reflection, inasmuch as they date before the creation of our race. If it is, as it surely professes to be, a serious conveyance of truth, it can only be a communication from the Most High; a communication to man and for the use of man, therefore in a form adapted to his mind and to his use. If, thus considered, it is true, then it carries stamped upon it the proof of a divine revelation; an assertion which cannot commonly be sustained from the nature of the contents as to this or that minuter portion of Scripture at large.

If, when thus considered, it proves not to be true, we then have to consider what account of it we are in a condition to give. I cannot say that to me this appears an easy undertaking. "If," says Professor Dana with much reason, " it be true that the narration in Genesis has no support in natural science, it would have been better for its religious character that all the verses between the first and those on the creation of man had been omitted." [1]

It has indeed been advanced by some, as a mode of obviating any difficulty arising from supposed conflict with scientific results, that the credit of Holy Scripture is not involved in statements which have reference to physical adjustments, but only in moral or spiritual subject-matter and purpose; to which, as a revelation from God, it is exclusively related.

This is a highly important proposition; especially when it is considered that we are professors of a religion which rests not so much on abstract principles, as on matters of fact. It may be true that the Bible is not a revelation upon physics; and yet it may be also true that physical facts may stand in immediate connection with other facts in the high-

[1] " Creation." By Professor Dana. Oberlin, O., 1885; p. 202.

est sense moral and spiritual, and that this connection cannot be severed.   Let us suppose a case
such as the Incarnation, or the Resurrection. Here
there is a spiritual power declared to have been at
work, which lies at the very heart of our religion ;
but its operation issues in a physical fact.   In such
cases the credit of the revelation is attached to
a physical fact, because that fact is inseparable
from the revelation itself. It is plain, therefore, that
the proposition cannot be accepted in its full
breadth.   It has at once to undergo an important
limitation, and to be confined to physical facts
which are not annexed to a moral or spiritual purpose.   But then arises the further question, are
there, in the Holy Bible, apart from mere phrases
and forms of expression, any announcements of
physical fact, except such as are associated with a
purpose of that nature ?

It must be borne in mind that we have not now
to do with errors incidental to transmission or
translation.   Or with the use of poetical figure,
such as when it is said that " God is gone up with

a shout" (Psa. 47 : 5). Nor with familiar phrases which have only a relative truth, such as the sunrise and the sunset. Nor with the case of parable, such as the magnificent vision of the dry bones in Ezekiel: for, in a parable, no truth is understood to be conveyed in the parts, but only in their relation to one another. In none of these cases, speaking generally, do we understand the sacred writer to be recording matters of fact. It may almost be said that it is of the nature of a parable to be allegorical, that is to say to borrow its particulars from a foreign subject-matter. If so, the great chapter which opens the Bible would be a strangely incongruous parable, for there is no lesson to be taught except the lesson that is conveyed in and by the particulars themselves.

It will be generally felt that none of the parallels or illustrations which have been cited will avail for the purpose of covering the Creation Story, which forms in itself an elaborate and carefully constructed whole, dealing throughout with matters of fact, and bearing every mark that as a whole it

4

was meant by those who recorded it to be believed. I will presently endeavor to show its inseparable association with moral and religious purpose. At present I will only contend that if we found physical expositions of this kind in Scripture which were not thus associated we should have to ask ourselves how and why they came there; and should, with Professor Dana, wish them away.

If then there be difficulties presented to us, as I admit that of late years has been extensively supposed, I for one must decline to accept a mode of escape which is hardly susceptible of definition, and which will hardly bear a close examination. We may find a happier issue to the argument in the truth, as well as the majesty, of the narrative itself.

But the truth, or trueness, of which I speak, is truth or trueness as conveyed to and comprehended by the mind of man; and, further, by the mind of man in a comparatively untrained and infant state. I cannot, indeed, wholly shut out from view the possibility that casual imperfections may have crept into the record. Setting aside, however, that possibility, let us consider the conditions of the case, in its heart and substance, as they are exhibited to us by reasonable likelihood; for, if the communication were divine, we may be certain that it would on that account be all the more strictly governed by the laws of the reasonable.

In an address[1] of singular ability, on " The Discord and Harmony between Science and the Bible," Dr. Smith, of the University of Virginia, has drawn some very important distinctions. In the department of natural science, and in the department of Scriptural record, the question lies " between the present interpretation of certain parts of the Hebrew Scriptures, and the present interpretation of certain parts of nature."[2] " We must not too hastily assume that either of these interpretations is absolute and final." " The science of one epoch is to a large extent a help, which the science of the next uses and abandons." Dr. Smith points out as an example that, down to the early part of the present cen-

[1] New York : Hatcham.   The Address is dated July 27, 1882.

[2] *Ibid.*, p. 3.

tury, Newton's projectile theory of light seemed to be firmly established, but that it has given place to the theory of undulation, " which has now for fifty years reigned in its stead." Hence, he observes, we should not be too much elated by the discovery of harmonies, nor should we receive with impatience the assertion of contradictions. Throughout, it is probable, and not demonstrative, evidence with which we are dealing. There should always be a certain element of reserve in our judgments on par-ticulars; yet probable evidence may come indefi-nitely near to demonstration; and even as, while fall-ing greatly short of it, it may morally bind us to action, so may it, on precisely the same principles, bind us to belief. What we have to do is, to deal with the evidence before us according to a rational appreciation of its force. It may show on this or that particular question the concord, or it may show the discord, between alleged facts of nature and alleged interpretations of Scripture; or it may leave the question open, for want of sufficient evidence, either way, on which to ground a conclusion.

It is by these principles, and under these limitations, that I desire to see the question tried in the terms in which I think it ought to be stated; namely, not whether the recitals in Genesis at each and every point have an accurately scientific form, but whether the detailed statements of the Creation Story, as a whole, appear to stand in such a relation to the facts of natural science, so far as they have been ascertained, as to warrant or require our concluding that the statements have proceeded, in a manner above the ordinary manner, from the Author of the creation itself.[1]

Those who maintain the affirmative of this proposition have, by opponents, been termed Reconcilers; and it is convenient, in a controverted matter, to have the power of reference, by a single word, to the proposers of any given opinion. The same

---

[1] See the attractive paper of Professor Pritchard, in his " Occasional Thoughts," Murray, 1889. He says, on p. 261, " I cannot accept the Proem as being, or even as intended to be, an exact and scientific account of Creation," but adds that it " contains within it elements of that same sort of *superhuman aid or superintendence, which is generally understood by the undefined term of inspiration.*"

rule of convenience may perhaps justify me in des-
ignating those who would assert the negative by
the name of Contradictionists.   The recorder of the
Creation Story in Genesis I may designate by the
name of Moses himself, or the Mosaist, or the Mosaic writer.   This would not be reasonable, if there
were anything extravagant in the supposition that
there is a groundwork of fact for the tradition which
treats Moses as the author of the Pentateuch.   But
such a supposition, in whole or in part, is sustained
by many and strong presumptions, and I bear in
mind that even the modern criticism does not always
refuse to acknowledge that there is a strong Mosaic
element in the Pentateuch.[1]

It does not seem too much to say, that the conveyance of scientific instruction as such would not,
under the circumstances of the case, be a reasonable object for the Mosaic writer of this chapter to
pursue; for the condition of primitive man, as it is

[1] Bleek, " Einleitung in das Alte Testament (1878), sec. 18 ; edited
by Wellhausen, who contributes introductory sections (1-3) and other
passages, sometimes of dissent, without expressing any dissent from
this fundamental proposition.

portrayed in the Book of Genesis, did not require, perhaps did not admit of, scientific instruction. On the other hand, it could not but be a reasonable object then to convey to the mind of man, such as he actually was, a moral lesson drawn from and founded on that picture, that assemblage of created objects, which was before his eyes, and with which he lived in perpetual contact. We have, indeed, to consider both what lesson it would be most rational to convey, and by what method it would be most rational to stamp it, as a living lesson, on the mind by which it was to be received. And the question finally to be decided is not, whether, according to the present state of knowledge, the recital in the Book of Genesis is at each several point altogether precise or complete. It may be like the construc- tion of the human eye, which is said not to con- form with absolute strictness to the pure theory of science, but which is still held to be the construction best adapted to the service which the organ has to perform. It may here be general, there particular; it may here describe a continuous process, and it may there make large omissions, if the things omitted were either absolutely or comparatively immaterial to its purpose; it may be careful of the actual succession in time, or may deviate from it, according as the one or the other best subserved the general and principal aim; so that the true question, I must repeat, is no more than this: Do the propositions of the Creation Story in Genesis appear to stand in such a relation to the facts of natural science, so far as they are ascertained, as to warrant or require our concluding that these propositions proceeded, in a manner above the ordinary manner, from the Author of the visible creation?

What, then, may we conceive to have been the moral and spiritual lessons which the Mosaist had to communicate, and not only to communicate, but to infuse or to impress? I do not presume to attempt an exhaustive enumeration. But it is not difficult to specify a variety of purposes which the narrative was calculated to promote, and which were of great and obvious value for the education of mankind.

Some important distinctions have to be drawn

between the first verse of the chapter, and the narrative which follows. Much of that narrative falls within the compass of the thought of man. It also may be said to fall within the sphere of his experience; inasmuch as the facts of the material creation are before us. Reasoning upon them, with various degrees of probability or certainty we travel on parallel lines with the Mosaic story, and have to examine whether what we thus learn confirms or impugns it. These considerations do not apply to the sublime announcements conveyed in the first verse of the chapter. Creation in itself is eminently (to use a modern phrase) unthinkable. And it cannot be tested or called to account by any knowledge we have obtained, or may obtain, of things created, being essentially anterior to them all. The more we contemplate, the more we examine, this proem to the Book of Genesis, the more we shall perceive it to be the great foundation-chapter of the entire Scripture, New as well as Old. But the first verse seems to be the foundation of this foundation-chapter. We may well ask, why it is that the objections of the sceptical school, covered with the name and the profession of natural science, have been taken in detail to geological or biological particulars, and have not been aimed at the challenge conveyed in the opening words:

"IN THE BEGINNING, GOD CREATED THE HEAVENS AND THE EARTH."

For here is enunciated a proposition of which it may be justly said that, if it be false, we have no need either to impugn it or to defend the statements of a document discredited *ab initio.* But on the other hand that, if it be true, its truth includes in principle and carries along with it the truth of all those statements of the Holy Scriptures which most seriously strain the enfeebled faculty of modern belief, for there is no conceivable manipulation of, or transaction with, matter, nearly so marvellous as the stupendous conception of calling it out of nothing into existence. This idea, made familiar by revelation to Jews and Christians, was the one idea that the unaided intellect of man proved totally incompetent to conceive. Of relations between matter and spirit, and of every sort of change ensuing upon those relations, it could conceive in a measure, and that readily enough ; but to the idea of pure and sheer creation it does not seem to have been at any time able to ascend. Why should belief in the transformation of water into wine be difficult for those who believe already that there was once a condition of things, when none of the elements out of which each is compounded had any existence at all ?   And we may observe that, in this matter of creation, there is no room for the fallacy often applied to the things which God did not (as such) create, but only made : the fallacy which beguiles men into thinking that by graduating a process we alter its essential character, and into thus establishing a false antithesis between evolutionary and creative power.   One single step in the work of creating out of nothing is equal to a thousand.   It is an operation unfathomable in idea, but so definite in result that it stands ever before us in its virgin integrity.   It must be accepted or refused : it cannot be tampered with.

And if accepted it draws after it, as far as regards possibility, not only what may be called the minor miracles of Scripture, but also those greatest miracles which are the corner stones of the Christian Creed, the Resurrection, and, above all, the Incarnation. He, who calls out of nothing both matter and life, must surely be beyond questioning by us as to the conditions which his wisdom may be pleased to establish between them and his own Divine Essence, or the manner in which he may determine to impress himself upon them. Not that such high processes are hereby brought within the reach of our understanding, for no one of the countless operations either of material or immaterial change can radically enter within those narrow bounds : but no rational objection can lie against them from those who have already admitted into their categories of belief what lies above and beyond them all. Thus, then, the first chapter of Genesis is the foundation-chapter of the Bible, and the first verse is its foundation-verse.

Let us now pass on to the detailed narrative.

I have said that the mind of man did not, by its unaided powers, ascend to the idea of creation out of nothing. This conception, maintained all along by the Jewish and the Christian tradition, has become to us part of the very alphabet of religious thought, and taken its place among those elementary and familiar ideas which, like certain vital functions of the body, remain within our knowledge, but pass beyond our habitual consciousness. Yet this idea, now the property of " babes and sucklings," was entirely beyond the competency of the most instructed heathen to embrace. Not only before, but after, the publication of the Hebrew Scriptures to the world through the vehicle of the Greek language, the mind of cultivated man failed to grasp the idea of Creation, and was unable to advance beyond the manipulation of pre-existing matter. It seems obvious that Ovid, when he wrote the proem to his Metamorphoses, had himself been drawing, whether directly or through others, from the Septuagint. He evidently conceives the first making of the world to have been only a modification of forms, and hence finds it to be an appropriate preamble to the series of transformations which furnished the subject of his poem. And hence the Greek tongue, with all its wealth and resource, had no word to express creating as distinct from moulding, shaping, or framing; and while our Bible, following the Hebrew in its primitive record, tells us (Gen. 2:3) that God rested from "all he had created and made," the Greek version drops the distinction, and speaks only of the things that he fashioned. But, on the one hand, if our translators have been faithful to their original, it is worthy of remark with what uniformity the sacred books apply the word "create" to the origin, and not to any mere modification of existence. And, on the other hand, the Greek tongue itself applied distinctively one of its own words, different from that which signifies moulding or fashioning, to discharge imperfectly the office which is perfectly fulfilled (as we are told) by the Hebrew in the first chapter of Genesis.

It is probable that that chapter, and even the

first words of that chapter, are absolutely the parents of the idea of Creation, that is to say of summoning into existence: unless it can be shown that it came into the possession of man from some other source also. Into the possession of the most intellectual and cultivated portion of man we know that it did not so come. And I own it appears to me that those believers in revelation who depose the opening chapter from the position of authoritative Scripture because it relates to physical matters, place themselves in this dilemma, that the great conception of Creation properly so called, although it has been humanly announced, has never been revealed. Yet it is the idea, which lies at the very root of the relation between the Almighty and mankind, and supplies the basis and the measure of the duties which we owe to the Fountain of our being.

Secondly, it is plain that this chapter presented to the mind of man the fact that he had a common origin with the rest of Nature, both animate and inanimate, and thereby that he was constituted in a definite relation to all created things. As we know through subsequent communications from the same high source, this is a relation partly of dominion. But is of dominion regulated by duty: and duty governing our conduct generally governs that part of it which concerns the animal creation by an appropriate law. We are to use those which are appointed to our use, whether for labor or for food, with the obligation to avoid excess in the one, and infliction of unnecessary pain in the other. We are to destroy those which are noxious to human subsistence. And we are to avoid all wanton injury, as to the greatest, so also to the least among them. In those men or women who are by nature tenderly disposed, Nature itself may supply the needful dispositions. But one of the sad and afflicting incidents in our nature as it actually stands is the widespread proneness, even in childhood, to cruelty: to a cruelty not systematic or reasoned, but what may be termed a cruelty of indifference, which treats the inferior creatures as without any interest or feeling that should be taken into account, and which instinctively feels delight in the exercise of power although without an object. And among the consequences probably due to this proclamation of fellowship between man and beast are those enactments of the Mosaic law which make provision on behalf of laboring animals. "Thou shalt not muzzle the ox when he treadeth out the corn" (Deut. 25 : 4). A thing probably unexampled in the early history of man.

There is, however, a larger sense of the fellowship with Nature in which it extends to the inanimate, and has a positive and no longer a merely negative character. There is no idea I think more foreign to classical literature than that God is the God of animals as well as of man, and the God of lifeless nature as well as of animals. But these noble ideas took root in the comparatively undeveloped minds of the Hebrews. "The lions, roaring after their prey, do seek their meat from God," and "When thou hidest thy face they are troubled; when thou takest away their breath

they die, and are turned again to their dust"
(Psa. 104 : 21, 22). Then we may pass to things
inanimate, which not only amaze, but also gladden
the soul of the Psalmist. "Thou, Lord, hast made
me glad through thy works: and I will rejoice in
giving praise for the operations of thy hands. O
Lord, how glorious are thy works: thy thoughts
are very deep." And again, "I will consider thy
heavens, even the works of thy fingers, the moon
and the stars, which thou hast ordained" (Psa.
92 : 4, 5, and 8 : 3). Thus the train of ideas, which
flowed downward through the ages from the great
chapter, opened to the Hebrews a rich treasury of
thoughts by placing them in communion with universal Nature, a great book of God.

And it is a singular reflection that this book of
Nature was opened to them alone, so far as we
know, among the kindred races of the ancient
world; at any rate, it was absolutely closed to Greeks
and Romans as regarded any duty or piety connected with it. Some have even gone so far as to
contend that the ancients of the two classic penin-

sulas had no perception at all of beauty in the landscapes, which were so lavishly spread before their eyes. And if this statement cannot be sustained in its full breadth,[1] yet it is I believe undeniable that they most rarely and feebly touched that boundless field of observation which has not only added a vast department to modern art, but has enriched our literature in prose and verse, and has found food for the nurture of such a genius as Wordsworth, never to be forgotten while British poetry holds its place in the grateful recollection of our race.

It was not then for nothing that primitive tradition was directed into a divergence from the usual course ordained for it, and that in this one place only of all the Bible it supplies us with a detailed and systematic statement of a great series of physical facts, with which we cannot lightly tamper, inasmuch as they hold on to high educative pur-

[1] We seem to find instances in Virgil such as (probably) in Georg. II. ; more certainly in Æn. I. But we have the same idea conveyed a thousand or more years before Virgil in the Odyssey of Homer (**IV.** 606) with reference to the scenery of Ithaca.

poses closely akin to the general aims of the sacred volume.

To the foregoing considerations we may subjoin some further lessons conveyed to the primitive man by the Creation Story as it stands in Genesis.

It presented to his mind, and by means of detail made him know and feel, what was the beautiful and noble home that he inhabited, and with what a fatherly and tender care Providence had prepared it for him to dwell in. There was a picture before his eyes. That picture was filled with objects of Nature, animate and inanimate. I say, one of its great aims may have been to make him know and feel by means of detail; for wholesale teaching, teaching in the lump, or abstract teaching, mostly ineffective even now, would have been wholly futile then. It was needful to use the simplest phrases, that the primitive man might receive a conception, thoroughly faithful in broad outline, of what his Maker had been about on his behalf. So the Maker condescends to partition and set out his work, in making it a picture.

But He proceeds further (and this is the climax) to represent himself as resting after it. This declaration is in no conflict with any scientific record. It, however, implies a license in the use of language, which for its boldness was never exceeded in any interpretation, reconciled or other, which has been applied to any part of the text of Genesis. But it draws its ample warrant from the strong educative lesson that is to be learned from it ; for it invests both with majesty and authority the doctrine of a day of rest. Now, this doctrine was of the highest importance to the higher and inner life of man, while it was one which the daily cares of his existence were but too likely, as experience too amply proved, to efface from his recollection.

I contend then, finally, that the Creation Story was intended to have a special bearing on the great institution of the day of rest, or Sabbath, by exhibiting it in the manner of an object lesson. Paley, indeed, has said that God blessed the seventh day and sanctified it (Gen. 2 : 3), not at that time but for that reason. He is a writer much to be respected, and for many reasons; but, in dealing with Holy Scripture, he was somewhat apt to rest upon the surface. And now we have learned from Assyrian researches how many and how sharply traced are the vestiges, long anterior to the delivery of the law, of some early institution or command, which in that region evidently had given a special sanctity to the number seven, and, in particular, to the seventh day.

Man then, child-like and sinless, had to receive a lesson which was capable of gradual development, and which spoke to something like the following effect: It has not been by a slight or single effort that the nature, in which you are moulded, has been lifted to its present level; you have reached it by steps and degrees, and by a plan which, stated in rough outline, may stir your faculties, and help them onwards to the truth through the genial action of wonder, delight, and gratitude. This was a lesson on the facts of creation, perhaps quite large enough, so it seems to me, for the primitive man;

and one which, when he had heard and had begun to digest it, might well be followed by a rest for generations.

And it further seems to have been vital to the efficiency of this lesson, from such a point of view, that it should have been sharply broken up into parts, although there might be in nature nothing, at any precise points of breakage or transition, to correspond physically with those divisions. They would become intelligible, significant, and useful on a comparison of the several processes in their developed state, and of the vast and measureless differences, which in that state they severally present to contemplation. As, when a series of scenes are now made to move along before the eye of a spectator, his attention is not fixed upon the joints which divide them, but on the scenes themselves, yet the joints constitute a framework as it were for each, and the idea of each is made more distinct and lively than it would have been if, without any note of division, they had run into one another.

There is, however, another purpose, not yet named, and more remote yet perhaps even more vital, which appears to be powerfully served by the Creation Story of the Bible. In the prehistoric time, polytheism was very largely engendered by national distinctions, rivalries, and amalgamations. By a ready and ingenious compromise each people became habituated to recognize a deity all-sufficient for its own wants, but unconcerned with those of others. In the course of time and of successive change, many of these deities might find themselves inducted into one and the same thearchy, or mythological system, such as that of Assyria or of Olympus, and sitting there side by side. When this happened, the polytheistic idea had reached its full development. But the road to it lay principally through the erection of separate thrones, each for the god of some particular national organization; and it was narrowed within the limits thus imposed upon the earlier and more proper conception of a Divine Governor. But, wherever the Creation Story of Genesis was truly received, the door was effectually closed for all thinking men against these co-equal and purely national gods. And how? Because the God of Israel was the Maker of the world, and so of all the nations in it. It was his creation; and its inhabitants, whether terrestrial or celestial, were his creatures. Thus the narrative of this great chapter was nothing less than a Great Charter of monotheism; and though, in Israelitish practice, Baal and Ashtoreth might find their way into popular worship, and spread around them an infinity of corruption, the lines of the dogma, as a dogma, never were obscured, and the standard of authoritative reform still lifted up its head to heaven from the first day of idolatry to the last, when, under the pressure of the Exile, that form of mischief was finally submerged.[1]

This great idea, the universal authorship of creation, lost rather than dilapidated elsewhere, was impressed upon the Hebrew mind with a force which found its way into the solemn worship of

[1] For the further elucidation of the subject of this paragraph, see the Postscript to "The Creation Story."

the temple. It was not in Palestine alone that the orders of animals depended upon the providence of God, and that hill and valley, land and water, showed forth his image. It was the entire heavens which declared the glory of God, the entire firmament which showed forth his handiwork. The sun proclaimed the glory of its Maker from the uttermost part of the heavens unto the end of it again; and the sound of things created is gone out into all lands, and their words into the ends of the world. . . . The sun cometh forth as a bridegroom out of his chamber, and rejoiceth as a giant to run his course (Psa. 19 : 1-6). But this glorious sun, in his predestined course, was himself doing homage to his Lord and Maker. And the great chapter visibly reappears in the verse "One day telleth another, one night certifieth another" (Psa. 24 : 1). This is without doubt noble poetry, but it is also nobler than any poetry. Mute Nature is instinct with life and vocal with worship, and all Creation, in its humblest orders giving a lesson to its loftiest, ministers to the glory of the Most High.

In order, then, to approach any attempt at comparison between the record of Scripture and the record of Natural Science, we must consider first, as far as reasonable presumption carries us, what is the proper object of the scientist, and what was the proper object of Moses, or of the Mosaic writer, in the first chapter of Genesis.

The object of the scientist is simply to state the facts of nature in the cosmogony as and so far as he can find them. The object of the Mosaic writer is broadly distinct; it is, surely, to convey moral and spiritual training. This training was to be imparted to human beings of child-like temperament and of unimproved, unopened understanding. It was his business to use those words which would best carry home the lessons he had to teach, which would carry *most truth* into the minds of those he taught. This observation has not the honors of originality. "He emphasized," says Rabbi Grossman,[1] in his interesting tract on Maimonides, "as very proper and wise, the Talmudic

[1] Page 12. Putnam : New York and London. 1890.

maxim, that the Torah employs such diction as is likely to be most communicative."

In speaking of the Mosaic writer, I would, without presumption, seek to include any divine impulse which may have prompted him, or may have dictated any communication from God to man, in whatever form it may have been conveyed. With this aim in view, words of figure, though literally untrue, might carry more truth home than words of fact; and words less exact will even now often carry more truth than words superior in exactness. The truth to be conveyed was, indeed, in its basis physical; but it was to serve moral and spiritual ends, and accordingly by these ends the method of its conveyance behooved to be shaped and pictured.

I submit, then, that the days of Creation are neither the solar days of twenty-four hours, nor are they the geological periods which the geologist himself is compelled popularly, and in a manner utterly remote from precision, to describe as millions upon millions of years.   To use such language as this is simply and properly to tell us that we have no means of forming a determinate idea upon the subject of the geologic periods. I set aside both these interpretations, as I do not think the Mosaist intended to convey an idea like the first, which would seem to be false, or like the second, which for his auditory would have been barren and unmeaning. Unmeaning, and even confusing in the highest degree; for large statements in figures are well known to be utterly beyond comprehension for man at an early intellectual stage; and I have myself, I think, shown[1] that, even among the Achaian or Homeric Greeks, the limits of numerical comprehension were extremely narrow, and all large numbers were used, so to speak, at a venture, and with only a clouded comprehension.

It seems to me that the "days" of the Mosaist are more properly to be described as CHAPTERS IN THE HISTORY OF THE CREATION. That is to say, the purpose of the writer, in speaking of the days, was

[1] "Studies on Homer and the Homeric Age," Vol. III., Section on Number.

the same as the purpose of the historian is, when he divides his work into chapters. His object is to give clear and sound instruction. So that he can do this, and in order that he may do it, the periods of time assigned to each chapter are longer or shorter, according as the one or the other may minister to better comprehension of his subject by his readers. Further, in point of chronology, his chapters often overlap. He finds it needful, always keeping his end in view, to pursue some narrative to its close, and then, stepping backwards, to take up some other series of facts, although their exordium dated at a period of time on which he has already trespassed. The resources of the literary art, aided for the last four centuries by printing, enable the modern writer to confront more easily these difficulties of arrangement, and so to present his material to a reader's eye, in text or margin, as to place the texture of his chronology in harmony with the texture of the action he has to relate. The Mosaist, in his endeavor to expound the ordinary development of the physical world, had no such resources. His expedient was to lay hold on that which, to the mind of his time, was the best example of complete and orderly division. This was the day; an idea at once simple, definite, and familiar. As one day is divided from another, not by any change visible to the eye at a given moment, yet effectually, by the broad chasm of the intervening night, so were the stages of the creative work several and distinct. Even if, like the lapse of time, they were without breach of continuity, yet the work of each, when viewed in its completeness, was broadly separated from that of every other. Each had its work, each had the beginning and the completion of that work, even as the day is begun by its morning, and completed and concluded by its evening.

And now to sum up. In order that the narrative might be intelligible, it was useful to subdivide the grand operation. This could most effectively be done by subdividing it into periods of time. And further, it was well to choose that particular circumscription or period of time which is the most definite

and best understood.   Of all these, the day is clearly
the best, as compared with the month or the year :
first, because of its small and familiar compass ;
and, secondly, because of the strong and marked
division which separates one day from the days
which precede and follow it, while the months and
the years run into one another.

Hence, we may reasonably argue, it is that not
here only, but throughout the Scripture, and even
down to the present time in familiar human speech,
the day is figuratively used to describe periods
of time, perfectly undefined as such, but defined,
for practical purposes, by the lives or events to
which reference is made.   And if it be said there
was a danger of its being misunderstood in this
particular case, the answer is that such danger of
misapprehension attaches in various degrees to all
use of figurative language ; but figurative language
is still used.   And with reason, because the mischiefs arising from such danger are rare and trivial,
in comparison with the force and clearness which
it lends to truth on its passage, through a thickened

atmosphere of folly, indifference, and prejudice, into the mind of man. In this particular case, the danger and inconvenience are at their minimum, the benefit at its zenith; for no moral mischief ensues because some have supposed the days of the creation to be pure solar days of twenty-four hours, while the benefit has been that the grand conception of orderly development, and ascent from chaos to man, became among the Hebrew people a universal and familiar truth, of which other races appear to have lost sight.

I may now part from the important and long-vexed discussion on the Mosaic days. But I shall further examine the general question, what is the true method, what the reasonable spirit, of interpretation to be applied to the details of the Creation Story? I will state frankly my opinion that, in this important matter, too much has sometimes been conceded in modern days to the scientist and to the Hebraist, just as in former days too much was allowed to the unproved assumptions of the theologian. Now it is evident that the proper

6

ground of the scientist and of the Hebraist respectively is unassailable, as against those who are neither scientists nor Hebraists.   On the meaning of
the words used in the Creation Story, I, as an *igno-*
ramus, have only to accept the statements of Hebrew
scholars, with gratitude for the aid received ; and in
like manner the pronouncements of men skilled in
natural science on the nature and succession of the
orders of being, and on the transitions from one to
the other.   Not because their statements are inerr-
able, but because they constitute the best working
material in our possession.   Still they are the statements of men whose title to speak with authority
is confined to their special province ; and if we
allow them without protest to go beyond it, and
still to claim that authority when they are what
is called at school " out of bounds," we are much
to blame, and may suffer for our carelessness.

I will now endeavor to illustrate and apply
what has been said.   The Hebraist says, I will conduct you safely (as far as the case allows) to the
meaning of the Hebrew words.   And the scientist

makes the same promise in regard to the facts of the created orders, so far as they are exhibited by geological investigations into the crust of the earth. At first sight it may seem as if these two authoritative witnesses must cover the whole ground, each setting out from his own point of departure, the two then meeting in the midst, and leaving no unoccupied space between them. But my contention is that there is a ground which neither of them is entitled to occupy in his character as a specialist, and on which he has no warrant for entering, except in so far as he is a just observer and reasoner in a much wider field. And what is the residuary subject-matter still to be disposed of? Not the meaning of the Hebrew words. The Hebraist has already given us their true equivalents in English. We now learn, for example, that the "whales" of Genesis 1 : 21 are not whales at all, but that they are aquatic monsters[1] or great crea-

---

[1] Rev. Ver., the great sea-monsters. "It seems, on the whole, most probable, that the creatures here said to have been created were serpents, crocodiles, and other huge saurians, though possibly any large monsters of sea or river may be included" (Bp. Browne *in loc.*

tures; while we learn from the biologist that the whale is a late mammal. So geology has acquainted us what are the relative dates of the water and of the land populations, and has supplied much information as to reptiles, birds, and beasts. But there remains a great uncovered ground, and a great unsolved question. It is this. Given the facts as the geologist is led to state them, given the Hebrew tongue as the instrument through which the relator has to work, what are the terms, and what is the order and adjustment of terms, through which he can convey most of truth and force, with least of incumbrance and of impediment, to the mind of man, in the condition in which he had to deal with it? Let me be permitted to say that the only specialism, which can be of the smallest value here, is that of the close observer of human nature; of the student of human action, and of the methods which

" Speaker's Commentary "). Possibly a word signifying, whether wholly or *inter alia*, crocodiles, would convey a pretty clear idea to the mind of the Hebrews, after their sojourn in Egypt. On the other hand, it may be asked what reason can be given for construing the word in this limited sense.

Divine Providence employs in the conduct of its dealings with men. Certainly I can lay no claim to be heard here more than any other person. Yet will I say, that any man whose labor and duty, whether for several scores of years or for a shorter term, has included as their central point the study of the means of making himself intelligible to the mass of men, is *pro tanto* perhaps in a better position to judge what would be the forms and methods of speech proper for the Mosaic writer to adopt, than the most perfect Hebraist as such, or the most consummate votary of natural sciences as such.

I will now endeavor to try some portions of the case which turn upon verbal difficulty. At the outset of the narrative the relator says, that "the earth was without form and void" (Gen. 1 : 2) and that "the spirit of God moved upon the face of the waters." Nay, how is this? says the Hebraist. The Hebrew word for earth means earth, and the word used for water never means anything except water. But according to the beautiful theory, which has during the last half-century won so largely the adhesion of the scientific world, and which seems to be mainly called the nebular theory, at the commencement of the process which Genesis describes, and in its early stages, there was no earth, and there were no waters. Is the relator here really in fault? It seems to me that it might be quite as easy to cavil at the phrase nebular theory, though it be one in use among scientific men, as it is to find fault with these words of Genesis. For nothing can be more different than a *nebula* or cloud from a vast expanse of incandescent gaseous matter. In truth, we seem to have for our point of departure a time when all the elements and all the forces of the visible universe were in chaotic mixture, whereas there could hardly be any sort of *nebula* until they had begun to be disengaged from one another. How then are we to judge of the employment of the word "earth" by the Mosaic writer? Is it not thus? He is dealing with an Adam, or with a primitive race of men, who have the earth under their eyes. He wants to give them an idea of its coming into

existence. And he says what we may fairly paraphrase in this way: that which has now become
earth, and was then becoming earth, the solid well-
defined form you see, was as yet without form and
void; epithets which I am told might be improved
upon, but this is a matter by the way.

So again with respect to water. The men for
whom the relator wrote knew, perhaps, of no fluid
except water, at any rate of none vast and practically measureless in volume. What was the idea
he had to convey? It was not the special and distinctive character of the liquid called water; it was
the broad separation between solid as such, familiar,
firm, immovable under his feet, and fluid as such,
movable and fluctuating at large in space. No
doubt the idea conveyed by the word "waters" is an
imperfect idea, although waters are still waters at
times when they may be holding vast quantities of
solid in solution. But it was an idea easy, clear,
and familiar up to the point of expressing forcibly
the contrast between the ancient state of things,
with its weltering waste, and the recent and defined

conditions of the habitable earth. Could we ask of the relator more than that he should employ, among the words at his disposal, that which would come nearest to conveying a true idea? And had he any word so good as water for his purpose, though it was but an approximation to the actual fact? Dr. Driver[1] describes the scene as that of a "surging chaos." An admirable phrase, I make no doubt, for our modern and cultivated minds; but a phrase which, in my judgment, would have left the pupils of the Mosaic writer exactly in the condition out of which it was his purpose to bring them; namely, a state of utter ignorance and total darkness, with possibly a little ruffle of bewilderment to boot. Another description claiming high authority is, an "uncompounded, homogeneous, gaseous condition" of matter; to which the same observation will apply. Even now, it is only by rude and bald approximations that the practiced intellects of our scientists can bring home to us a conception of the actual process by which *chaos*

[1] In an article contributed to the "Expositor," January, 1886.

passed into *kosmos*, or, in other words, confusion became order, medley became sequence, seeming anarchy became majestic law, and horror softened into beauty. Before censuring the Mosaist, who had to deal with grown children, let the adverse critic try his hand upon some little child. I believe he will find that the method and language of this relator are not only good, but superlatively good, for the aim he had in view, if once for all we get rid of standards of interpretation other than the genuine and just one, which tests the means employed by their relation to the end contemplated and sought.

I now approach a larger head of objection, which is usually handled by the Contradictionists in a tone of confidence rising into the pæan of triumph. But let me, before presuming to touch on objections to particulars of the Creation Story, guard myself against being supposed to put forward any portion of what follows as unconditional assertion, or final comment on the text. The general situation is this: Objectors do not hesitate to declare dogmatically that the great chapter is in contradiction with the laws and facts of Nature, and that attempts to reconcile them are futile and irrational. It is thus sought to close the question. My aim is to show that the question is not closed, and that the condemnation pronounced upon the Mosaist is premature; and that a very different contention has to be considered, namely, whether this chapter does not in itself supply proof of a divine revelation. For this purpose I offer conjecturally, and in absolute submission to all that biology and geology, or other forms of science, have established, replies which are strictly provisional; yet replies which I consider that the Contradictionist ought, together with other and weightier replies, to confute, or legitimately to consider, before he can be warranted in asserting the contradiction. But I proceed.

How hopeless, is the cry, to reconcile Genesis with fact, when, as a fact, the sun is the source of light, and yet in Genesis light is the work of the first day, and vegetation of the third, while sun, moon, and stars appear only on the fourth! Nay, worse still. Whereas the morning and the evening depend wholly on the rotation of the earth upon its own axis, as it travels round the sun, the Mosaist is so ignorant that he gives us not days only, but the mornings and the evenings of days before the sun is created. And so his narration explodes, not by blows aimed at it from without, but by its own internal self-contradictions. It is hissed, like a blundering witness, out of court. Not that this is the opinion of astronomers in general. Mr. Lockyer,[1] for example, cites, with apparent approval, a passage from his very distinguished predecessor in the science, Halley, who says that the diffused lucid medium he had found, disposed of the difficulty which some have moved against the description Moses gives of the Creation, alleging that light could not be created without the sun.

The first triad of days, says Professor Dana,[2] sets forth the events connected with the inorganic history of the earth. The second triad, from the fourth day to the sixth, is occupied with the events

---

[1] Nineteenth Century, Nov., 1889, p. 788.

[2] Dana's " Creation," p. 207.

of the organic history, from the creation of the first animal to man. He finds in the general structure of the narrative a considerable degree of elaboration, an arrangement full of art. The passage from verse 14 to verse 19 is, in one sense, a qualification of the order he thinks to have been laid down, inasmuch as the heavenly bodies belong to the inorganic division of the history. From another point of view, however, this arrangement contributes in a marked manner to the symmetry of the narrative. The first triad of days begins with the first and gradual detachment of light from the "surging chaos;" the second, at the stage in which light has reached its final distribution. The central mass had now assumed with a certain amount of regularity (for, according to heliologists, the process does not even yet appear to be absolutely completed) its spherical and luminous figure, after shedding off from itself the minor masses, each to find for itself its own orbit of rotation. Or, if we are to assume that the photosphere or vapor-envelope of the earth itself had obstructed the vision of the sun, we have, further, to assume[1] that this obstacle had now disappeared or ceased to be impervious, and that the visibility of the sun was established. So that light, or the light-power, while diffused, ushers in the first division of the mighty process; the same light-power, concentrated by the operation of the rotary principle, and for practical purposes become such as we now know it, is placed at the head of the second division, the division that relates to organic life.

It is remarkable that the subject of light is the only one which is dealt with in two separate sections of the narrative. The gradual severance, or disengagement, of the earth from its present vesture, the atmosphere, and of the solid land from the ocean, are continuously handled in verses 6-10. Each of these processes may have been gradual, and may have passed through many stages. But, at verses 6 and 9, they are respectively summed up by a few peremptory words of command, as if they had been convulsive or instantaneous. Only the

---

[1] Guyot, " Creation," Chap. XI., p. 92.

grand result is made known. The avoidance of all attempt to explain the process seems to me only a proof of the wisdom which guided the formation of the tale. To the primitive man it would have become a barren puzzle; the wood might have been lost in the trees. As it now stands, mental confusion is avoided, and definite ideas are conveyed.

There seems, however, to be a special reason for the introduction of the heavenly bodies at this particular place. It was evidently needful at some place or other to give a specific account of the day, or compartment of time, which is employed throughout the chapter to mark the severance of the different stages of creation from each other. At what point of the narrative could this account be most properly and most accurately introduced? In order to answer this question, let us consider the situation rather more at large.

It may be convenient, before entering into the fuller discussion, to set out some brief and synoptical account of the contents of the (detailed) Creation Story properly so called, which begins with the commencement of the first chapter, and ends with the third verse of the second.

It may be divided first into two portions, the first of six days and the second of the seventh day only: the first presenting an account of the creation and fashioning of the world, and dealing with work done. The second is negative with respect to work done, and simply records the issue of a command, together with the grand analogy on which that command is based.

When we turn to the creative work of the six days, we cannot limit it to the earth, as the operations of the fourth day are concerned with the heavenly bodies; nor can we extend it to the *kosmos* properly so called, or material universe, for we cannot tell how far the signification of the word "stars" in verse 16 may be meant to extend. It may refer to the creation of our own solar system, but we are not warranted in propounding this as a definition of its extent. Keeping in view the manner in which the whole narrative addresses itself

to practical ends, the word "stars" may be thought
to include all those heavenly bodies of which the
earliest astronomy took note. But the terms employed define nothing as to time, except as regards
the sun and moon, making only the general assertion that the Almighty was also the Creator of the
stars. When speaking of the creation of the world,
I employ the phrase in the sense thus indicated.

It does not appear that the six days can be separated into portions by any perfectly clean division.
The first four are mainly cosmological, but they
include the beginning of vegetation on the surface
of the earth. The two last of the days are zoölogi-
cal. But the sixth day, like the third, is mixed,
and contains operations not homogeneous. Of
geology, as it is commonly understood, the chapter
takes no notice. It is confined to the air, the
sea, and the earth surface. But the researches of
geology into the changes which that surface has
undergone in the lapse of time have most bene-
ficially enlarged our knowledge of the chapter, and
our means of appreciating its wonderful construc-

tion. The mixture of cosmic with terrestrial history in the third day, and the return to cosmic narrative on the fourth, are readily to be accounted for by the aim of the chapter which apparently governs its sequences. But on account of this mixture I do not attempt subdivision of the days of creation, and simply bring together the leading operations in what is, I hope, a simple and intelligible form.

Verse 1. First we have the creation of the material universe, described as "the heavens and the earth." This takes place in the beginning. But it is not stated of *what* it was the beginning. This is in the first verse; and there is no link of time between it and the second, which resumes the narrative independently of the first.

So far as form is concerned, the chapter might have commenced with verse 2. But then we should not have possessed the pronouncement or dogma of universal creation.

Verse 2. This verse proclaims first the formless condition of the earth. Now, as no earth can prop-

7

erly be said to exist except with form, the words amount to a declaration that the materials for the formation of the earth existed, but that the earth was not yet formed.   Motion is then announced, and assigned to the divine actuating power.   The Spirit of God moved upon the face of the waters! That motion was imparted to these "waters" is not directly mentioned; but such a mention would have conveyed no rational conception to the primitive man, who had nothing in his experience to correspond with it.

I shall assume that what is known as the nebular theory of creation stands good as a working hypothesis.   We have then to observe, not that the Mosaic narrative is tied to it so as to be consistent with no other, nor that it gives a complete exposition of it, but that, moving as it were on parallel lines, one chapter is so constructed as at no point to clash with it.

Verses 3-5.   Accordingly motion is at once followed by the disengagement of light.   And this light is divided from the darkness.   According to the nebular theory, the rotation is followed by the formation of a central mass, and the detachment from it of minor masses, which as they continue to rotate expose successively the different portions of their surface to, and then remove it from, the central light. Thus the light is parted from the darkness and the basis of diurnal division laid.

Verses 6-8. The first grand severance having thus been made, and something in the nature of a globular figure constituted, by rotation and gravitation, which was to become the earth, and the next grand severance is that of the earth from its atmospheric vesture described as the firmament or expanse, a portion of space accommodated as we now know to the conditions of animal life. This firmament "divides the waters from the waters," humidity being gradually condensed beneath into what we know as water, and also above our heads collected without such condensation into the clouds from whence proceed our supplies of rain.

Verses 9,10. The second grand severance is followed by a third. Moisture being no longer diffused through the parts of space without sensible distinction, and the principal part of it being condensed into water, this water becomes a mass limited to a certain portion of space, beneath the firmament of air. Then this mass, local, circumscribed, becomes the sea, filling the great cavities of the earth surface, and leaving the portions not thus occupied to become comparatively dry. Thus land and sea are constituted. This severance, like the others, is described so to speak in the large, and leaves unnoticed all the particular arrangements for the successive production and deposition of the rocks; for it adheres throughout to its principle, which confines its statements within the limits of what is suitable for the instruction of the primitive man.

Verses 11, 12. Land and sea being thus constituted, and light having been their precursor, with heat, its twin-brother, which from other sources we know to have been produced as its concomitant through motion, we are possessed of the necessary antecedents of vegetation and vegetation follows.

The mode in which it is described will be presently considered.

The acts of the fourth day are cosmological in themselves; but they form a chapter of cosmology which is here treated in reference to the earth, as the sun and moon are to be the time-markers for mankind. In this view then we may be justified in saying that from henceforward the narrative only concerns itself with terrestrial arrangements.

Verses 14-19. These verses have evidently the making of the sun and moon for their principal subject. It is subjoined without any particulars that God made the stars also. They are in such conjunction with the moon that they seemed fit for mention; but their relation to man at large is comparatively slight, and accordingly the mention is without detail.

Verses 20-23. The fifth day introduces us to animated life: an onward stride in the evolution of the world of so distinct a character, that it is marked by the use for the second time only of the Hebrew word which we are told denotes creation. The

work of this day is in two stages, and it is ushered
in by a double command.   First it is ordained that
the waters shall bring forth abundantly the moving
creature that hath life, and in verse 20 the command, as it is stated in the Authorized Version,
seems to cover the fowl that were to fly in the
firmament of heaven.   But the Revised Version
completely separates the two portions of the fiat,
(1) that the waters should bring forth, and (2) that
the fowl should fly.   Thus verse 20 is placed in
complete harmony with verse 21, where in the
Authorized as well as in the Revised Version the
successive divine acts that produce the water and
the air populations respectively are placed in regular sequence.

Verses 24-28.   The work of the sixth day embraces in its entirety the earth-population of
animals and men.   Animals are described with
some variation of phrase, but apparently none of
meaning. In verse 24 they are " the living creature
after his kind," " cattle and creeping thing and beast
of the earth after his kind."   In verse 25 they are

" the beast of the earth after his kind," and "cattle after their kind, and everything that creepeth upon the earth after his kind."   Such is in general out-line the animal kingdom of the earth-population.

Verses 26-31.   We now come to the grand con-summating act, the creation of man ; and here, for the third time, the Hebrew term indicative of crea-tion proper is used.   The production of man is an-nounced under a form of consultation ; the distinc-tion of male and female is included in the opera-tions of the day ; this eminent being is created in the image of God (26, 27), is endowed with general dominion over all living creatures, and with a title to all seed-bearing herbs and fruit-bearing trees for food (29), while the grasses are assigned to the in-ferior orders.   Finally, a solemn benediction from the Creator inaugurates the great mission of man (28) upon the earth, and so the work of the six days stands complete in outline before us.   Then follows in 2 : 1-3 the benediction of the seventh day.

Having the whole process placed thus synoptically before us, we proceed to the discussion in detail.

The supposition is, that we set out with a vast seething mass, of such a nature as to contain all the elements which are to become the solids and liquids, the moist and dry, the heat and the non-heat or cold, the light and the non-light or darkness, that so largely determine the external conditions of our present existence. By degrees, according to the rarity or density of parts, the centripetal or the centrifugal force prevails. And accordingly, while the huge bulk of the sun con-solidates itself in the center, so likewise aggre-gations of matter (rings, according to Guyot,[1] which afterwards become, or may become, spheres), are detached from it to form the planets, under the agency of the same mechanical forces. All or some of these, in their turn, dismiss from their as yet ill-compacted surfaces other subaltern masses either to revolve around them as satellites, or other-wise, according to the balance of forces, to take

[1] " Creation," pp. 67, 73.

their course in space. Meantime, the great cool-
ing process, which is still in progress at this day,
has begun. It proceeds at a rate determined for
it by its particular conditions, among which mass
and motion are of essential consequence ; for, other
things being equal, a small body will cool faster and
a large body will cool slower ; and a body moving
more rapidly through space of a lower temperature
than its own will cool more rapidly ; while one
which is stationary, or more nearly stationary, or
which diffuses heat less rapidly from its surface
into the colder space, will retain a high temperature longer. Owing to these perhaps with other
causes, the temperature of the earth-surface has
been adapted to the conditions of human life, and
of the more recent animal life, for a very long time.
It had already been made suitable to those of the
earlier animals, and of vegetation in a series of
progressive orders, for we know not how much
longer; while the sun, though gradually losing
some part of his stock of caloric (whatever that
may be), still remains at a temperature inordinately

high, and with a globular formation comparatively incomplete.

Considering, then, what are the relations between the conditions of heat and those of moisture, and how the coatings of vapor, " the swaddling-band of cloud,"[1] might affect the visibility of bodies, may it not be rash to affirm that the sun is, as a definite and compact body, older than the earth? or that it is so old? or that the Mosaist might not properly treat the visibility of the sun, in something like its present form, as best marking for man the practical inception of its existence? or that, with heat, light, soil, and moisture ready to its service, primordial vegetation might not exist on the surface of a planet like the earth, before the sun had fully reached his matured condition of sufficiently compact, material, and well-defined figure, and of visibility to the human eye? May not, once for all, the establishment of the relation of visibility between earth and sun be the most suitable point for the relator in Genesis to bring the two into con-

[1] Dana, p. 210.

nection? And here again I would remind the reader that the Mosaic days may be chapters in a history; and also that, not in despite of the law of series, but with a view to its best practicable application, the chapters of a history may overlap.

The priority of earth to sun, as given in the narrative, carries us so far as this: that vegetative work (of what kind I shall presently inquire) is stated to be proceeding on the surface of the earth before any relation of earth with sun is declared. It is then declared in the terms, "and God *made* two great lights" (v. 16.) Now the *making* of earth is nowhere declared, but only implied. And who shall say that there is some one exact point of time in the continuous process which (according to the nebular theory) reaches from the first beginning of rotation down to the present condition of the solar system, to which point, and to which alone, the term "making" must belong? But, unless there be such a point, it seems very difficult to convict the Mosaic writer of error in the choice he has made of an opportunity for introducing the heavenly bodies into his narrative.

I suppose that no apology is needed for his mentioning the moon and (more slightly) the stars as accessories in the train of the sun, and combining them all without note of time, although their several "makings" may have proceeded at different speeds. But here again we find exhibited that principle of relativity to man and his uses, by which the writer in Genesis appears so wisely to steer his course throughout. We are told of "two great lights" (v. 16); and one of them is the moon. The formation of the stars is interjected soon after, as if comparatively insignificant. But the planet-stars individually are in themselves far greater and more significant than the moon, which is denominated a great light. In what sense is the moon a great light? Only in virtue of its relation to us. For its magnitude, as it is represented on the human retina, is far larger than that of the stars, and in certain states of atmosphere even seems to approach that of the sun. Its office also makes it the queen of the nocturnal heaven. So, then, the general upshot is, that the mention of the sun is introduced at that point in the cosmogonic process when, from the condition of our form and atmosphere, or of his, or of both, he had become so definite and visible as to be finally efficient for his office of dividing day from day, and year from year; that the planets, being of an altogether secondary importance to us, simply appear as his attendant company; and that to the moon, a body in itself comparatively insignificant, is awarded a rather conspicuous place, which, if objectively considered, is out of proportion, but which at once falls into line when we acknowledge relativity as the basis of the narrative; by reason, first, of its visual magnitude in the heavens, and, next, of the great importance of the functions which this satellite discharges on behalf of the inhabitants of the earth.

Next, it is alleged that we have days with an evening and a morning before we have a sun to supply a measure of time for them. Doubtless there could be no approach to anything like an evening and a morning, so long as light was uniformly diffused. But under the nebular theory, the work of the first day implies an initial concentration of light; and, from the time when light began to be thus powerfully concentrated, would there not be an evening and a morning, though imperfect, for any revolving solid of the system, according as it might be turned towards, or from, the center of the highest luminosity? To put it in the briefest words. When light begins, motion begins. When motion begins, there begins also a concentration of light. When light is concentrated, a relation of day and night, and of evening and morning, or gradual night and gradual day, is established. So the distinction of days begins at the right place (v. 5), and could not rightly have begun at any other place.

But we have not yet emerged from the net of the Contradictionist, who lays hold on the vegetation verses (11, 12) to impeach the credit of the Creation Story. The objection here becomes twofold. First, we have vegetation anterior to the sun; and secondly, this is not merely an aquatic vegetation for the support of aquatic life, nor merely a rude and primordial vegetation, such as that of and before the coal-measures, but a vegetation complete and absolute, including fern-grass, then the herb yielding seed, and lastly the fruit-tree, yielding fruit after its kind, whose seed is in itself. Here is the food of mammals and even of man provided, when neither of them was yet created. Nay, when neither of them was on the eve of existence, or was to take its place in the created order, until after many a long antecedent form of lower life had found its way into creation and undertaken its office there.

First, as regards vegetation before the sun's performance of his present function in the heavens is announced. There were light and heat, atmosphere with its conditions of moist and dry, soil prepared to do its work in nutrition. Can there be ground for saying that, with such provision made, vegetation could not, would not, take place?

Let us, for argument's sake, suppose that the sun could now recede into an earlier condition, could go back by some few stages of that process through which he became our sun; his material less compact, his form less defined, his rays more intercepted by the "swaddling-band" of cloud and vapor. Vegetation might be modified in character, but must it therefore cease? May we not say that a far more violent paradox would have been hazarded, and a sounder objection would have lain, had the Mosaic writer failed to present to us at least an initial vegetation before the era at which the sun had obtained his present degree of definiteness in spherical form, and the conditions for the transmission of his rays to us had reached substantially their present state?

But, then, it is fairly observed that the vegetation as described is not preparatory and initial, but full-formed; also, that any tracing of vegetation anterior to animal life in the strata is ambiguous and obscure. In the age of Protozoa, the earliest living creatures, the indications of plants are not determinable, according to the high authority of Sir J. W. Dawson. It is observed by Canon Driver "that the proof from science of the existence of plants before animals is inferential and *à priori*."[1] Guyot, however, holds a directly contrary opinion, and says the present remains indicate a large presence of infusorial protophytes in the early seas.[2] But suppose the point to be conceded. Undoubtedly, all *à priori* assumptions ought in inquiries of this kind to be watched with the utmost vigilance and jealousy. Still there are limits beyond which vigilance and jealousy cannot push their claims. Is there anything strange in the supposition that the comparatively delicate composition of the first vegetable structures should have given way, and become indiscernible to us, amidst the shock and pressure of firmer and more durable material ? The flesh of the mammoth has, indeed, been preserved to us, and eaten by dogs in our own time, though coming down from ages which

[1] "The Cosmogony of Genesis," in The Expositor, January, 1886, p. 29.   [2] "Creation," X., p. 90.

we have no means of measuring; but then it was not exposed to the same pressure, and it subsisted under conditions of temperature which were adequately antiseptic. But has all palæozoic life been ascertained by its flesh? or do we not owe our knowledge of many (perhaps of all) among the earlier forms of animated life altogether to their osseous structures? And, in cases where only bone remains, is it an extravagant use of argument *à priori* to hold that there must at some former time have been flesh also? And, if flesh, why should not vegetable matter also have subsisted, and have disappeared? Canon Driver, indeed, observes[1] that from a very early date animals preyed upon animals. Still the first animal could not prey upon himself; there must have been vegetable *pabulum*, out of which an animal body was first fed and so developed. "Before the beasts," says Sir George Stokes, "came the plants, plants which are necessary for their sustenance."[2]

[1] The Expositor, January, 1886, p. 29.
[2] Letter to Mr. Elflein, Aug. 14, 1883.

Next, with respect to the objection that the vegetation of the eleventh and twelfth verses is a perfected vegetation, and that there existed no such vegetation before animal life began. But why are we to suppose that the Mosaic writer intended to say that such a vegetation did exist before animal life began? For no other reason than this: having mentioned the first introduction of vegetable life, he carries it on, without breaking his narrative, to its perfection. In so proceeding, he does exactly what the historian does when, for the sake of clearer comprehension, he brings one series of events from its inception to its close, although in order of time the beginning only, and not the completion, belongs to the epoch at which he introduces it. What I have called the rule of relativity, the intention, namely, to be intelligible to man, seems to show the reason of his arrangement. If his meaning was, "The beautiful order of trees, plants and grasses which you see around you had its first beginnings in the area when living creatures were about to commence their movements in the waters and on the earth, and all this was part of the fatherly work of God on your behalf"—such meaning was surely well expressed, expressed after a sound and workman-like fashion, in the text of the Creation Story as it stands.

I will next notice the objection that the Mosaic writer takes (according to the received version) no notice of the great age of reptiles, but proceeds at once from the creation of marine animals (v. 20) to the fowl that may " fly above the earth in the open firmament of heaven."   He thus passes over without notice the amphibians, the reptiles proper, the insects, and the marsupial or early mammals, on his way to the birds.   It is added that he brackets the birds with the fishes, and thus makes them of the same date.

It is requisite here to observe, with respect to birds, that Professor Dana[1] writes of the narrative in Genesis as follows: Speaking of the relation between the Mosaic narrative and the ascertained facts of science, he uses these words: " The accord-

[1] "Creation," as before, p. 215.

ance is exact with the succession made out for the earliest species of these grand divisions, if we except the division of birds, about which there is doubt."

Owen, however, in his "Palæontology,"[1] places animal life in six classes, according to the following order, namely:

1. Invertebrates.	4. Birds.
2. Fishes.	5. Mammals.
3. Reptiles.	6. Man.

In the more recent "Manual" of Professor Prestwich (1886), the order of seniority stands as follows:

1. Cryptogamous Plants.	4. Mammals.
2. Fishes.	5. Man.
3. Birds.	

In the "Manual"[2] of Etheridge we are supplied with the following series, after fishes: 1. Fossil reptiles. 2. Ornithosauria; *flying animals, which combined the character of reptiles with those of birds."* 3. The first birds of the secondary rocks, with

[1] Second edition, 1861, p. 5.

[2] Phillips's "Manual of Geology," Part II., by R. Etheridge, F.R.S., Chap. XXV., pp. 511–520.

" feathers in all respects similar to those of existing birds." 4. Mammals.

It thus appears that much turns on the definition of a bird, and that in this point, as in others, it is hard, on the evidence thus presented, seriously to impeach the character of the Creation Story. Largely viewed, the place of birds, as an order in creation, is given us by our scientific teachers, or, at the very least, as I have shown, by many and recognized authorities among them, between fishes and the class of mammals. It is a gratuitous assumption that the Mosaist intends to assign to them the same date as fishes; he places them in the same day, but then we have to bear in mind that he more than once gives several actions to the same day. He sets them after the fishes; and the fairer construction surely is, not that they were contemporaneous, but that they were subsequent. In verse 21, if not in verse 20, the emergence into life of the one order is absolutely severed from that of the other. He forbears, it is true, to take separate notice of amphibious reptiles, insects, and marsupials. And why? All these, variously important in themselves, fill no large place—some of them no place at all—in the view and in the concerns of primitive man; and, having man for his object, he forbears, on his guiding principle of relativity, to encumber his narrative with them.

If it be true that the demarcation of the order of birds in creation is less sharply drawn than that (for example) of fishes and of mammals, may we not be permitted to trace a singular propriety in the diminution, so to speak, of emphasis, with which the Mosaist gives to their introduction a more qualified distinctness of outline, by simply subjoining them (v. 20) to the aquatic creation? Does not that diminution of emphasis accompany, and correspond with, an inferior breadth of distinction in the things themselves?

I must not, however, be understood to assert that the great reptile kingdom is omitted from the narrative. I find there are Hebraists who find nothing in the *Tannin*, which seems to be unhappily rendered by the word "whales," to exclude the great reptiles from the scope of its meaning. In this view, this charge of omission, small as its significance would be if proven, falls to the ground.

I have now made bold to touch on the principal objections popularly known. They run into details which it has not been possible fully to notice, but which seem to be without force, except such as they derive from the illegitimate process of holding down the Mosaic writer in his narration, so short, so simple, so sublime, by restraints which the ordinary historian, though he has plenty of auxiliary expedients, and is under no restraint of space, finds himself obliged to shake off if he wishes to be readily and popularly understood. On the introduction of the great or recent mammals, and of man, as the objector is silent, I remain silent also.

It would be uncandid, however, not to notice the "creeping thing" of verses 24, 25, and 26. In these verses the "creeping thing" is distinguished from cattle, and undoubtedly appears upon the scene as if it were a formation wholly new. If the Mosaist really intended to convey that this was the first appearance of any creeping thing in creation, there is, I suppose, no doubt that he is at war with the firmly established witness of natural science. Guyot, indeed, says[1] that these creeping things are not reptiles, but are the smaller mammals, rats, mice, and the like. If, however, the common rendering be maintained, it may be just worth while to suggest a possible explanation. It is as follows. These creeping things were a very minor fact in the scheme of creation; so that the purpose of the relator, and the comparative importance of the facts, may here, as elsewhere, have an influence upon the mode of handling them. It is fit to be observed that he never mentions insects at all, as if they were too insignificant to find a place among the larger items of his account; as if he advisedly selected his materials, and sifted off the less important among them. And there does seem to be some license or looseness in his method of treating these creeping things; for while he severs them from fish, fowl, and beast, in the verses I have

[1] " Creation," p. 120.

named, and again in verse 30 from fowl and from
beast, yet in verse 28, when the great charter of
dominion is granted to man, he sums up in three
divisions only, and makes man the lord " over the
fish of the sea, and over the fowl of the air, and
over every living thing that moveth upon the
earth." Reptiles appear to have passed out of his
view, either wholly, or so far as not to deserve separate mention, and it may seem likely that he did
not think their importance such as to call for a particular and defined place, and, while according to
them incidental mention, did not mean to give
them such a place, in the chronological order of
creation. Let the Contradictionist make the most
he can out of this secondary matter: it will not
greatly avail.

If, on the whole, such be a fair statement of arguments and results, we may justly render our thanks
to Dana, Guyot,[1] Dawson, Stokes, and other scien-

[1] In the preface to Guyot's " Creation " will be found some account
of the recent literature of this subject. I must also mention a valuable pamphlet entitled " The Higher Criticism," by Mr. Rust, Rector
of Westerfield, Suffolk. It sets forth the scope of the negative criti-

tific authorities, who seem to find no cause for supporting the broad theory of contradiction. I am well aware of my inability to add an atom of weight to their judgments. Yet I have ventured to attempt applying to this great case what I hold to be the just laws of a narrative intended to instruct and to persuade, and thus finding a key to the true construction of the chapter. For myself, I cannot but at present remain before and above all things impressed with the profound and marvellous wisdom, that has guided the human instrument, whether it were pen or tongue, which was first commissioned from on high, to hand onwards for our admiration and instruction this wonderful, this unparalleled relation. If I am a "reconciler," I shall not call myself a mere apologist, for I aim at a positive, not merely a defensive result, and claim that my reader should feel how true it is that in this brief relation he possesses an inestimable treasure. And I sub-

cism at large, and recommends (p. 30) to " have patience for a while, and wait to see the issue." Similar advice has, I understand, been given in the recent Charge of the learned Bishop of Oxford.

mit to those, who may have closely followed my remarks, that my words were not wholly idle words, when, without presuming to lay down any universal and inflexible proposition, and without questioning any single contention of persons specially qualified, I said that the true question was whether the words of the Mosaic writer, in his opening chapter, taken as a whole, do not stand, according to our present knowledge, in such a relation to the facts of Nature as to warrant and require, thus far, the conclusion that the Ordainer of Nature, and the Giver or Guide of the Creation Story, are one and the same.

POSTSCRIPT TO THE CREATION STORY.

Mankind have traveled not by one but by several roads into polytheism. It took a thousand years from the institution of the Mosaic legislation to place the chosen people, as a whole, in a state of security from this insidious mischief. But all along a powerful apparatus of means had been at work, which was strengthened from time to time as

Divine Providence saw fit. The foundation, however, had been laid in the Creation Story. It was
impossible for those who received it either to travel
or to glide into polytheism by either of the two
widest roads then open, the system of Nature-wor-
ship, and the deification of Heroes. No one could
make the sun his God, who really believed that
there was a God who created the sun. Even more
perhaps was it needful that the line should be
clearly and sharply drawn between Deity and
humanity, and that a barrier not capable of being
surmounted should exclude kings and heroes from
deification. In the Homeric or Olympian system,
the worship of inanimate nature was studiously
shut out; but the beginnings of deification are
visible in the case of Heracles,[1] whose very self
($\alpha\dot{v}\tau\dot{o}\varsigma$) sits at the banquets of the Immortals ; also
of the twin brothers, Castor and Pollux, who live
and die on alternate days, and who, when they
live, receive honors like the gods. In the height
of their civilization, the Romans set up their living

[1] Od. XI., 302–305.

emperors as divinities. But neither they nor the Greeks believed in the creation of man by the Almighty. The old cosmogonies of the heathen placed matter and other impersonal entities in a position of priority to their gods, who merely take their turn to come upon the scene. Only (I believe) in the Hebrew story is the Deity anterior, without which condition he cannot be supreme.

Besides being anterior, he is separate. Did we find in the pages of the Old Testament a story of deification, we should at once know it to be spurious, because in contradiction, alike as to letter and as to spirit, of the entire context.

It is, I hope, not presumptuous to proceed a step further, and to say that this broad and effectual severance was necessary, not only for the old dispensation, but for the new: not only for the exclusion of idolatry in all its forms, but for the establishment of the Incarnation. A marriage would be no marriage, unless the individuality of the parties to it were determinate and ineffaceable. The Christian dogma of the two natures in one

Person would be in no sense distinctive, if it had been habitual in the preparatory dispensation, as in some of the religions outside it, for man properly so called to pass into proper deity. Reunion was to be effected between the Almighty and his prime earthly creature by the bridge to be constructed over that flood, the flood of sin, which parted them; and, to sustain that bridge, it was needful that the natures to be brought into union should stand apart like piers perfectly defined, each on its own separate and solid foundation. And the firm foundations of those piers were laid, to endure throughout all time, by the great Creation Story.

III.

THE OFFICE AND WORK OF THE OLD TESTAMENT IN OUTLINE.

We may often hear it said, that the Old Testament is an introduction to the New. Much more is contained in these words than an irreflective recital may enable us to grasp. Yet they do not seem to cover the whole ground. It seems necessary to glance first at the conjoint function of the two Testaments, in order to measure fully the exalted mission of the earlier. As the heavens cover the earth from east to west, so the Scripture covers and comprehends the whole field of the destiny of man. The whole field is possessed by its moral and potential energy, as a provision enduring to the end of time. But it is marvellous to consider how large a portion of it lies directly within the domain of the Old Testament. The interval to be bridged

over between the prophet Malachi and the Advent
is not one of such breadth as wholly to abolish a
continuity, which was also upheld by visible institutions divinely ordained, and possibly even by the
production of certain of the Psalms themselves.
It is further narrowed in so far as something of a
divine *afflatus* is to be found in the books which
form the Apocrypha, which are esteemed by a large
division of Christendom to be actually a part of the
Sacred Canon, and which in the Church of England
have a place of special, though secondary honor.
At the more remote end of the scale, it is difficult
to name a date for the beginning of the Sacred
Scriptures. The corroborative legends of Assyria,[1]
ascertained by modern research, concerning the
Creation and the Flood, to which we know not
what further additions may still progressively be
made, carry us up,[2] it may be roughly said,

> "*To the* FIRST *syllable of recorded time.*"

[1] These legends will be separately noticed later in the present series
of essays.

[2] See No. VI. of this series for the ground of the argument, which,
as here presented, can only have in a certain measure the character
of an assumption.

Historic evidence does not at present warrant our carrying backwards the probable existence of the Adamic race for more than some such epoch as from 4000 to 6000 years before the advent of Christ. And if, as appears likely, the Creation Story has come down from the beginning, and the Flood legend is also contemporary, the Christian may feel a lively interest in observing that, during by far the larger portion of human history, the refreshing rain of divine inspiration has descended, with comparatively short intervals, from heaven upon earth, and the records of it have been collected and transmitted in the sacred volume. Apart from every question of literary form and of detail, we now trace the probable materials of the oldest among our sacred books far back beyond Moses and his time. And so we have a marvellous picture presented to us, not only all-prevailing for the imagination, the heart, and the conscience of man, but also, as I suppose, quite unexampled in its historical appeal to the human intelligence. The whole human record respecting Adam and his descend-

ants is covered and bound together in that same
unwearied and inviolable continuity, which weaves
into a tissue the six Mosaic days of gradually
developed creation, and fastens them on at the
hither end to the gradually advancing stages of
Adamic, and, in due course, of subsequent history.

We find then, that, apart from the question of
moral purity and elevation, the Scriptures of the
Old Testament appear to distinguish themselves
from the sacred books possessed by various nations
in several vital particulars. They deal with the
Adamic race as a whole. They begin with the
preparation of the earth for the habitation and use
of mankind. They then, from his first origin, draw
downwards a thread of properly personal history,
with notices, most remarkable in their character,
though contracted in space, of divergent families of
men. As, from being personal, the narrative becomes national—that is to say, from the Exodus
onwards this thread is enlarged into a web ; and
eventually it includes the whole race of man. Our
Scriptures are not given once for all, as were the

works of Confucius or Zoroaster in their respective spheres. They do not deliver a mere code of morals or of legislation, but their character is pre-eminently historical, while they purport to disclose a penetrating and continuing superintendence from on high over human affairs. And the whole is doubly woven into one formation. First, by a chain of divine action, and of human instructors acting under divine authority, which is sustained and represented by national institutions, and is never broken until the time when political servitude, like another Egyptian captivity, has well-nigh become the fixed destiny of the Hebrew nation. Secondly, by the Messianic bond, by the light of prophecy shining in a dark place, and directing onwards the minds of devout men to the "fulness of time" and the birth of the wondrous Child, so as effectually to link the older sacred books to the dispensation of the Advent, and to carry forward their office through an action both of and in the Church, until the final day of doom. May it not boldly be asked, what parallel to such an outline as this can be supplied by any of the sacred books preserved among any other of the races of the world? So far, then, the office and work of the Old Testament, as presented to us by its own contents, is without a compeer among the old religions. It deals with the case of man as a whole. It covers all time. It is alike adapted to every race and region of the earth.

And how, according to the purport of the Old Testament, may that case best be summed up? In these words: it is a history first of sin, and next of redemption.

Our Lord has emphatically said, "They that be whole need not a physician, but they that are sick" (Matt. 9 : 12); and this saying goes to the root of the whole matter. Is there, or is there not, a deep disease in the world, which overflows it like a deluge, and submerges, in a great degree, the fruit-bearing capacities of our nature? Are we, as a race, whole, or are we sick, and profoundly sick?

I think that, to an impartial eye and to a thoughtful mind, it must seem strange that there should be a doubt as to the answer to be given to this question. It seems more easy to comprehend the mental action of those whom the picture of the actual world, as it is unrolled before them, tempts, by its misery, guilt, and shame, into doubt of the being of God, than of persons who can view that picture, and who cannot fail to observe the dominant part borne by man in determining its character, and yet can make it a subject of question whether man is or is not morally diseased. Veils may have been cast between our vision and the truth of the case by the relative excellence of some select human spirits; by the infinitely varied degrees and forms of the universal malady; by the exaggerations and the narrownesses of outlying schools of theology; and lastly by the remarkable circumstance, that races, above all the extraordinarily gifted race of the ancient Greeks, have lived on into large developments of art, of intellect, and of material power, without creating or retaining any strong conception of moral evil, under the only aspect which reveals its deeper features; that aspect, namely,

which presents it to the mind as a departure from
the supreme and perfect standard, the will of God.
But these disguises are pierced through and
through by ever so little of calm reflection. We
can conceive how generations, blinded by long
abuse to the character of moral evil, could well
contrive to blink and pass by the question. But
we, who inherit the Christian tradition, ethical as it
is not less than dogmatic, cannot, I think, deny the
prevalence, perhaps not even the preponderance, of
moral evil in the world, without some subtle and
preliminary process of degeneracy in our own
habit of mind. We shall find that, in renouncing
that tradition, we return to a conception which
admitted to be evil only that which was so vio-
lently in conflict with the comfort of human society
as to require condemnation and repression by its
self-preserving laws. The gap between these two
conceptions of our state, the one furnished by disordered nature, the other by divine grace, is immeasurable.

And I think it will not be denied that, in describing vividly the fact of sin in the world, the Scriptures of the Old Testament proceed upon lines, which have also been clearly drawn in the general consciousness at least of the Christian ages. This sense of sin, which lies like a huge black pall over the entire face of humanity, has been all along the point of departure for every preacher, writer, and thinker within the Hebrew or the Christian fold. And it is the gradual and palpable decline of it, in the literature and society of to-day, that is the darkest among all the signs now overshadowing what is in some respects the bright and hopeful promise of the future.

Nor can any one, who believes in the existence of God, wonder that sin is described as a deviation from the order of nature, as a foreign element, not belonging to the original creation of divine design, but introduced into it by special causes. At this point we come to what is known as the Fall of man, and to the narration of that fall as it is given in the Book of Genesis.

For the moment, let us simply note what is

unquestionable: that the Old Testament, from the beginning to the end, deals with the conception of sin, and of its opposite, as forming one side of its special work, and in this capital respect entirely differs from all the other documents of profane antiquity.

Against the narrative of the Fall, the negative criticism has been actively employed. The action ascribed to the serpent is declared to be incredible; the punishment of Adam, disproportioned to the offense, which consisted only in an action not essentially immoral, but only wrong because it was prohibited; the punishment of all mankind, for the fault of one, is denounced as intolerably unjust.

Now let us set entirely aside, for the moment, the form of this narrative, and consider only its substance. Let us deal with it as if it were a parable; in which the severance between the form and the substance is acknowledged and familiar. In proposing this, I do not mean to make on my own part any definitive surrender of the form as it stands, or any admission adverse to it. There is, it may be, high and early Christian authority even for surrendering the form. I only seek to pass within it, and to put the meaning and substance of the Fall Story upon their trial.

In this relation, we find a certain aggregate of objects, which we are now asked to treat as if they were simply significant figures. There are presented to us the man, with the woman, in a garden; the serpent, with its faculty of speech and subtle thought; the two trees, of knowledge and of life respectively; a fruit forbidden by divine command, but eaten in defiance of it; and, after certain reproofs and intimations, ejectment from the garden in consequence. In this ejectment is involved a great deterioration of outward state. But it is not a matter of outward state alone. A deterioration of inward nature is also exhibited, in the derangement of its functions. A new sense of shame bears witness to the revolt[1] of its lower against its higher

---

[1] See Delitzsch, who, in accordance with patristic authorities, writes as follows: "The first consequence of the Fall was shame. The nakedness of mankind is no longer the appearance of their innocence. Their corporeity has fallen from the dominion of the spirit.

elements; and, for the first time, exhibits it to us as a disordered, and therefore a dishonored thing. Together with all this, there is the outline of a promise that, from among the progeny of the fallen pair a Deliverer, born of woman, shall arise, who at the cost of personal suffering, shall strike at the very seat of intelligence in the creature set before us as the living emblem of evil, and so shall destroy its power. In this relation, on the one hand, many modern objectors have discovered an intolerable folly, and, on the other hand, the Christian tradition of eighteen centuries has acknowledged a profound philosophy, and a painful and faithful delineation of an indisputable truth.

Now what is the substance conveyed under this form? The Almighty has brought into existence a pair of human beings. He has laid upon them a law of obedience, not to a Decalogue or a code, setting forth things essentially good, and the reverse of them, but simply to himself; and as

Their beholding has become a sensuous imagining, and the flesh excites their fleshly passions " (" Old Testament History of Redemption," p. 23. Edinburg: Clark, 1881).

uttered by him, to a rule of feeding and not feeding. The point, at which this representation first
brings into view an independent or objective law,
lies in the prohibition to feed upon a tree which
imparts the knowledge of good and evil. That is
to say, the pair, as they then were, were forbidden
to aspire to the possession of that knowledge. The
dispensation under which for the time they lived,
was a dispensation of pure obedience.

The question whether this was reasonable or
unreasonable cannot be answered upon abstract
grounds, but resolves itself into another question,
whether it was appropriate or inappropriate to the
state of the beings thus addressed, and to their
relation towards Him who gave the command.
Some may assume that Adam was what so great a
writer as Milton has represented him to be—

"For contemplation he and valor formed," [1]

and not for contemplation only, but for intricate
inquiry and debate on subjects such as tax all the
powers of a cultivated intellect. And indeed, if we

[1] "Paradise Lost," IV. 297.

take the developed man, such as we know him in Christian and civilized society, it seems plain that to lay down for him a law of life which did not include the consideration of essential good and evil, would not only stunt and starve his faculties, but would shock his moral sense.

It may be said that a single act of disobedience, even after full warning, could not so deprave a character as reasonably to entail upon the offender a total change of condition.

Now, I observe, in the first place, that this objection, so stated, unwarrantably assumes that the same rule must govern the case of the developed, and of the undeveloped or infant man. The effect of a single action upon the entire being may, for all we know, have been far greater when the moral organism was simple and homogeneous, than it would be now when that organism has become highly complete, elaborate, and diversified.

Further, I would observe that the school of critics which is apt to take this objection is the very school which, utterly rejecting the literal form of the narrative, is bound to look at it as parable. When so contemplated, its lesson is that rebellion, deliberate and wilful (and this is nothing less), against just and sovereign authority, fundamentally changes for the worse the character of the rebel. It places him in a new category of motive and action, in which the repetition of the temptation ordinarily begets the repetition of the sin; and from this point of view it is mercy, not cruelty, which meets this deterioration of character, not with a final and judicial abandonment, but with a deterioration and reduction of state, such as to teach the lesson of retribution, and to serve as an emphatic warning against further sin.

Scripture will lie before us in a true perspective, when we come to understand that everywhere the will of God is in accord with the righteousness of God. So that what is promised or inflicted by command is also, under an invariable law, promised or inflicted by self-acting consequence, according to the constitution of the nature we have received. Religion and philosophy thus join hands,

and never part them. When, therefore, we are
told that Adam after his sin was shut out from
Eden, we are not entitled to say, how hard that he
could not be allowed to return, and then perhaps
to amend. What is inflicted as penalty from without is acted and suffered in character within. There
is no record of the repentance of Adam; and even
if there were, yet repentance is not innocence.
There must be a remedial process; and, until that
process has been faithfully accomplished, the anterior state and habit of mind cannot be resumed.

I do not argue with those who say this is a bad
constitution of things, under which sin engenders
sinfulness; some wiser one might surely have been
devised. This is to say, "Had I been in the
Creator's place, I would have managed the business
of creation better." It is for us not merely as
Christians, but as men of sense, to eschew speculations which, not to mention their overweening
presumption, even their authors must see to be
wholly devoid of practical effect. We shall do
better to assume the great moral laws, and the

constitution of our nature, as ultimate facts, as boundaries which it is futile to attempt to overstep.

To my mind, then, the narrative of the Fall is in accordance with the laws of a grand and comprehensive philosophy, and the objections taken to it are the product of narrower and shallower modes of thought. Introducing us to Adamic man in his first stage of existence, a stage not of savagery but of childhood, it exhibits to us the gigantic drama of his evolution in its opening. In the Paradise of the Book of Genesis, it reduces to a practical form that noble legend of the Golden Age, which was cherished especially in prehistoric Greece. It wisely teaches us to look to misused freewill as the source of all the sin, and mainly of the accompanying misery, which still overflow the world, and environ human life like a moral deluge. It shows us man in his childhood, no less responsible for disobedience to simple command, than man in his manhood for contravention of those laws of essential right and wrong, which remain now and forever clothed with the majesty of divine authority. It teaches us how sin begets sin; how the rebellion of the creature against the Creator was at once followed by the rebellion of the creature's lower appetites against his higher mind and will. It impresses upon us that sin is not like the bird lightly flying past us in an atmosphere, which closes on it as it goes, and carries no trace of its passage. It alters for the worse the very being of the man that acts it, and leaves to him a deteriorated essence. This he in turn, by the inexorable laws of his constitution, transmits to his descendants; and this again in them exhibits, variably, yet on the whole with clear and even glaring demonstration, the evil bias, which it has received; and which, in the course of nature, it retains until it shall be happily corrected and renewed by those remedial means, which it was the office of the Old Testament to foreshadow, and of the New to establish. Everywhere, then, in this narrative of the Fall, we find that it is instinct with the highest principles of the moral and judicial order.

For the present I pass by the Flood (Gen. 6-8),

10

and the Dispersion (Gen. 10), which may be most conveniently considered in connection with what is termed profane history; and I touch next upon the call of Abraham.

This call imports the selection of a peculiar and separate family, which was afterwards to grow into a people. They were to be in a special degree the subjects of God's care, the guardians of his Word, and the vehicles of his promises. Of all great and distinctive chapters in the Biblical history of the human race since Paradise, we have here perhaps the greatest and the most distinctive.

The selection of a family may be regarded from many points of view.

When sin had come into the world, it developed itself in the forms of infirmity and of apostasy: if it be allowable to describe rudely by these general terms the forms of character which distinguished the race of Cain from the race of Seth. What we see of the former is, as described in Genesis 4: 16-24, its rapid advance, and apparently its marked precedence, in arts and powers. It disappears entirely with the story of the Flood; and we are left to infer that it may have had a principal share in calling down that great retribution inflicted upon revolt from God.

After the Deluge, in the time of Peleg, fifth from Noah, selection again appears, and is carried down in Genesis 11 to Abraham, from whom an unbroken thread runs onward into the period when the chosen family had become a chosen nation.

This choice of a particular family or race may be advantageously contrasted with the heathen method of selection or preference, by the deification of individuals. Of the first, it is obvious that it reached over all time; that in this way it tended to assert the unity, alike of the divine revelation and of the Adamic race; and that it was never exclusive,[1] as it from the first (not to mention other proofs) invited to partake of its benefits the

[1] That is to say, never according to the Mosaic law as contained in the Old Testament. After the return from Babylon, the ruling authorities among the Jews gave a greatly enhanced stringency to the law of intermarriage. See Graetz, "History of the Jews" (1891), Vol. I., pp. 398–401.

"stranger" with whom it had come into contact. The rival method of deification broke communion rather than established it, and was based on no rational principle of choice. It was corrupt as well as arbitrary; for the deified were not the best. But what I would here chiefly press is, that the continuous selection of a family was a bar to deification, because deification was essentially founded on individualities; instead of that headship in series, the members of which presented to humanity, as its chiefs, a lineage. Of this lineage every one had its destiny as it were locked into that of the rest by an essential parity. This kind of selection did not favor idolatry, like the other, but, on the contrary, built up a wall against it; for it was not possible effectively to deify a race. And so it came about, as we have seen, that, even when idolatry invaded and possessed the people, it never tainted the traditional religion.

This selection of Abraham and his progeny, if we speak after the manner of men, we might perhaps describe as follows: The original attempt to plant a species upon our planet, which should be endowed with the faculty of free-will, but should always direct that will to good, had been frustrated through sin; and the tainted progeny had, after a trial of many generations, been destroyed by the Deluge. In the descendants of Noah, man was renewed upon a far larger scale. Different branches of the race (Gen. 10) were sent, or were allowed to go forth, and to people different portions of the earth, each carrying with them different gifts, and different vocations according to those gifts; the notes of which, in various prominent cases, we cannot fail to discern written large upon the page of history. After a brief period, choice was made not of a nation, but of a person, namely, Abraham, who with his descendants became the subject of a special training. He and his posterity lived, according to the record in the Bible, not like other men generally, dependent upon the exercise of their natural faculties alone, but with the advantage from time to time, and with the continuing responsibility, of supernatural command and visitation.

But this remarkable promotion to a higher form of life did not invest them with any arbitrary or selfish prerogative.   On the contrary, as the legislation of Moses was distinguished from other ancient codes by its liberal and likewise elaborate care for the stranger; so also, from the very outset, and before the family could blossom into the nation, nay, even in the very person of Abraham, the gift imparted to him was declared to be given for the behoof of mankind at large.   "In thee and in thy seed shall all the families of the earth be blessed" (Gen. 28: 14).   The prerogative of the Jew was, from its very inception, bound up with the future elevation of the Gentile.

This divine election doubtless carried with it the duty and the means of reaching a higher level of moral life than prevailed among the surrounding Asiatic nations.   These nations, sharing with the chosen race a common infirmity and deterioration of nature, differed in this, that they at once carried the reflection of their own sinfulness into their creed respecting the unseen, and made religion itself a direct instrument of corruption. Yet those, whom we call the patriarchs, were not exempted from the general degeneracy of morals; and even Abraham, the general strain of whose life appears to have been so simple and devout, on going down into Egypt to escape from famine, advisedly exposed his wife to the risk of an adulterous connection with the king of the country, lest, if she were known to be his wife, his personal safety should be compromised. On the moral standing of the nation sprung from Abraham, as compared with that of contemporary races, there will be more to say hereafter. Meantime, it may be observed that the sins and follies of the favored people, as well as of their priests and rulers, are told in the narrative frankly, and without attempting to excuse them. This frankness of narration extends also to the calamities which befell the Israelites; and, as an evidence of the integrity of the Hebrew penmen, it suggests a presumption that such plain speaking, in the face of national and ancestral self-love, is, to say the least, highly in accordance with the belief that the record generally was framed under special guidance from above.

The selection of Abraham and his posterity was at the least a boon to some, while it was a privation to none.   In its immediate effect, it withdrew nothing from the nations outside the Hebrew pale.   It bestowed, indeed, upon the parallel line of Ishmael a preferential but inferior blessing.   This dispensation, however, it is no part of the present purpose to consider, further than to say that the Mohammedan religion may be regarded, in its conflict with the idolatry which it first confronted, and again in the present day among the tribes of Western Africa, as having been, if not permanently yet for a time, the communication of a relative good.   And the Old Testament abounds with passages which demonstrate the care, and even the special care, of the Almighty for nations other than the Jews.[1]

But the object, which now demands our attention, is the promise of a blessing in and by the seed of

[1] See, for example, the two first chapters of Amos, and the whole book of Jonah.

Abraham to all the nations of the earth. The first-fruits of this blessing may be said to have been perceived in the translation of the books of the Old Testament into Greek during and after the third century before the Advent. At the time when the language of the Greeks was mounting to its supremacy, in the East through the conquests of Alexander the Great, and in the West through appreciation by the Roman and Italian genius, in some respects allied to their own, the Greek race itself was on its decline, both as to its intellect and as to its practical energy. Such a decline may, perhaps, have rendered the world more receptive of the influences, which the substance of the Hebrew books was calculated to exercise.

There can hardly be a doubt that, among all the forms of Hellenic thought exhibited in the different schools of philosophy, that of the Stoics was the highest in respect of its conception of the Deity, of its emancipation from idolatry, and of its capacity of moral elevation. In the hands of Seneca, of Epictetus, and of Marcus Aurelius, Stoic ideas attained so high a level as to have been used by some in disparagement of the exclusive claim of the gospel to the promulgation of truths powerful enough to regenerate the world. Without asserting that the early Stoics derived their inspiration through the Greek version, called the Septuagint, from the Hebrew Scriptures, it may be observed that, as a matter of fact, philosophy rose to its highest level through the Stoics at a time when the Greek mind was declining; and further, that Stoicism made its first appearance, and began its advance at the epoch when those Scriptures had become accessible. Also it arose and flourished not in Greece itself, but at points such as Citium, in countries such as Pontus, in schools of learning such as Alexandria, which were seats of Jewish resort and influence.[1] For my own part I cannot but incline to believe that both the translated Old

[1] See "Encyclopædia Britannica." 9th ed. Art. "Stoics." It states that " the school is mainly to be considered as the first-fruits of that interaction between West and East, which followed the conquests of Alexander. Zeno was of Phœnician descent; Cyprus, Silicia, Syria, the main countries of its origin. Citium, Alexandria, Heraclea,

Testament, and the silently diffused ether, so to speak, of Christianity, in the Roman atmosphere, had to do with the high moral elevation of the later Stoicism.

It was an advance of a different order, and of a wider range towards the fulfilment of the Abrahamic promises, when the Apostles, charged with the commission of our Lord, went forth into all the world, and preached the gospel to every creature (Mark 16 : 15). Then, indeed, an enginery was set at work, capable of coping with the whole range of the mischiefs brought into the world by sin, and of completely redeeming the human being from its effects, and consecrating our nature to duty and to God. It is impossible here to do so much as even to skirt this vast subject. But at once these three things may be said as to the development, through the gospel, of the Abrahamic promise. First, that in a vast aggregate of genuine

Pontus, were prominent among the places furnishing and rearing its teachers. Most of the Stoics were from lands of Hellenistic (as distinct from Hellenic) civilization. It was the growth of the Hellenized East." Further, see Huidekoper's " Judaism at Rome," New York, 1877.

believers, the recovery of the divine image has been effectual, and the mainspring of their being has been set right before their quitting the world, by the dedication of the will to God. Secondly, that the social results of the change have been beneficial and immense, in the restriction of wars, in the abolition of horrible practices publicly sanctioned; in the recognition of essential rights; in the elevation of woman (whose case most and best of all represents the case of right as against force); in the mitigation of selfish and cruel laws; in the refinement of manners; in the utter proscription of all extreme forms of sin; and in the public acknowledgment of standards of action nearer to the true. I may perhaps add in the abolition of slave-trading and of slavery, and in the law of nations, and the mitigating rules of war. Thirdly, that Christendom is at this moment undeniably the prime and central power of the world, and still bears, written upon its front, the mission to subdue it. In point of force and onward impulsion, it stands without a rival, while every other widely spread religion is in decline. Critical, indeed, are the movements which affect it from within. Vast are the deductions which on every side are to be made from the fulness of the divine promises, when we try to measure their results in the world of facts. Indefinitely slow, and hard to trace in detail, as may be, like a glacier in descent, the march of the times, the Christianity of to-day has, in relation to the world non-Christian, an amount of ascendency such as it has never before possessed; and, if only it can sufficiently retain its inward consistency, the sole remaining question seems to be as to the time, the circumstances, and the rate of its further, perhaps of its final, conquests.

I know that it is far beyond the scope of a few pages such as these to make good in detail the claims of the great Abrahamic promise. Still, I think that even what has been said may in some measure suffice for the purpose which I have immediately in view. That purpose is to establish in outline the strictly exceptional character of the books of the Old Testament; and with this aim to show that they bear upon them the stamp of a comprehensiveness which concerns, which penetrates, and which also envelops the history of the world as a whole. The promise, given to Abraham nearly two thousand years before the Advent, finds its correlative marks in the general train of subsequent history. These marks demonstrate that it was given by a divine foreknowledge. And if so, then the venerable record in which it is enshrined surely seems here, as it did in the Creation Story, to carry the seal and signature of a divine authorship.

Now let us consider from another point of view the selection of the Hebrew race, and the peculiar standing of the Mosaic legislation, so intimately allied with the whole of its singularly checkered fortunes. And, in order to effect something towards ascertaining what was probably the cause determining the divine selection and procedure, we may do well first to refer to some aims which might at first sight have been thought probable. It might conceivably have been the design to provide a complete theology; or to reward with honor, wealth, and power a peculiarly virtuous people, whose moral conduct was to be of a nature likely to make them an edifying and attractive example to the nations of the earth. Human speculation might have been forward to anticipate that one or both of these aims might have been contemplated by a plan so exceptional as the selection and isolation of one particular line and people. But the facts appear to show that any such anticipation would have been entirely mistaken.

By a complete theology, I mean simply such a theology as would confront and make provision for all the leading facts of the moral situation. Among these a prominent place had from the date of the first traditions been given to the entrance of sin into the world, and to the promise of redemption from its power. Now it is evident that there was no attempt, in the legislation of the Pentateuch, at this theological completeness. Its theology is summed up in clear declarations of the being of God, of his great attributes, and of duty and love to him and to our neighbor. With these are directly associated, in the Decalogue, the main items of man's duty to other men, and, both there and elsewhere, a doctrine of rewards and punishments. The race also inherited the narrative of what is termed in Christian theology the Fall of Man. This, however, was part of the anterior tradition; and, though implied in the Mosaic system, was neither directly set forth in its terms, nor made a common subject of allusion in the historic books, however it may have been involved in the sacrificial system.

But these rewards and punishments are of a temporal nature; and the Mosaic legislation is thought to give no indication of a future state, or of an Underworld. This is the more remarkable, because, not to mention other indications, even the earliest chapters of Genesis, although they usually contain but the merest outline of history, are not without such indication (Gen. 5 : 24). Enoch, at the end of his 365 years, "was not, for God took him."

These remarkable words are substituted for the formula given in the cases of the other patriarchs, whose record closes with the phrase, "and he died" (Gen. 5 : 5, and *passim*). Here there seems to be a clear manifestation of the state into which Enoch is declared to have entered, without passing through the gate of death. It is indeed obvious to remark that, under the Mosaic system, long life was the reward of virtue, and that unless a future life was believed in, the translation of Enoch would have been the record of a punishment inflicted on him for his superior goodness.

Again, we now know, from the Egyptian Book of the Dead and otherwise, that the religious system of that country not only included, but was greatly based upon, the conception of a future life. It seems absolutely impossible that the Israelites, even had they not been aware of it already, could have dwelt for many generations in the land of Egypt without coming to know of it. Our Lord himself affirms that they knew it in his time (Matt. 22 : 32 ; Mark 12 : 27). And we have it

11

presented to us in the Psalms (for example, Psalms 16 : 10; 49 : 15), which exhibit the interior and spiritual life of chosen souls.   There are other indications to the same effect.   I have stated the instances of belief in a future state among the early Hebrews somewhat more largely in an article published in the Nineteenth Century for October, 1891.   But the argument is capable of still wider development.

It has, perhaps, been too much the practice to assume that the Mosaic law is to be regarded as an enlargement of the patriarchal religion.   Without doubt it is at least a very large and important supplement to that religion.   But a supplement differs from an enlarged and reconstructed edition : it is less, as well as more.   It need not, and indeed it hardly can, contain everything contained in that to which it is a supplement.   Here is a great and vital particular, in which the Mosaic law cannot be said even to have republished the patriarchal religion; and which both preceded and survived the law, yet did not find a place in it.   Accordingly, among the Jews of the Advent, the school which most rigidly adhered to the letter of the law, namely, that of the Sadducees (Acts 23 : 8), denied the future state, and held "that there is no resurrection, neither angel nor spirit."

We are not, therefore, to suppose that Israel was without the hope of a future life, which St. Peter on the Day of Pentecost himself demonstrated out of the sixteenth Psalm (Acts 2 : 25); but only to perceive that the Mosaic legislation was limited to its proper purpose; that, namely, of setting apart a nation from the rest of mankind, and providing it with peculiar means and guarantees for the fulfilment of its mission as a nation. It erected a walled precinct, within which the ancient belief of the fathers was to find shelter and to thrive, while it was wofully dwindling and perishing among all the kindred nations of the world. It supplied an impregnable home for personal religion. But personal religion, taken by itself, is conspicuously weak in the means of transmission from age to age. The sons of Eli were wicked persons, and the evil

Manasseh at once succeeds the pious Hezekiah. It is not without the aid of fixed and solid institutions, which take hold upon masses of men collectively, and unite them in a far-reaching chain, that the sacred fire is kept alive among us.   Hence our Lord did not merely teach his holy precepts, and fulfil his divine career in his own person, but founded his Church on earth, to carry his work onwards even to the day of doom.   And hence, under the guidance of the Most High, Moses was commissioned to establish a system which, without being in itself complete, provided for the double purpose, first, of building up a fortress (so to call it) within whose wall true spiritual religion might in singular fulness flourish and abound; and, secondly, of establishing a firmly knit national system of doctrine and worship, intended to secure the permanent purity of belief in the one self-existent God, and the continuing practice of a ritual which set forth in act the existence of sin, and made intelligible and familiar to the people at large some need of deliverance from it by reconciliation.   And so, through the long ages from the Exodus to the Advent, there lived on the two systems together, distinct but accordant. The one was the religion of interior devotion, powerfully upheld and stimulated, as occasion offered, by the Prophets, and continually exercised and developed in the public ritual by the Psalms. The other was the religion of exterior worship. This ritual was full of significance. It had a command over the entire people. It was incorporated in public laws and institutions, and was associated at every point with the national life. And these outer means so operated as to exempt the higher and interior treasure from the risks inherent in dependence on short-lived individual fervor, and provided a secure vehicle for its transmission from age to age.

We have in the institution of the prophetic schools the setting forth of a profound lesson, which reminds us that the Mosaic system was alike in itself necessary, and of itself insufficient.

From another, and possibly even more commanding, point of view, we perceive the insufficiency of Mosaism to fill up worthily the outlines of the divine dispensations. Sin, in the form of disobedience to divine command, had entered into the world, and had utterly marred the fair order which, at the outset, the Almighty had noted in his Creation. The mischief was not left to stand alone; and the promise of a Redeemer from it was immediately bestowed. Thus far, the Mosaic system helps us; yet, in helping us, it surely prompts us to look beyond itself. By its system of sacrifice, it threw into distinct relief the idea that offense had been committed, and that our standing was not upright before God. Now with this were associated in Genesis the further ideas that from this offense there would be a way of reconciliation and recovery, and that this way would be found in a member of the human race, a portion of the seed of the woman. On these further ideas Mosaism so far threw light, that it pointed through sacrifice to pardon; but it added nothing of force or clearness to the original promise that this recovery should be wrought out in and through a Redeemer having the form and the nature of man. This prophecy of the Incarnation, though a vital portion of the ancient tradition of the patriarchs, did not receive any supplement or new enforcement from the construction of the Hebrew laws and institutions. It remained, and it propagated itself, mainly in the Psalms and in the Prophets, while its root was pre-Mosaic. Some rays of the light of that promise may perhaps be traced, outside the Hebrew precinct, in particular traditions of the heathen world. There may be vestiges of it, for example, in that close vital association between Deity and humanity, which marked the Greek or Olympian religion; but which, as the fundamental conception of sin more and more faded away, lost by degrees all its moral force. Mosaism did essential and infinite service in deeply sculpturing (so to speak) the idea of sin in the human consciousness; but it was not favorable to that theanthropy, or union of the divine and human, of which the human side had been so strongly foreshadowed in the original charter of redemption. Perhaps by the rigid prohibition of images, which was so necessary for its direct purpose, it rather tended to widen the distance at which man stood as a being worshipping his Maker.   Already idolatry, such as prevailed in the East, was associated with the human form, and the necessity of shutting out that idolatry may have carried with it, in this respect, a certain religious incompleteness as a consequence, which becomes manifest to us when we stand, as Christians, in the full light of the Incarnation.

I now come to the second supposition; and I ask whether the selection of the Hebrew race was grounded on their moral superiority.   Within narrow limits, the answer would be affirmative.   They were appointed to purge and to possess the land of Canaan on account of the terrible and loathsome iniquities of its inhabitants.   The nations, whom they were to subdue, had reached that latest stage of sensual iniquity, which respects neither God nor nature.   The sensual appetite within man, which rebelled against him when he had rebelled against God, had in Canaan enthroned its lawlessness as law, and its bestial indulgences had become recognized, normal, nay more, even religious if not obligatory. And there are those in the present day who, admitting the facts, find in them a subject of pleasurable contemplation, as if they simply exhibited an innocent and free exercise of natural propensities. The propensities were due indeed to nature; but only to nature in a condition of disorder and disease.

The vicious practices of these nations, indicated rather than described in the Old Testament, and veiled, apparently for decency's sake, in the translations, are too sadly attested by the character of the remains, which, in later times, archæology has recovered from their hiding-places. They are also attested by the poems of Homer. In these poems, the Phœnicians represent Syrian religion, and we find the goddess Aphroditè, whose debased worship it seems plain that they were gradually importing into Greece, to have stood for a symbol of lawless lust in combination with the highest power of animal attraction. This is "Ashtoreth, the goddess of the Zidonians" (1 Kings 11 : 5, 33), to whom both Solomon and the people bowed down themselves.

I find it much more difficult to answer the question, whether the Hebrew race were planted in the land of promise, which flowed with milk and honey, by reason of, or in connection with, their moral superiority to the nations of the world taken universally. It is, down to the present day, extremely difficult to make any trustworthy estimate of the comparative moral standing even of any two contemporary peoples. It may be admitted that the form of human nature has with the modern conditions grown far more manifold and complex. But, on the other side, in answering the question I have just put, we have the difficulty not only of remoteness in time, but, as to most cases, of extreme scantiness of information.

I shall assume that the mass of the children of Israel at large were trained mainly by Mosaism, and little in comparison by the more highly spiritual tradition conserved and enshrined within it. Speaking of the nation generally, we may consider that the Old Testament gives us more than a sketch, if less than a picture, of their social and moral state. I am aware of only one other race with respect to which we have any account possessing a tolerable fulness. That is the race of the Achaian Greeks, painted with marvellous truthfulness, and not less remarkable completeness, by Homer. The poet describes the manners of one generation; the books of the Old Testament, say from Abraham to the Captivity, range over many. Still, numerous as these are, they present a considerable unity of color. I carefully reserve the case of that inner and elect circle among the Hebrews, to whom we owe the possession down to this day of inestimable spiritual treasures. But comparing, as well as I am able, ordinary or average life, among the ordinary Hebrews on the one side, and the ordinary Greeks of Homer (whom I take to have lived long after Moses, but considerably before the age of David), on the other, I cannot discern that these last were in a moral sense inferior.

I am sensible, however, that in such a proposition as has just been uttered there must be, to the general reader, some appearance of paradox; and likewise that such an appearance will not be effectually removed by reference to the Scriptural complaints of the stiff neck, or the hard heart, of the Israelites. I must therefore make further endeavors to get at the truth of the case before us.

I do not feel that even the patriarchal history is designed to convey to us the idea that the privileged race stood uniformly at a great moral elevation, as compared with other and ordinary portions of mankind.

The subject is a painful one, and I shall not dilate upon its details. But it seems undeniable that, in the history of the selected line, we find from time to time the development of wickedness in its extreme forms. Such are the sin of Onan (Gen. 38 : 8, 9), the incest of the daughters of Lot (Gen. 19 : 32), and the brutal insensibility of Ham, the son of Noah, to the claims of natural decency (Gen. 9 : 22).

Nor are the women exempt, as we learn from the incest devised and effected by Tamar (Gen. 38:6-30). And the wife of Lot cast a yearning look on the hell of Sodom (Gen. 19 : 26). The first three cases, and the last, are not in the line of the ultimate succession; but Pharez, the son of Tamar, is the recorded ancestor of King David and his descendants (Matt. 1 : 3-5). Now, among the Achaian Greeks of Homer we find a sensitive delicacy, altogether peculiar, as to all exposure of the person. Nor is there anywhere in the Poems, among the Achaian Greeks, any extreme form of sensual indulgence. Among the Hellenized Bœotian immigrants from the East, that is from the Syrian coast, there occurred at an early stage of their history in the Peninsula, a case of incest;[1] but this was always regarded by the indigenous tradition as involuntary, and, what is more, a curse clave on account of it to the race of Kadmos, and brought about its early extinction.

While incest is thus regarded as a monstrous

[1] Od., XI. 271-274.

perversion of nature among the Greeks, there are in the Homeric poems, as I think, sufficiently clear indications that it was practiced without shame among the Phœnicians,[1] the coast neighbors of Syria, and partners with that country in manners, if not also probably in race.

Let us now turn to two others among the great moral constituents of human character, and compare the cases in point of humanity as against cruelty, and of truth as against fraud.

Let us take the two instances, first of the deceit practiced by Jacob upon his brother Esau and his father Isaac; secondly, of the base and unnatural conduct of the sons of Jacob towards their brother Joseph. As there is nothing recorded in favor of the Homeric or Achaian Greeks which approaches in moral beauty to the forgiveness freely accorded by Joseph, so there is nothing recorded against them which so wickedly tramples down the laws of nature, as those flagrant iniquities of the sons of Jacob, to which attention has just been called.

[1] Od., X. 7, and less flagrantly, VII. 64-68.

The conduct of the suitors of Penelopè in the Odyssey, and the actions of Paris (a foreigner), supply the worst exhibitions of human nature which come before us in the Poems. Both there and in the Old Testament retribution follows guilt, but what I now speak of is the depth of guilt, not its treatment. There is nowhere in Homer a case, between relatives, of deceit like that of Jacob, or of cruelty like that of his sons.

When we come to the Palestinian period, it would appear that the Israelites were subjected to a force and diversity of temptations, such as perhaps no people ever had to encounter. Successful war had stimulated their vindictive passions. Triumph everywhere had waited on their arms. They were entitled to esteem themselves the directly chosen ministers of God. They were likely to regard the heathen, among whom they came, with hatred and contempt. They passed from a life, wandering, uncertain and ill supplied, to settlement and to abundance. The temples or emblems of seductive lust everywhere met their eyes; and the vile example, by which they were solicited in the mass and in detail, pretended plausibly to hallow itself by close association with religion. There is scarcely an evil passion that finds entrance into the human breast which was not powerfully stirred by the circumstances of the Israelitish conquest. We find in the sacred text indications of the severity of some of their temptations. Take, for instance, Deuteronomy 6 : 10-16; and again in 31 : 20 it is written,

> "For when I shall have brought them into the land which I sware unto their fathers, that floweth with milk and honey; and they shall have eaten and filled themselves, and waxen fat; then will they turn unto other gods and serve them, and provoke me, and break my covenant."

The general indication seems to be first the perpetuation of a chosen seed, at the very heart of the nation, high in the knowledge of interior religion; secondly, a decided ethical superiority of the Hebrew line over the Asiatic nations in their neighborhood; as indeed it was from Asia that the extremes of corruption flowed into the Greek Peninsula in the earliest historic times. Yet the loveliest picture of womanhood in all the early sacred books is that of Ruth; and Ruth was of the children of Moab, who was the incestuous offspring of one of the daughters of Lot (Gen. 19 : 36, 37).

Humanity, or mercy, is certainly not the strong point of the Achaian Greeks. With them not only no sacredness, but little value, attached to human life; and the loss of it stirs no sympathy unless it be associated with beauty, valor, patriotism, or other esteemed characteristics. Yet here, again, the forms of evil are less extreme. We do not find, even in the stern, relentless vengeance of Odysseus on his enemies, or in the passionate, almost frenzied, wish of Achilles, that nature would permit what it forbade, namely, to devour the hated foe who had slain his bosom-friend, a form of cruelty and brutality so savage as is recorded in the case of the Levite with his wife and concubine at Gibeah, and of the war which followed it (Judg. 19-21).

The temptations of lust were even more formida-

12

ble than those of cruelty and revenge. According to the sacred text, this danger was foreseen from the first; and the very earliest Mosaic legislation (Exod. 22 : 16), after that of the Commandments, begins to denounce a portion of the indescribable practices which were rife among the older occupiers of the promised land. It was subsequently carried into further particulars, and we know that, down the whole course of the historic period before the Captivity, the filthy idolatry not only encircled the chosen people, but at times so invaded it, as to reduce to a remnant among the ten tribes the untainted portion of the community, the true worshippers of God. Even pious monarchs were sometimes afraid to destroy its constituted and, in a perverse sense, consecrated emblems.

On the other hand, we must not view the case of the earliest Greeks in the spirit of optimism. War and its devastations were with them habitual and almost normal; property was little respected; cunning, as well as skill, was sometimes held in honor.

Yet it remains a broad and indisputable truth that honor and truth, as well as valor, were prevailingly respected, that family ties were very sacred, that the law of nature was simply and profoundly revered, and that the extreme forms of vice and sin, the widest and most hopeless departures from the law of God, are nowhere to be found in any of their forms.

Enough has perhaps been said to show that we are by no means permitted to claim as a thing demonstrable a great moral superiority for the Hebrew line generally over the whole of the historically known contemporary races. This, however, leaves ample room for the belief that there was an interior circle, known to us by its fruits in the Psalter, and also in the prophetic books, of a morality and sanctity altogether superior to what was to be found elsewhere, and due rather to the pre-Mosaic, than to the Mosaic, religion of the race. But it remains to answer with reverence the question, Why, if not for a distinctly superior morality, nor as a full religious provision for the whole wants of man, *why* was the race chosen, as a race, to receive the promises, to guard the oracles, and eventually, to fulfil the hopes, of the great Redemption?

The answer may, I believe, be conveyed in moderate compass. The design of the Almighty, as we everywhere find, was to prepare the human race, by a varied and a prolonged education, for the arrival of the greatest among the epochs of history. The immediate purposes of the Abrahamic selection may have been to appoint, for the one necessary task of preserving in the world the fundamental bases of religion, a race, which possessed qualifications for that paramount end decisively surpassing those of all other races. We may easily indicate two of these fundamental bases. The first was the belief in one God. The second was the knowledge that mankind at large had departed from his laws; without which knowledge how should they welcome a Deliverer, whose object it was to bring them back? It may be stated with confidence that among the dominant races of the world the belief in one God was speedily destroyed by polytheism, and the idea of sin faded gradually but utterly away. Is it audacious to say that what was wanted was a race so endowed with the qualities of masculine tenacity and persistency, as to hold over in safe custody these all-important truths until that fulness of time, when, by and with them, the complete design of the Almighty would be revealed to the world? Superior fitness for the performance of this indispensable but very special function may not have implied by necessary consequence a universal superiority in moral qualities. A long experience of trials beyond all example has proved since the Advent that the Jews, in this one essential quality, have all along surpassed every other people upon earth. A marvellous and glorious experience has shown how, among their ancestors before the Advent, were kept alive and in full vigor the doctrine of belief in one God, and the true idea of sin. These our Lord, when he came, found ready to his hand, as essential pre-conditions of his teaching. And, in the exhibition of this great and unparalleled result of a most elaborate and peculiar discipline, we may perhaps recognize, sufficiently for the present purpose, something of the office and work of the Old Testament.

IV.

THE PSALMS.

I.—THEIR HISTORIC PLACE IN THE DEVOTION
OF ALL AGES.

John Bright has told me that he would be content to stake upon the Book of Psalms, as it stands, the great question whether there is or is not a divine revelation. It was not to him conceivable how a work so widely severed from all the known productions of antiquity, and standing upon a level so much higher, could be accounted for except by a special and extraordinary aid calculated to produce special and extraordinary results; for it is reasonable, nay needful, to presume a due correspondence between the cause and the effect. Nor does this opinion appear to be otherwise than just. If Bright did not possess the special qualifications of the scholar or the critic, he was, I conceive, a very capable judge of the moral and religious elements in any case that had been brought before him by his personal experience.

It was in truth a noble distinction of the Hebrew race to have produced persons imbued with such qualities and gifts, as made them capable of composing the Book of Psalms.

Twice in his Epistles (Eph. 5 : 19; Col. 3 : 16) does St. Paul admonish Christians with regard to musical services as a fitting vent for the devout mind and heart. In both cases he employs the same phraseology, and enjoins the use of "psalms and hymns and spiritual songs," each time giving the first place in the enumeration to Psalms. I find it difficult to dismiss the idea that in this word the use of the Psalter was intended; especially as there are early testimonies to the effect that antiphonal singing was in use from the origin of the Church.[1]

Upon the most superficial survey of the Psalms in their general aspect, it seems difficult or impos-

[1] As to the last-named point, see Wordsworth and Alford, *in loco.*

sible to regard them as simply owing their parentage to the Mosaic system. Some, indeed, of their
features may well be referred to it; especially the
strong sense of national unity which they display,
and the concentration of that sense upon a single
centre, the city of Jerusalem and the temple.

It may also be noted that the Mosaic law incul-
cated in its utmost breadth the principle of love to
God. "Thou shalt love the Lord thy God with all
thine heart, and with all thy soul, and with all thy
might" (Deut. 6 : 4, 5). Yet may it not be said,
from the place in which it occurs, that this is rather
exhortation than statute? Further, it is not un-
folded in the detail of the legislative Torah; and,
even in the Decalogue, service is enjoined without
the mention of love. The early books do not
exhibit, like the Psalter, the close, inner contact of
the individual soul with the Deity; and, as water
does not rise above the source from which it flows,
it is hard to ascribe to them alone the wonderful
development of that principle which pervades the
body of this unparalleled collection. We seem

compelled to assume for them some loftier fountain-head of instruction. This, I would submit, is in part supplied, and in part suggested, by the Book of Genesis. I say suggested, inasmuch as the outlines of a primeval religion drawn in that book are not less slight than they are significant. So slight, indeed, that I have long been unable to resist the impression that there were at the outset supplementary communications, divine in their origin, over and above those contained in Holy Writ, and perhaps traceable, here and there, in later portions of the Old Testament and of the Apocryphal Books. Much, however, is supplied, if something also is only suggested: inasmuch as the story of the Fall involves in full the idea of our restoration in character as well as condition, which is nowhere enunciated in the Law; and further, inasmuch as the Book of Genesis sets forth, at least down to the time of Abraham, a personal intercourse, habitual and direct, with the Deity, and one pointing onwards to the great Redemption.

In a preceding essay I have represented that the

Mosaic law was not the promulgation of a new and complete religion, but a code of provisions intended for the particular purpose (1) of building up a wall of effectual separation between the Jewish community, and the corruption of the nations whose land they were to conquer and to possess ; and (2) of preserving in vitality and freshness, within that precinct, the fundamental conceptions of the divine unity and righteousness, and of the duty and the sinfulness of man. These all-important propositions were the necessary pre-conditions of any plan for the restoration of peace in a disordered world. But they were, nevertheless, in process of extirpation from the general and public religion of all those Gentile races, whose history is given us in Scripture, or in the classical books of profane antiquity.

Thus the Mosaic system, while it was defensive against the surrounding iniquity, was also something more, and something higher. That system, both institutional and doctrinal, fenced in, as it were, a clear space, a free and secure domain, for the fuller development of a religion, inward and personal, devotional and spiritual, the materials for which it could hardly have supplied by presenting, as it did, God as ruler and judge, and man as a servant who continually either sinned, or was on the brink of falling into sin.

In the inner sanctuary, thus provided for the most capable human souls, was reared the strong spiritual life, which appears to have developed itself pre-eminently in the depth, richness, tenderness, and comprehensiveness of the Psalms. To the work they have here accomplished, there is no parallel upon earth. For the present I put aside all details, and am content to stand upon this fact —that a compilation, which began (at the latest) with a shepherd of Palestine, three thousand years ago, has been the prime and paramount manual of devotion from that day to this; first for the Hebrew race, both in its isolation, and after it was brought, by the translation of its sacred books, into relations with the Gentile world; and then for all the Christian races, in all their diversities of character and circumstance. Further, that there is now, if possible, less chance than ever of the displacement of these marvellous compositions from their supremacy in the worship of the Christian Church. And beyond doubt it may be also said that their function has not been one of ritual pomp and outward power either mainly or alone. They have dwelt in the Christian heart, and at the very centre of that heart; and wherever the pursuits of the inner life have been most largely conceived and cultivated, there, and in the same proportion, the Psalms have towered over every other vehicle of general devotion. We have a conspicuous illustration of their office in the fact that of two hundred and forty-three actual citations from the Old Testament found in the pages of the New, no less than one hundred and sixteen are from the single Book of Psalms; and that a similar proportion holds with most of the early Fathers.[1]

[1] Canon Cook, in the Speaker's Bible, Vol. IV., p. 146. There is a minor, but still not unmeaning, indication to the same effect, which it would be unseemly to couple with that given in the text, but which I venture to name for its recency, and because it is eminently asso-

The Bishop of Derry has published the result of a careful examination made by himself. It is, that reference is made to the Psalms, either by quotation or otherwise, in no fewer than two hundred and eighty-six passages of the New Testament.[1]

We have thus before us the fact that the Psalms, composed for the public worship of the Hebrews from two to three thousand years ago, constitute down to the present day for Christians the best and highest book of devotion. A noteworthy fact even on the surface of it; more noteworthy still, when we go below the surface into the meaning. The Hebrews were Semitic, Christendom is (chiefly) Aryan; the Hebrews were local, Christendom is world-wide; the Hebrews were often tributary, and finally lost their liberties and place among the nations; Christianity has mounted over every obsta-

ciated with the general course of modern life. In a manual, not of hymns, but of devotions prepared for public use in the mixed congregations on board a great line of packet ships from Great Britain to North America, I find that, out of 254 pages, 137 are occupied by selections from the Psalms; the chief part of the remainder being a collection of hymns.

[1] " The Witness of the Psalms." Note A, p. 291.

cle, and has long been the dominating power of the world. The Hebrews had no literature outside their religion, nor any fine art; Christendom has appropriated, and even rivalled both the literature and the art of the greatest among the ancients. This strange book of Hebrew devotions had no attraction outside Hebrewism, except for Christians; and Christians have as yet found nothing to gather, in the same kind, from any of the other religions in the world. The stamp of continuity and identity has been set upon one, and one only, historic series; one and one only thread runs down through the whole succession of the ages; and, among many witnesses to this continuity, the Psalms are probably one of the most conspicuous. This stamp purports to be, and to have been all along, divine; and the unparalleled evidence of results all goes to show that it is not a forgery.

The wonderful phenomenon thus presented to us can hardly be said to admit of enhancement; and yet it is, perhaps, enhanced, when we bear in mind that the long period of this perpetual youth, exhibited by the Psalms, has been one broken by the promulgation of a new religion, together with all the changes of fact, and developments of principle, which transformed the heathen world.

Moreover, we should remember that the shapings of all language merely human are essentially short-lived, and forms of speech succeed one another as wave follows upon wave. But herein seems probably to lie one of the ways in which the divine revelation asserts itself. It appears to have the faculty of giving to things mutable the privilege and the power of the immutable, and to endow innumerable fashions of speech, when they belong to the heart's core of human nature, with a charter that is to endure throughout all time.

I submit, then, that the fact of so wonderful a power as was thus exercised by the Psalms, in such diversities of time, race, and circumstances, is not only without parallel, but is removed by such a breadth of space from all other facts of human experience in the same province, as to constitute in itself a strong presumption that the cause also is one lying beyond the range of ordinary human action, and may most reasonably be set down as consisting in that speciality of divine suggestion and guidance, which we term revelation.

II.—THEIR ANTIQUITY.

The antiquity of the Book of Psalms, like that of the other books of Scripture, does not directly or necessarily involve the essence of the case concerning them, which I apprehend is more dependent upon their character and their results. Yet it counts, for importance, in the next order of considerations, since the form and substance are here more intimately allied than in the terms used for the recital of events in a historical book.

It is also to be assumed that the incessant use of the Psalms in the service of the temple, and the comparatively wide knowledge of them thus conveyed to the people, were in the nature of special securities for their faithful and exact transmission.

When we speak of the Psalms of David, we use

13

a popular and general form of expression, which names the whole from the largest or most weighty, and, originally, most conspicuous, among the parts. The phrase is sufficiently shown not to be absolute and precise by the beautiful 137th Psalm, which describes the condition of the Hebrews in Babylon, five centuries after the death of the minstrel king. Seventy-three Psalms[1] in all are ascribed to him. This is not the assumption or opinion of conservative writers only. Bleek, whose work was republished and (I must conceive at least generally[2] sanctioned) in 1878 by Wellhausen, admits it to be a matter of the highest probability that no inconsiderable number of the Psalms are due to his authorship.[3] He also, with others, largely accepts the inscriptions which are prefixed to them. According to Canon Cook, a judicious and able writer, it

---

[1] Cook's Introduction, p. 150.

[2] It has been erroneously asserted (Academy, Jan. 31, 1891) that Wellhausen has limited his responsibility to certain passages written by him. He evidently makes no such limitation : but only specifies his authorship of those passages.

[3] " Einleitung in das alte Testament." . . . Besorgt von J. Wellhausen. Sect. 221. Berlin, 1886.

was never held that the entire Psalter was the work
of the king; and he says that, in the time of the
Maccabees, the completion of the Book was ascribed
to Nehemiah. He thinks that a large proportion
of the two closing books (out of the five books
composing the Psalter) belong to the period of or
following the Exile.[1] But of the three Psalms most
pointedly referable to the Messiah, two (22, 110)
are Davidic. He shows how the conclusive objections to the theory which refers the Psalms to the
Maccabean age are sustained by various advanced
German writers, and Bleek holds that no Psalm
can be shown to be later than Nehemiah. Ewald,
we have seen, to the last held that no part of the
Psalter was of the Maccabean period. Indeed, as
the language of the people had then come to be
Aramaic, and the old text read in Hebrew was
explained in the synagogues by interpretation, it is
not easy to see how new Psalms could be afterwards composed in pure Hebrew, and added to

[1] Cook's Introduction, p. 156. The books are Psalms 1-41, 42-72,
73-89, 90-106, 107-150.

the collection.   The Psalms themselves were para-
phrased into Chaldee or Aramaic after the Captivity,
in order that the people might understand them.
This fact of itself overthrows the modern destructive supposition that the Psalms only came into
existence at that period.   But the master idea of
the whole argument is not so much that such and
such Psalms were produced at such and such an
era, as that the Book at large is the product of that
influence which stamps it, like the other books of
Holy Scripture, as embodying a Divine revelation.

On this point of antiquity, it is more than enough
if a large portion of the Psalms are ascribable to
King David.   I venture, however, to offer two suggestions.   First, the Psalms come to us through a
channel supplied by the kingdom of Judah, not the
kingdom of Israel.   If they had been largely composed after the severance of the ten tribes from the
two, would they not have presented some more
definite indication of that severance?   Now, the
name of Israel is the name under which in the
Psalms the chosen people are commonly described.

We have this name repeated sixty-two times.[1] The
name of Judah was likely, it may be supposed,
after the schism, to become the prevailing and distinctive name.   It would probably so continue even
after the captivity and dispersion of the ten tribes,
at any rate as long as their remnants continued to
represent a corporate existence separate from that
of the southern kingdom.   Yet, throughout the
Psalter, we never find the name of Judah mentioned
in this paramount sense.   Jerusalem is mentioned
seventeen times, and Sion thirty-eight; together
fifty-five times.   But the name of Judah only occurs
ten times, and never with this pre-eminent significance.   It is mentioned either together with Israel
(Psa. 76 : 1; 114 : 2), or in conjunction with other
tribes, as with Ephraim and Manasseh in Psa. 60 : 7,
and 108 : 8, or with Sion; but always locally or

[1] Psa. 14 : 7 (twice); 22 : 3, 23; 25 : 22; 41 : 13; 50 : 7; 53 : 6 (twice);
59 : 5; 68 : 8, 26, 34, 35; 69 : 6; 71 : 22; 72 : 18; 73 : 1; 76 : 1;
78 : 5, 21, 31, 41, 55, 59, 71; 80 : 1; 81 : 4, 8, 11, 13; 83 : 4; 89 : 18;
98 : 3; 103 : 7; 105 : 10, 23; 106 : 48; 114 : 1, 2; 115 : 9, 12; 118 : 2;
121 : 4; 122 : 4; 124 : 1; 125 : 5; 128 : 6; 129 : 1; 130 : 7, 8; 131 : 3;
135 : 4, 12, 19; 136 : 11, 14, 22; 147 : 2, 19; 148 : 14; 149 : 2.

tribally. Could this have been so, if the Psalms had mainly been composed when Judah was the only acknowledged name for the elect people, and Israel was habitually a stranger, often an enemy, always the symbol of a rival and apparently, from the character of its priesthood and otherwise (1 Kings 12 : 31; 13 : 33), a degraded worship?

Secondly: the one great deliverance commemorated in the Psalms (as also, I understand, in the later Jewish Liturgies), is the deliverance from Egypt. See, for example, Psalms 68, 72, 80, 81, 105, 106, 114, 135, 136. Could this have been the case, if the Book was unknown until the time when, between the people and their earlier past, there arose up a frightful spectre? I refer to the lacerating experience of the Captivity in Babylon.

And yet, surely, there were incidents attendant upon that Captivity, which might have carved upon the Jewish mind recollections yet deeper in some respects than those of Egypt. In that country, if their treatment had been cruel and degrading, yet they must upon the whole have flourished, inasmuch as they grew there from a family into a people. But the Babylonish Captivity entailed, firstly, the loss of what was not only an ancestral home, but the local seat of the divine promise to their race; secondly, the loss of the worship divinely ordained, and attached to the temple of Jerusalem; thirdly, the loss of the kingly line, and of the visible form of that prized nationality, in and by which they were preferred before all the nations of the earth. Is it then conceivable, if the Psalms in general owed their origin to the time of the Captivity, that the composers of them should, in numerous and conspicuous cases, have dwelt so long and so often on the details of the Egyptian bondage, and should never but once and briefly have made reference, specific indeed but narrow, to the one recent catastrophe, choosing rather to go back to the centuries dimmed, in comparison, by the interval of a thousand years?

It seems more than possible that this argument may be decisively supported by that portion of the Book of Jeremiah, which distinctly prophesies, not

long before the Captivity, that a time is coming
when the servitude in Egypt shall cease to be the
one commanding recollection of the Hebrews, and
its place shall be taken by the Exile in Babylon.

" Therefore, behold, the days come, saith the Lord, that
it shall no more be said, The Lord liveth, that brought up
the children of Israel out of the land of Egypt;

" But, The Lord liveth, that brought up the children of
Israel from the land of the north, and from all the lands
whither he had driven them: and I will bring them again
into their land that I gave unto their fathers " (Jer. 16:
14, 15).

The arguments, drawn from general features and
from historical probability, respecting the antiquity
of the books of the Old Testament, are in some
degree common to the Torah, or Books of Moses,
and the Psalms.   The Psalms have, however, the
benefit of the admission which at no distant period
received countenance from the leader of the negative school in our own day, that a considerable
number are probably from the pen of David.   And
there are also points in which reasoning, available

to show the antiquity of the Torah, has even an enhanced force for the Psalms.

We see, for example, that the history of the Israelites, from the conquest of Canaan to the Captivity, is upon the whole a history of decaying faith. This is exhibited in the original demand for the change to a monarchy from that earlier form of government by Judges, which powerfully suggested the presence and providence of the Almighty, by leaving unoccupied the place upon earth most symbolical of him. It was shown by the increased wickedness of the Kings, and by the enlarged and developed office of the Prophets. For these were like an army of reserve in support of the divine dispensation, which takes its position on the field of battle in the hour of need.

It is also observed by Sack,[1] that in the period succeeding the Exile the original creative force of the Hebrew spirit died out, and that, as formalism

---

[1] " Die altjüdische Religion in übergange vom Bibelthume zum Talmudismus," von Israel Sack. Berlin, 1889. Einleitung, pp. 13 *seqq.*

advanced, the sectarian lines of party were sharpened and deepened. In both these tracts of history, the spirit and voice of the Book of Psalms appear to throw us back upon antiquity, and even upon a distant antiquity. They seem to be, when taken at large, the product as of a school, so probably of an age, of living, energetic faith. And they are not less eminently notable for the harmony which all along pervades the religious community. " Jerusalem is built as a city that is at unity in itself" (Psa. 122 : 3).

III.—THEIR CONTENTS.

Let us now look for a moment at the contents of this Book, which are such as to fasten our wonder upon them, and to leave little room for any surprise that they should have established for themselves, in collective worship and in personal devotion, the place to which no parallel is elsewhere to be found in the experience of the human race. And, on the other hand I shall not fail to notice in their proper place the objections which some have urged against the Book of Psalms.

The multiplication of divinities, under the system which we term polytheism, had tended to establish everywhere a system of what are termed national gods. These act within the sphere of a particular race or country; they are open to the competition of other deities, when through migration or conquest these spheres happen to overlap. They do not claim the allegiance of other races, or show care or, so to speak, responsibility, for their welfare.

I do not indeed deny, but should be forward to assert, that while, in the early stages of historic antiquity, this nationalizing process seems to harden more and more with the gradual accretions of legendary tradition, we can trace among the mythologies, in various degrees of faintness or clearness, the older idea of a supreme God; of a belief in one Ruler of the universe, anterior and superior to these multiform powers. We find in many cases disguised resemblances of that original belief; but

it is most commonly with such dislocation of its
elements ; with such exaggerations, such intrusion
of ideas foreign to it, as often to defy all attempts,
at least in the present state of knowledge, to ascend
the channel upwards to the source. The schemes
become so complex, as to defy any rational account
of the original deviation: even when their basis is
found to lie in the several powers of external nature, which were not known to be connected by
any common tie, but which received the names of
gods, and were combined into religious systems.
These popular gods became realities in two senses:
first, subjectively, because as they were accepted in
the minds of men, the associations connected with
them became a source and spring of human action;
secondly, in an objective sense, because the images,
under which they came to be represented, gave
them a real existence at least in the material and in
the traditionary sphere. It is, therefore, natural
that the Psalms, in phrases concerning deity, should
not be confined to the One God, but should say, for
example that among the gods there is none like

unto him, or should exhort the worshippers to give thanks unto the God of gods (Psa. 86:8; 136:2. See Exodus 15:11).

Yet no reader of the Psalms can fail to see that they are strictly, unconditionally, and exclusively monotheistic. God is undoubtedly the God of Israel, and the worshippers properly describe him in the terms which most closely correspond with his relation to themselves. There seems to be a great mixture of the terms of Elohim and Jehovah, and in none of the five Books is the use of the properly Hebrew name exclusive.[1] But, without drawing any argument from this intermixture, the Psalms make it plain, in a multitude of places, that the God whom they adore is from everlasting, and is the God, not of Palestine alone, but of the whole world: "Sing unto God, O ye kingdoms of the earth; O sing praises unto the Lord; who sitteth in the heavens over all from the beginning" (Psa. 68:32, 33). And his eye and care are over all men. "O praise the Lord, all ye heathen: praise him, all

[1] Cook's Introduction, p. 149.

ye nations. For his merciful kindness is ever more and more towards us; and the truth of the Lord endureth for ever" (Psa. 117).

No doubt the "Lord" is represented as having special relations with and special care for Israel. But these are relations of affection, not of exclusion. A Psalm declares indeed—

"He shall choose out an heritage for us; even the worship of Jacob, whom he loved."

But the very same Psalm had already sounded the trumpet note—

"O clap your hands together, all ye people; O sing unto God with the voice of melody: for the Lord is high, and to be feared; he is the great king upon all the earth" (Psa. 47: 4, and 1, 2).

Among the notes, then, of the supreme position of the Psalms, and of the religion to which they belonged, we find this idea of the one God, who is also the universal God, and the universal Governor of men, and who thereby stands broadly distinguished from what we find to be the character of the polytheistic systems and of their heads; namely, divinity restrained by limits of the races or countries of antiquity.

But the form of the Almighty, thus divested of the limitations of mere nationality, and exhibited in the majesty of perfect Oneness and Omnipotence, revealed itself through the Psalms in other and more tender aspects. His care for the poor and for the stranger might be learned from the books of the law, and may be traced in other religions among the remnants, as is probable, of true theism. Still, that is a function of government only, though of benevolent government, and it is compatible with the idea of a Deity immeasurably remote. But in the Psalms is developed with singular force and beauty the idea of Omnipotence in the attitude of nearness to man: and, more conspicuously still, of nearness to the individual man. In Heaven, and in the Underworld, and at the extremities of earth, "even there also shall thy hand lead me, and thy right hand shall hold me" (Psa. 139: 6-9).

The presence thus brought near is not, as in

Exodus (chap. 19: 12, 13, 21), a consuming, but a
soothing and sustaining presence (Psa. 23).   When
thus brought near, the Almighty is invested in
relation to us with all those capacities of action
and of sympathy, which fill in human nature the
department of the affections.   In the mouth of the
objector, this is termed anthropomorphism.   I do
not presume to say that there is not in it some
prefiguration of the Messiah, made in all such
things like as we are made.   But that there is no
deflection from the loftiness of the monotheistic
idea we know from this, that the same people, who
gave utterance to the Psalms, have been the most
rigid and lofty in their definitions of the Godhead.
As when it is said by Maimonides, in the best and
loftiest strain of Judaism, that with God "there is
neither folly nor wisdom, like the wisdom of a wise
man; neither sleep nor waking; neither anger nor
laughter; neither joy nor sorrow; neither silence
nor speech, like the speech of the sons of men." [1]

[1] Maimonides, "Yad Hachazakah."   Transl. Bernard (Cambridge,
1832), p. 39.   Declarations not less remarkable are to be found in the

Yet it is he that is not only the guardian of his people, but as it were their sentinel; and not of his people only, but of every one among them, as truly and as much as of the whole. In truth, the two threads of national and of personal Providence are so intertwined in the Psalms, that they scarcely can be disentangled. "He will not suffer *thy* foot to be moved, and he that keepeth *thee* will not sleep;" and then in the very next verse, by a transition not less gentle than complete, "Behold, he that keepeth Israel shall neither slumber nor sleep." There is no detail too minute for describing the closeness of this protection: "He is thy defence upon thy right hand;" "The Lord shall preserve thy going out, and thy coming in: from this time forth for evermore" (Psa. 121: 3, 4, 5, 8). But no mere selection can rightly convey a picture of the close and intimate care, which this and so many others of the Psalms describe in setting forth the attitude of the Almighty towards his worshippers.

More Nebuchim, or "Guide of the Perplexed." See also the work of Dr. Ginsburg on the Kabbala, pp. 87-89 (London: Longmans, 1864)

14

I will not quit this portion of the subject without quoting a remarkable testimony to the elevation of the Psalter from a recent critic generally negative, but one who makes his affirmative declarations with an exemplary sincerity and fervor. He speaks of the Psalter as follows: "It is, as a whole, the expression and fruit of the principles of the Jewish religion, as they existed in the minds of pious Israelites. Its one great theme is the clinging of the human spirit to God. In joy and sorrow, in victory and defeat, in moods of saintliness or sin, the spirit of the poor earthly wayfarer here pours out its plaint and prayer to the God of its life. . . . What exultation is here, for high days of victory and joy! What touching moans of penitence! What child-like cries for help! What entreaties from the soul that can only say, ' out of the depths I have cried unto thee!' What delightful confidences between the trustful spirit, and the Shepherd who leadeth by the green pastures and the still waters!"[1]

[1] Seven Lectures by the Rev. J. P. Hopps, VII., p. 33.

I must not altogether pass by the Messianic Psalms. These are the songs which show, by the adaptation of their language to him and to his office, either that their composers had a prevision of his coming, or that such prevision was conveyed into their strain by the higher influence which prompted it. It is not necessary here to debate the number of these Psalms. Suffice it to specify Psalms 2, 21, 22, 45, 72, 110. And it is sufficiently plain that the principle of prophecy, which is involved in them, whether conscious or unconscious in the mind of the composer, is the same which belongs to the other predictions and prefigurations in the books of the Old Testament. But they differ from, and go beyond, the rest in this important particular. The primitive religion descends through them, as it were by an inner conduit. The great and cardinal facts of the lapse of man from righteousness, and of the need and promise of a Redeemer, were embodied by the Psalms in the perpetual public worship of the Temple; they thus became part of the open, common inheritance of all; and were systematically forced, so to speak, upon the attention of the people, that they might come into personal and conscious appropriation of this most precious and absolutely central part of their covenanted privileges. Great as was the Torah, the Psalter, in this capital respect, was greater still.

When the foot of the Greek first, and afterwards of the Roman, trod the streets of Jerusalem; when the treasures of the Hebrew books were unlocked to the Gentile world through the Septuagint; then there happened, we may justly assume, one of two things. There was, as we know upon strong heathen testimony, before the advent of our Lord, a universal and traditional expectation in the East that a great power was to arise in Judæa and to subdue the world. How came it that so remarkable a conception, foreign to the cultivated communities of the Greek and the Italian peninsulas, and apparently menacing the continuance of the Roman dominion, should at this time have been prevalent in the East? The East had, indeed, through a

long series of centuries, supposed itself entitled to
the mastery of the world: hence the wild expe-
dition of Darius into Scythia, and the repeated
conflicts of Persia with the Greeks.   It is not
strange that this heritage should in some shape or
other be reclaimed, for ideas of this kind are tena-
cious of life, and easy of revival.   But what is at
first sight most strange is the choice of the spot
from which deliverance was to proceed.   It was
not from any of the seats of ancient power, the
fame of which was still on record; but from among
the small, isolated, and undistinguished people who
inhabited Palestine, and whose brief appearance
on the stage of human affairs as conquerors, in the
time of King David, was so slight in extension
and in duration, as to have inscribed no mark upon
the page of general history.   It had passed away
without visible record, as might, until a few years
back, have been said of the old empire of the Hit-
tites. The Jews were also a people, whose manners
and institutions repelled rather than attracted the
sympathy of the world. One supposition, explana-

tory of this remarkable expectation, might be that
it had lived on from prehistoric times in feebleness
and obscurity, but had come to the front when the
East felt the hard hand of power pressing on it
from Rome, and welding it for the first time by
a permanent system into uniformity of servitude
or inferiority, from which it panted for deliverance. But it seems more probable that the Jewish
Scriptures, which had for two centuries become
known by translation into Greek, were themselves
the fountain-head of this most remarkable anticipation ; and in that case its popular promulgation
would seem in all likelihood to have been due, in
an eminent degree, to the Messianic Psalms, which
were, of all the available evidence, the part most
likely to be prominent in the eye and mind of the
people.

Such being, in outline, the presentation of God
to man in the Book of Psalms, let us consider in
its turn the manner in which they present man to
God.   Now this may be set forth in a multitude of
particulars, but they are all capable of being

summed into one. For we have seen that the Psalms are a book of spiritual communion, not only between God and man, not only between God and his Church, or especially chosen people, but also, and even pre-eminently, between God and the individual man.

As it is the fashion of the day to assert for the sacred books of other religions a kind of parity with the Old Testament, I ask the reader to spend a few moments on this subject.

No doubt there are points, at which resemblance may be traced between the Hebrew devotions and those of the outer world: not those of the outer world generally, for from the Greek mind, as represented by the Greek literature, devotion, properly so called, has disappeared; the rise of intellect, sad and strange as this may sound, was the fall of piety. But let it be granted that in the Vedas, for example, and in the Babylonian Hymns, there are points of contact with the Psalms. Do those points of contact run along the whole line? Are they continuous, or are they isolated? Is it coincidence, or is it a sort of tangential contact only, or one which reminds us of the definition of a point as that which has position but not magnitude in space?

May not those hymns be described as belonging only to the idea of dependence upon the Deity; to the power and grandeur which exist on one side, the misery, want, and weakness on the other? This is perhaps what is called the religious sentiment, the religion of which we have a subjective need, and which we are now constantly (and doubtless in good faith) assured is not to disappear on the submergence of positive religion and its institutions. But does this give us anything near a true conception of the Psalms? They are based upon the idea, not of dependence only, but of sympathy and communion. Yes, for the work of spiritual discipline, the human soul is there almost lifted upwards, as St. Paul was, into the third heaven, and meets the Creator as son meets father, face to face. It is not possible, perhaps, to carry this idea farther than it is carried in the Psalms. It is certainly not woven

into a closer tissue in the "Imitatio Christi," after
fourteen centuries of Christian ideas and practices.
We approach to it especially in the Prophets; as
when, through Isaiah, the Almighty invites us to
a pleading (Isa. 1: 18), "Come now, and let us
reason together."[1] But can we, even in idea, press
it further, or lift it higher, than in that marvellous
expostulation of the forty-fourth Psalm? It defies
the test of extract or quotation. From the fifth
verse to the end it is a sustained note of moving,
sorrowing appeal, lifted as far above the level of
any merely human effort known to us, as the flight
of the lark, "hard by the sun," is lifted above the
swallow, when it foresees the storm and skims
the surface of the ground. Such, as set forth in
the Psalms, are the inward exercises of the individual soul.

Not that the stamp set upon the Psalms is
uniform; it is highly diversified. Take the noble
first Psalm, which opens the Book. It sets forth in
one part (verses 3 and 4) with a tender beauty, in

[1] See further (*e.g.*) Ezek. 18: 25, 29.

another with strong and stern denunciation, the positions of the righteous and of the wicked before God. But it sets them forth, as it were, from the outside. So, again, many of the Psalms, dealing with the Israelites as a whole, have for their theme national deliverance and glory. But let us turn to the penitential Psalms, and most of all to the fifty-first, in which King David[1] sounds the lowest depths of sorrow and shame for sin, and has provided for the penitent of every age and every character the auxiliary medicine that his case required. On these Psalms as a whole, on this Psalm in particular, and, again on the thirty-eighth Psalm, most of all in its first moiety, let us fasten our attention for a moment. Have modern learning and research succeeded in extracting from all the sacred books of all the ancient religions of the world anything like, I do not say a parallel, but an ever so remote approach to them? The great discourse of our Lord to Nicodemus, in the third chapter of St. John, might

---

[1] Some critics argue, not without some reason on their side that the two last verses are an Exilic addition.

find in these compositions a basis broad enough to sustain the whole of His startling doctrine, "except a man be born again, he cannot see the kingdom of God" (John 3: 3).

Penitence thus lying at the door of the process by which man is appointed to ascend to holiness, this golden book supplies, beyond all others, the types and aids for attaining it in all its stages. All that special class of virtues, which were unknown to the civilized world at the time when the Apostles preached them, had been here set forth in act a thousand years before, and stored up for use, first within the narrow circle of the Jewish worship, and then in the Church, which claims, and which may yet possess, the wide world for its inheritance. Another standard of virtue indeed, and in itself a glorious one, the Greek and the Roman world possessed. They had their code of Justice, Fortitude, Temperance, and Wisdom. But this list of virtues contained no recognition of the terrible and world-wide fact of sin, and opened no road to the acquisition of powers capable of contending against it,

and of casting down its strongholds to the ground.
That road was to be opened by the Beatitudes of
the Sermon on the Mount, and by the Faith, Hope,
and Charity of St. Paul.   Now, is there one of those
Beatitudes which has not been, in its blossom or its
germ, anticipated by the Psalms?   Take the sancti-
fication of sorrow in verse 4: so the Psalm instructs
us, "Thy loving correction shall make me great"
(Psa. 18: 35).   Take the blessing of the meek
(v. 5).   So says the Psalmist: "Lord, I am not
high-minded.   I have no proud looks.   I refrain
my soul and keep it low.   My soul is even as a
weaned child" (Psa. 131: 1, 3).   These are principles, not only which the ancient philosophies did not
contain, but which they would have repudiated and
contemned.   Take again that blessing of satiety
which is promised to "hunger and thirst" after
righteousness; words which indicate such an adult
age, such a fulness of growth and stature in the
new man of the Christian system, that what was at
first lesson from without has come to be appetite
from within, and forms part of the untaught spon-

taneous working of a renewed humanity. But this idea is fully developed in the Psalms (42 : 1, 2): "Like as the hart desireth the water brooks, so longeth my soul after thee, O God. My soul is athirst for God, yea, even for the living God: when shall I come to appear before the presence of God?" Even the doctrine of forgiveness, of doing good to enemies, to the growth of which the conditions of Hebrew life were less favorable, finds expression in the Psalms. Take 35: 12, 13: "They rewarded me evil for good. Nevertheless, when they were sick I put on sackcloth, and humbled my soul with fasting." And again, "If I have rewarded evil unto him that dealt friendly with me: yea, I have delivered him that without any cause is mine enemy" (Psa. 7: 4).

There are, as I shall presently notice, other passages of a different strain. But it is, I submit, the general strain of the Psalms to which we should principally look. And who will deny that they habitually abound in humility, in penitential abasement, in the strong faith which is the evidence of things not seen, in fervor, self-mistrust, filial confidence towards God? These and all kindred qualities they develop in what, for want of a better word, I will term their innerness. Their tones come from the inmost heart, and, not with a rude familiarity, yet with a wonderful nearness, they seem to seek the response, if the phrase may be used without irreverence, from the inner heart of God himself.

All this is severed, as a whole, by an immeasurable distance from the language, ideas, and mental habits of pagan antiquity. What we find there of religion associated with intellectual culture turns upon the external relations between God and man, as between sovereign and subject, or master and dependant. The prehistoric verse of Homer abounds in prayers. They are not such commonly as we should use, yet they indicate fully these external relations. But in the life of later, of classical Greece, prayer seems wholly to have lost its force, and its place as a factor in human life.

Again, in the "Odyssey" of Homer we have remaining traces of the personal relation between man and God.   In the intercourse of Athenè with Odysseus, and reversely in her action on the minds of the guilty Suitors, there are distinct traces of the belief in a divine force working within the soul of man.   I do not remember to have found anything like this in the later classical literature. But the development of the principle and idea of a communion with God, operative on human feeling, thought, and action, is the standing and central thought of the Psalms.   And it is probable that, the more fixedly we regard them, the more of their distinctive marks we shall perceive, even as the stars in heaven multiply to the gazing eye.   The pervading idea of a living communion with the Most High, the communion which both gives and takes, exhibits and fulfils itself in many ways.   One of them is the use of intercessory prayer; a trait conspicuously absent from the numerous and interesting prayers of Homer.   Another is that, while full of warm personal interests, they persistently hold up the banner of a righteousness apart from and above all personal interests whatever.   Another is that the affections, alienated by sin, have returned to their allegiance, and are arrayed on the side of the Most High. The testimonies of God are the "very joy" of the Psalmist's heart. It is all his desire, that the divine will should have free course and be glorified upon earth. The glory of God has become to him a profound personal interest. There is a community of concern, purpose, and feeling, reciprocated between heaven and earth. "Set up thyself, O God, above the heavens; and thy glory above all the earth." Sentiments of this type are, I apprehend, hardly to be found outside the precinct of the Hebrew race.

I will only note, in passing, before quitting this subject, two remaining characteristics; the height of that sacredness which the Psalms attach to the claims of the poor; and their sense of the utter worthlessness of all ceremonial observances, though commanded, except in connection with the service of the will and purification of the heart.

IV.—THE OBJECTIONS TAKEN TO THEM.

Referring to what has been said elsewhere on the presence of a human element in Holy Scripture, I will now introduce a few words on the special objection which is lodged against the Psalms.

Let me first endeavor to reduce the question to its true dimensions. The criticism is not here, as it might be in some cases of books claiming to be sacred, that they are feeble, or fanciful, or remote from human interests, or that large veins of clay run through such true metal as they contain. The Psalms, in their sublimity and in their sympathy, so immeasurably divine and so intensely human, are proof against all such criticism, which would be no better than cavil. The only dart which really rings upon their coat of mail is the dart which carries the reproach of their severe and unmeasured denunciation of enemies.

And first, in order to disembarrass the question of matter which appears to be extreme and excep-

15

tional, I will refer to the verse which represents the *ne plus ultra* of the difficulty, as it stands in the Prayer-book Version of the Psalms; in respect to which we pay a certain price for its incomparable majesty and beauty, in the shape of occasional though rare shortcomings as to accuracy. The Prayer-book gives verses 21, 22, of Psalm 139, as follows:

" Do not I hate them, O Lord, that hate thee: and am not I grieved with those that rise up against thee?

" Yea, I hate them right sore: even as though they were mine enemies."

Which seems to say, " I have a reserved stock of special and superlative hatred for those who have not only sinned in general, but have sinned against me in particular." But this notion is completely put aside in the translation direct from the Hebrew as it stands in the Authorized, and also in the Revised Version, where the second of the two verses runs:

"I hate them with a perfect hatred; I count them mine enemies."

This seems not to set up the selfish feeling,

about offense personally received, above the sentiment of indignation and resentment against wickedness; but to say only, " All that I might feel
against a personal enemy, all that natural ex-
asperation would suggest, I discharge upon the
enemies of God." But the sentiment concerning
them has already been expressed in terms not
admitting of enlargement. " I hate them with a
perfect hatred." And this brings the objection to
a point. It is that such unmeasured detestation
and invocation of wrath by man even upon God's
enemies cannot be justified, and can by no means
be referred to divine inspiration.

Now let us notice, in the first place, that the
general tone of the Psalms concerning enemies is
not aggressive, but defensive. A sense of trouble
and danger from the might of experienced or im-
pending assault, and an appeal to God for protection, furnish the staple sentiment of the Book. I
quote a single instance, which is a fair sample of
the ground assumed in the whole of this class of
passages from Psalm 56 : 1, 2 :

"Be merciful unto me, O God, for man goeth about to
devour me : he is daily fighting and troubling me.

"Mine enemies are daily in hand to swallow me up:
for they be many that fight against me, O thou Most
Highest."

Let those who question the assertion I have
made, that this passage has a character typical of
the whole, refer (among other places) to Psalms 5 :
8; 6 : 7; 7 : 5; 18 : 27, *passim;* 56 : 9; 59 : 1; 69 :
4; 118 : 11, 12; 138 : 7; 143 : 9.

But undoubtedly a certain number of passages
are not defensive, they are denunciatory; such as
54 : 5, 7; 59 : 10; 92 : 11; 143 : 12. I will recite
this last verse in full, for it brings into view the
sentiment which forms the base of all these passages: "And of thy goodness slay mine enemies,
and destroy all them that vex my soul, *for I am thy
servant.*" If we put these words into paraphrase,
the Psalmist pleads that he is engaged in the service
of God; that in this service he is assailed and
hindered; that, powerless in himself, he appeals to
the source of power; and that he invokes upon the

assailants and hinderers of the divine work the divine vengeance, even to their extinction.

We have, then, to consider these denunciatory passages, first, as they were employed by their authors; secondly, as they are now presented to us for our own use in the services of the Church, or in private devotion.

Under the first head, let me observe as follows. There is not one of these passages which tampers with truth or justice; they are aimed only at sin, to blast and to wither it. "Lead me, O Lord, in thy righteousness, because of mine enemies" (Psa. 5 : 8). This is the universal strain. All these passages are strokes delivered with the sword of righteousness, in its unending warfare with iniquity. Nor is there one among them, of which it can be shown that it refers to any personal feud, passion, or desire. Everywhere the Psalmist speaks in the name of God, on behalf of his word and will; in behalf of righteousness, and against iniquity.

But it may still be urged, that such denunciations are excessive in degree, that they are too severe and

savage, and that they are not suitable for the mouth
of a being such as man; who in the sense of his
own shortcomings and sins should learn a lesson
of abstention from judgment upon his fellows.

With respect to their severity I suggest, and if
need be contend, that we, in our ignorance and
weakness, are not fit judges of the extent to which
the wisdom of the Almighty may, under given
circumstances differing widely from ours, justly
carry the denunciation, even by the mouth of man,
and the punishment of guilt.

Man, and even civilized man, contemplates with
much equanimity the taking of human life for the
occasions which he deems sufficient. He knows
that in all wars one party must be guilty, and that
in most or many wars neither have had a justification for the wholesale bloodshed, which floods
the path of destruction that they necessarily follow. Life, which man did not give and cannot
restore, he takes away, for the repression of crime,
with general, though not unanimous, approval. It
is also taken, even now, in most Christian coun-

tries, through duels for private injury or insult;
and it is but recently that public opinion in our
own country has become repugnant to the practice.
But the scruples, which for ourselves we so easily
thrust aside, become active, feverish, and even violent, when, in a world to the abundant wickedness
of which our own practice witnesses, the Ruler of
that world, who gave life for use, and who sees
and judges its abuse, is to be arraigned before our
mock tribunal; and we, who cannot and do not
rightly guide, each of us, our own action, are to
undertake to determine his. And this, when we
have not fully learned, and cannot measure, either
the deep and frightful depravity of the Canaanitish nations, or the purposes with which, from time
to time, penalty descends from on high. We know
not whether it comes in mercy to correct the
growth of evil before it shall become incurable;
and whether, or how far, when opportunity has
been exhausted here, resources may still have been
held in reserve on behalf of persons placed as
they were, to be expended for good in the great

Elsewhere. To pronounce verdicts upon these terrible denunciations may be impious; and is surely, at the least, unreasonable.

> "And who art thou, that on the bench would sit,
>   To judge what is a thousand miles removed,
>   With the brief vision of a single span?" [1]

There is certainly more claim to substance in the objection, which urges that these denunciations are unsuitable for man. But here I should interpose the question, To what man? The wonderful nature, in which we have been created, is in nothing more wonderful than in the diversity of the conditions under which it has to subsist and work, on its road from embryo to perfection. As those stages accumulate, the moral code becomes multiform and involved. In simpler forms of life, and in earlier stages of society, the roads between right and wrong were short, broad, and clear. Even so were then the dividing spaces of the battle-field, whereas contending hosts are now severed by miles, and almost leagues, from one another.

[1] Dante, "Parad." XIX. 81. Pollock's translation.

But, further, the Psalmists, and the nation to
which they belonged, lived under a different dispensation from ours. If we accept the Scriptures,
that nation held a divine commission to establish
the right and to put down the wrong, in a sense
in which no such commission is now given. For
us, it is enough to hope that at any given juncture
we may be doing the will of God. But what we
hope, they knew; and sight for them was mixed
with faith in a degree and mode very remote from
the spirit of our later, and, in this respect, perhaps
higher training. They were accustomed to what
may be termed short accounts with the divine
justice; and to reward or suffering as the immediate consequences, and, therefore, as the direct at-
testations, of the judgment of God upon the moral
conduct of man. The responsibility, which is for us
diffused and indefinite, was for them concentrated
and palpable. But, besides this, they had the
great standing institution of prophecy; and the
king in whose ears Nathan's words had thundered,
" Thou art the man," might well feel that his own

contact was a close one with the mind of the Almighty, and that he might upon occasion speak his very strongest words under guidance from on high.

I do not pursue farther these remarks, which are no more than tentative and approximate. But I cannot find myself justified in the assumption that we have in all cases a complete cognizance of the conditions under which the Psalms give judgment upon the unrighteous, or are intended to arrive at final conclusions on the question what the Jews might, and what they might not, suitably be commissioned by the Almighty to denounce.

More immediately are we concerned in the question as to the place held in Christian devotion, and especially in public ritual, by the denunciatory passages of the Psalms. It is one question what these denunciations were for the Jew; it is another, and entirely a distinct one, what they are for us. But the answer to this objection, I apprehend, lies near to hand. All scruple, at least all rational or plausible scruple in this matter, seems to rest upon the supposition that the passages are aimed at creatures who have characters mixed between good and evil, and who therefore are not presumptively fit subjects for unmixed, undiscriminating denunciation by their fellow-men. But can any one reasonably suppose that these declarations are, in the mind and sense of the Christian Church, directed against any human enemy? Our human enemies, if we are so unhappy as to have any, are not the most watchful, the most subtle, the most destructive of our foes. " For we wrestle not against flesh and blood, but against . . . the rulers of the darkness of this world" (Eph. 6 : 12). Both the Holy Scripture and the Christian religion teach, and our human experience largely testifies to a more formidable conflict. There are spirits whose meat and drink, so to speak, it is to extend the domain of evil, to deepen corruption, to destroy happiness by destroying innocence, which is its base ; to add, both in range and in intensity, to the misery and the sin which have made the world so sad. If this be so, then I contend that to pray for the abolition or paralysis of their work and of its agents, and this especially when we meet as Christians to set forth solemnly the collective as well as impersonal needs and aspirations of mankind, is a practice which speaks for itself, and requires neither justification nor apology.

Apart altogether from the question, what may be the value or completeness of the foregoing defensive suggestions, I would remind my readers that they relate not to the main body of the question respecting the Psalms, but to a portion of it which is limited and exceptional. The Psalms, like other productions, are to be judged by their general character. I do not perceive how, if we approach this question on the grounds and in the spirit of reason, it is possible for a person so approaching it to set aside the mass of evidence, which establishes the unparalleled and unapproached position of the Book in its antiquity and use, in its pure and noble theology, and in a moral and spiritual character witnessed afresh by the judgment and practice of each succeeding age.

And, if the several parts of this evidence link themselves into a compact and harmonious whole, it is
not reason, but unreason in the mask of reason,
which declines or omits to acknowledge the presumption thence arising, that the Book is at a level
indefinitely higher than has been reached by the
unassisted faculties of man, and that the power
which raised it to that level can only be divine.
Such a conclusion will survive even the approving
reference in Psalm 137 : 9, to a practice of savage
warfare. Were it true that the image of gold had
feet of clay, we might indeed be perplexed by the
combination; but would not this be just as we
often are perplexed by other combinations, presented to us in the providential government of the
world? And not only in the providential government of the world, but in the fulfilment of our
personal relations with other men. Yet we do not
put an end on that account to such relations : nor
do we cease to believe in God because we, such as
we are—God save the mark—cannot comprehend
the reason, or even discern the rightfulness, of all

he does. So neither, by parity of reasoning, can we refuse to admit sufficient evidence of an origin more than human for the Psalms on the ground that we see only through a glass darkly, and that they present incidental features of apparent difficulty, analogous in principle to those which in other departments our experience brings before us.

V.

THE MOSAIC LEGISLATION.

———————

The legislative books of the Pentateuch, from Exodus to Deuteronomy, may be contemplated in the light, either (1) of their credentials, or (2) of their character and contents.

The Christian Church, which had heretofore regarded them as an integral and instructive part of the divine revelation, is now challenged by the voices of numerous critics to defend them. Champions in this cause are not wanting; and it is not to be supposed that the learned in linguistic studies have arrived at unanimous and final conclusions in these grave matters. If we compare their studies, as to unanimity, continuity, and ascertained progress, with that of the natural sciences, the comparison will be not at all to their advantage. Their services are not, however, to be

unduly disparaged. What is understood to be at
issue is, the date and authorship of the books in
the form in which we now have them. These are
contested by the negative school on grounds of
language and style, upon which none can properly
attempt to follow or to judge them, unless when
equipped with the same special knowledge. They
also allege, as parts of the destructive argument,
that the books contain anachronisms, contradictions, statements disproved by history.

They have recently been challenged by Dr.
Cave[1] to set forth a plain and distinct statement of
these difficulties, such as might bring the allegations in some degree within the circles of knowledge and of judgment, for us, who are not experts,
but are a public supposed to be endued with ordinary intelligence. They are also invited to state
what meaning they assign to the standing phrase,
" And the Lord spake unto Moses," which with its
variants occurs, it may be observed, no less than
thirty times in the twenty-seven chapters of Leviti-

---

[1] Contemporary Review, April, 1890, pp. 537-551.

cus. And, finally, they are solicited by Dr. Cave to show in plain terms the reasons why it is unreasonable to suppose that the books (either in their present state or otherwise) were, from the time of Moses onwards, contemporaneous with the events described, and that they grew up one by one along with those events.

It seems but common equity that we, who stand outside the learned world, and who find operations are in progress, which are often declared to have destroyed the authority of these ancient books, should be supplied, as far as may be, with available means of rationally judging the nature and grounds of the impeachment. And it is unfortunate that this has been little thought of; and that, while we are, it may almost be said, drenched with the deductions and conclusions of the negative critics,[1] it is still so difficult, in multitudes of instances, to come at any clear view of the grounds

[1] These observations refer to the works of some Continental writers, notably Dr. Reuss ; and in no way to such works as the able volume of Dr. Driver on the Old Testament, published since the first edition of these essays.

16

on which they build. The matters of style and language we must contentedly take upon trust; but anachronism, contradiction of history, contradiction in the books themselves, ought to be more or less within our cognizance. And there are many arguments of historical verisimilitude and likelihood, which are in no sense the exclusive property of specialism.

Even within the compass of the Torah, a distinction has been drawn by some eminent critics (by Eichhorn, for example), in their writings on the canon of the Old Testament;[1] who have assigned the legislative portions generally to Moses himself, and the historical parts to scribes acting under his direction, or at a later time.

It does not appear easy to show why such a singular intermixture of the two should have been made, unless it were by or under the direction of the lawgiver himself. The tangled occupations of

[1] A most convenient summary of the history of critical opinion on the Pentateuch is supplied by Bleek *cum* Wellhausen in the *Einleitung* (Ed. 1886), sects. 13-17. Wellhausen adds another review at the close of the volume in this edition.

his evidently hard-pressed life would account for a
form of authorship, which is not in itself at all convenient. But the ordinary reader will not fail to
observe that it is the legislation, for which in the
sacred text itself the claim is constantly made of
being due to direct communication from above,
while no corresponding assertion in general accompanies the historical recitals.

Speaking at large, every imaginable difference
has prevailed among the critics themselves as to
the source, date, and authorship of the books. But
on the whole, the negative movement has become
bolder in its assertions as it proceeded, and has
brought them gradually towards later epochs: to
Samuel, to the age of David, to the severance of
the kingdoms, to Josiah, to the Captivity, and even
to those who followed it.   The affirmative side has
been also stoutly maintained,[1] not without the admission of particular additions and interpolations
in the received text.   The distinction between substantial authorship, and final editorship, has been

---

[1] Bleek, *Einleitung*, sect. 15.

largely recognized by writers of celebrity and weight. Bleek himself, apparently sustained by Wellhausen as late as 1886, held that Moses had a hand (*einen antheil*) in the legislative books. Many of the laws, they say at that date, are without sense or purpose, except in regard to circumstances which disappeared with the Mosaic period.[1] Several sections of this important work[2] are given to the indication of portions of the books which must have been Mosaic. Further, we have the following remarkable declaration. Though the entire Pentateuch in its present form should not have been the work of Moses, and though many laws are the product of a later age, still the legislation, in its spirit and character as a whole, is genuinely Mosaic;[3] and that, in dealing with the Pentateuch, we stand, at least as to the three middle books, upon historical ground;[4] evidently meaning upon ground which is historical as opposed to that which is unauthenti-

---

[1] Bleek, *Einleitung,* sect. 11.   [2] *Ibid.,* sects. 13-24.

[3] " *So muss doch die darin enthaltene gesetzgebung ihrem ganzen geiste und character nach echt mosaisch seyn.*"—*Ibid.,* sect. 22, p. 45.

[4] *Ibid.*

cated or legendary. Further, what is thus generally asserted of the spirit and character of the Penta-teuchal laws, is asserted, for an important share of them,[1] as to both the contents and even the form.

These statements—it would not be fair to call them admissions—go to the root of the whole matter, and seem to leave us in possession of that for which alone I contend; namely, that the heart and substance of the legislative and institutional system delivered to us in the Pentateuch is his-torically trustworthy. If this be so, it still remains highly important to distinguish by critical exami-nation what, if any, particular portions of the work in their actual form may be open to question, either as secondary errors, or as developments appended to the original formation; but the citadel, so long victoriously held by faith and reason, both through Hebrew and through Christian ages, remains unas-sailed, and the documents of Holy Writ emerge substantially unhurt from the inquisitive and search-ing analysis of the modern time.

[1] *Einleitung*, sect. 23, p. 46.

In more recent productions we find an extension of the field of debate and a change of tone.

There is a later work of Wellhausen's[1] which minutely subdivides the books into smaller portions, and refers these to their different authors, with a self-reliance which appears to be remarkable, but of which I am not a fit judge. I may observe, however, that this work has neither introduction nor conclusion, neither index nor table of contents, and that it resembles rather the promiscuous gatherings of a note-book, or rather, of two note-books crossing one another, discharged bodily into a printing-office, than a work of regular or scientific criticism. I must add that in certain cases, where the unity of the text is disputed upon grounds alike cognizable by us all, I find the conclusions of the author as disputable as they are confident. In other instances, numerous enough, assertions are made, as if they were oracles, without the slightest explanation, or any indication of their

[1] " Die composition des Hexateuch's und der Historischen Bücher." Berlin, 1889.

grounds. Examples of these methods may be found in the criticisms[1] on Genesis, and in the contradiction alleged to exist in the several accounts of Caleb and Joshua (Numb. 32 : 5, and Deut. 1 : 32-38).

A still more negative utterance, if I understand it rightly, is found in the " Prolegomena to the History of Israel," translated under the author's supervision, and accompanied with his article on Israel from the Encyclopædia Britannica.[2] This book, published since the edition of Bleek *cum* Wellhausen from which I have quoted, appears in a singular manner to contradict it, and announces that "the Mosaic history is not the starting-point of the history of ancient Israel, but for the history of Judaism."[3] The distinction may not be familiar to English readers, but the meaning seems to be that the Pentateuch had not, either in form or substance, any operative existence until after the Exile, when the ancient Israel is held to end, and Judaism

[1] Page 7.   [2] Edinburgh: A. & C. Black, 1885.
[3] Preface by Professor Robertson Smith, p. v.

to begin. A " Mosaic germ" only is admitted; and a germ is that which, like an unborn child, has no operative existence, but only the promise of producing one at some future date. According, then, to the showing of those who tender themselves as our guides, Israel lived on for nine hundred years, from the Exodus, and transmitted a peculiar faith, law, ritual, and nationality, without any legislative, or ritual, or institutional system to uphold any one of them. This very startling proposition appears to me to do violence to reason not less glaringly than any of the assertions ventured by the theologians in the days of their pride and power. Those writers are doubtless perfectly sincere, who represent this as a method of progressive revelation. But there are also persons who think that such a progressive revelation as this would for over two thousand years have palmed upon the whole Jewish and Christian world not only a heartless, but an impossible imposture. It is more immediately necessary to observe that the hypothesis is one reaching far beyond the province of specialism, and requiring to be tested at a number of points by considerations more broadly historical. Nor can I quit the subject without observing that it is extremely difficult to learn whether there exists any real standing-ground, which the present negative writers mean not only to occupy but to hold. Almost any representation of their views may be either supported or contradicted by citing particular expressions from their works. All we can do is to dive as best we may into their conception of what Wellhausen rather singularly calls "the secrets" of his art; as though he considered that its processes are akin to those of the occult sciences.[1] Upon the whole, and taking the article on Israel in the Encyclopædia Britannica as the fairest exposition of his views, I infer that the present fashion is to believe in Moses, but to question even his connection with the Decalogue;[2] to allow him to have given or suggested a something, totally indefinite in its character, to the Israelites; and to hold that

[1] *Einleitung*, Ed. 1886, Vorwort.
[2] Wellhausen, " Hist. Israel " (Black), pp. 436, 509.

the materials of the legislative books, as a whole, gradually grew up out of material supplied upon occasion by the priests (like the "Answers of Experts,"[1] which supplied a contribution to the Code of Justinian) into a state which enabled editors, generally post-Exilic, to reduce them to their present form. This scheme seems to be admirably represented by the words which Mr. Robertson Smith quotes, on his own very high authority, as its gist. And this is the scheme to which I desire, on historical grounds, to demur.

At the same time it is undeniable that, even if the outside negative conclusions were still such as they were stated to be so lately as in 1886, yet the impression they had created was not of a similarly limited character. Whether owing to the predispositions of the time, or to a spirit latent in some of the critics, or to the reaction which is usually perceptible when certain ideas long cherished on one side have been found to require modification, there have been, as it were, exhalations from the recent

[1] Gibbon (Milman's ed.), IV., 193.

inquiries, extending outwards in their effect much beyond the positive conclusions. An atmosphere has been diffused around us, and we habitually inhale it, which inspires a general uncertainty, leading to negation, with respect to the Mosaic books. This causes us, not, perhaps, to believe (for belief would imply and demand a rational process), but to feel towards these great foundation-books as if we believed, that, instead of being as to the heart and pith of them trustworthy, they were in the main untrustworthy; that they were compounded or composed at uncertain times, by uncertain authors, from uncertain materials; that even bad faith is to be traced in them; and that the question is not so much what particulars can be convicted of unauthenticity, as whether any particulars can be rescued from the general discredit of a mythical or legendary inception. It is against this vague, irrational, unscientific method of proceeding, that I would enter not a protest only, but a pleading. Whatever is to happen, let not Christians lose unawares either their faith, or that pillar of their faith which the great books of the Old Testament always have supplied.

I have already made it clear that I yield, as a matter of course, to the conclusions of linguists in their own domain, not only respectful attention, but provisional assent.   That domain includes not only criticism strictly textual, but all that relates to style, and, in a word, whatever properties of any given writings are developed through the medium of the particular tongue in which they are composed.   On the mere form of the books, they speak with a force which, as against us, the unlearned, is overwhelming. But, in the examinations directed to the matter as opposed to the form, their authority is of a less stringent character, and may even decline to zero. The historical aspects and relations which open out this field are not theirs exclusively, and we may canvass and question their conclusions, just as it is open to us to proceed with the conclusions of Macaulay or of Grote.

When it is attempted to bring down the date of the Pentateuch from the time of Moses, by whom

the books in various forms purport[1] to have been
composed, to the period of the Babylonian Captivity,
and this not only as to their literary form, but as
to their substance, the evident meaning and effect
of the attempt is to divest them of a historical, and
to invest them with a legendary character.

At the same time, it should be borne in mind
that those who have not seen reason to adopt the
negative theory above described leave entirely open
numerous questions belonging to the institutions
of the Israelites. It is not extravagant to assume
that laws given to them as a nomad people, and
then subjected to the varying contingencies of history during many centuries, may or even must have
required and received adaptation by supplement,
development, or change in detail, which the ap-

[1] For instance, as by the proem to Deuteronomy (1 : 1): the recited
orders of the Almighty to Moses that he should speak, followed by
the speeches—*e.g.*, Lev. 1 : 1, Num. 1 : 1, the constant verbal report
of words spoken to Moses when no other person (or in some cases
Aaron only) was present; and the remarkable and high-toned injunc-
tions in the later chapters of Deuteronomy, which all through seem to
have reference to a code of legislation preceding them.

pointed instructors of the people were authorized and qualified to supply; and all this not in derogation, but rather in completion and in furtherance of the work of Moses, which might still remain his in essence from first to last.

It is admitted, however, that the whole question must be tried on historical and literary grounds. On such grounds I seek to approach it, and to throw light upon it from some considerations of reason and probability, which appear to me to be of not inconsiderable cogency. By testing the subject in this way, we may come, in part at least, to learn by testing what in the main is fact, what in the main is speculation, and to a great extent fluctuating and changeful speculation.

First, it is never to be forgotten that our point of departure is from the ground of established historic fact. The existence of Moses is even better and far better established than that (for example) of Lycurgus. We know Lycurgus in the main from the one great fact of his very peculiar institutions. They, such as we find them in historic times, com-

pel us to presume his existence in a prehistoric
time. Not only their high and elaborate organization, but their practical efficacy in separating and
fencing off from the rest of Greece the Spartan
community, reduces to something near absurdity
any such supposition as that they were essentially
no more than a late growth reached by impercep-
tible degrees. We know Moses quite as well from
his institutions; which are by no means less peculiar, and which, as experience has shown, have
been very far more durable. In the case of Moses,
it happens that we have much evidence independent of, and anterior to, the institutions themselves
in their historic form. Yet no one doubts either
the existence of the Spartan lawgiver, or the general character of his personal work. If the form
of the books in which the Mosaic legislation
reaches us be open to the suspicion of manipulation by scribes or editors, or if it suggest some
suspicion of developments, how does this compare
with the case of Lycurgus? About or from him
we have no books at all; and yet it would be

deemed irrational to doubt either the existence of the man, or the substance of the work performed by him.

The exodus from Egypt, the settlement in Palestine, the foundation there of institutions, civil and religious, which were endowed with a tenacity of life and a peculiarity of character beyond all example; these things are established by Scripture, but they are also established independent of Scripture. They constitute a *trinoda necessitas*, a threefold combination of fact, which, in order to make them intelligible and coherent, in order to supply a rational connection between cause and effect, appears to require not only a Moses, but, in substance, such a Moses as the Scripture supplies. They build up a niche, which the Scripture fills. At all times of history, and specially in those primitive times, when[1] the men made the governments, not the governments the men, these great independent historic facts absolutely carry with them the assumption of a leader, a governor, a legislator. All this simply

[1] So Montesquieu, "Grandeur et Décadence des Romains," Chap. I.

means a Moses; and a Moses, such as we know him from the Pentateuch.

And thus we are led, I do not say to, but towards, the conclusion that, whatever be the disparaging allegations of the critics, they may after all according to likelihood be found reasonable only as to matters of form or of detail. It may still be fact that the substance of the history is in thorough accordance with the historic bases that are laid for us in secular as well as in sacred testimony. If this be so, then we have also to bear in mind that the phenomenon, which we have before us, is one so peculiar that it could only have been exhibited to the world as the offspring of a peculiar generating cause. A people of limited numbers, of no marked political genius, negative and stationary as to literature and art, maintain their absolutely separate existence for near a thousand years, down to the Captivity. They are placed in the immediate neighborhood, and subjected to the frequent attacks, of the great Eastern monarchies, as well as of some very warlike neighbors. These attacks

17

compromise their political independence, but do
not prevent it from being recovered. They receive
the impress of a character so marked, that not
even the Captivity can efface it; but, on the contrary, that searching trial helps to give a harder
and sharper projection to its features. It retains
its solidity and substance while everything else is
subjected to change, and even such a great political aggregation as the Hittite monarchy becomes
absolutely fused in the surrounding masses. It retains its obstinate and unconquerable peculiarities,
even when it has passed under the harrow of conditions such as at Babylon, apparently sufficient to
beat down and destroy the most obstinate national-
ism. Can it be denied that this great historic fact,
nowhere to be matched, is in thorough accordance
with, and almost of itself compels us to presuppose,
the existence from the outset of an elaborately detailed and firmly compacted system of laws and institutions, under which this peculiar discipline might
subsist and work, so as gradually to shape, determine, and mature the character of the people?

If, apart from all questions of form and expression, the substance of the Mosaic law was given to the Israelites on their settlement in Palestine, such a provision, it may fearlessly be said, was in full accordance with the moral exigency of the case, and with the laws of historical probability. If on the other hand there was no Moses, or only a Moses who left nothing palpable behind him, and who does not rank among the lawgivers of the world; if the legislative books represent only a gradual and mythical accretion due mainly either to class interests or to the magnifying effect of distance, and turned to account by invention either interested or credulous,—then the hypothesis presented to us is, it may surely be contended, in violent discord with what, on principles either of Providential government or of human good sense, the case would usually be held to have required.

In estimating the claim of the Old Testament to a divine origin, it is important to compare the legislation given by Moses with that of other ancient

lawgivers, such, for example, as Solon, who enjoyed
the light of a far more advanced civilization.   Still,
this comparison, if it stood alone, would not fully
bring out the reason of the case; we must also
match the Hebrew intellect, as measured by knowledge, art and manners, with the corresponding conditions among the other nations, whose laws may
be brought into the comparison.   For if, with inferior tools and materials, a superior work was
produced, it must surely be admitted that such a
result suggests, even perhaps of itself requires, the
supposition of some hidden aid which rectified the
disproportion, and placed the means in a due relation to the end.   Now, among the Hebrews of the
period, following the Exodus and settlement, there
is no sign as yet of intellectual predominance or
advancement; and that such a man as Moses
should have been raised up amongst them is a
fact, which of itself suggests and sustains the idea
of some altogether special and peculiar guidance
exercised by the Almighty over the selected
people.

I cannot but think that, wherever we turn, we seem to find the broad and lucid principles of historic likelihood asserting themselves in favor of the substance of the legislative books, apart from questions of detail and literary form.

In its great stages, we are entitled to treat the matter of the narrative books as history entitled to credit. An elaborate organization, with a visible head and a hereditary succession, is, after a long lapse of time, substituted for a regimen over Israel, of which the mainsprings had been personal eminence and moral force. It is represented in the Scripture, and it seems obvious, that the transition from this patriarchal republicanism to monarchy was in the nature of a religious retrogression. It showed an increasing incapacity to walk by faith, and a craving for an object of sight, as a substitute for the Divine Majesty apprehended by spiritual discernment, and habitually conceived of by the people as the head of the civil community. This view of the relative condition of· republican and of regal Israel is confirmed by the fact, on which I

have already observed, that with the monarchy
came in another regular organization, that of the
schools of the prophets.   Prophecy, which for the
present purpose we may consider as preaching,
instead of appearing from time to time as occasion
required, became a system, with provision for perpetual succession.   That is to say, the people could
not be kept up to the primitive, or even the necessary, level in belief and life, without the provision
of more elaborate and direct means of instruction,
exhortation, and reproof, than had at first been
requisite.

Notwithstanding the existence of those means,
and the singular and noble energy of the prophets,
the proofs of the decline are not less abundant than
painful, in the wickedness of most of the sovereigns,
and in the almost wholesale and too constant lapse
of the Israelites into the filthy idolatry which was
rooted in the country.   And again, it is not a little
remarkable that the enumeration by name of the
great historic heroes of faith, in the Epistle to the
Hebrews, ends in the person of King David (Heb.

11 : 32), with the first youth of the monarchy. The only later instances referred to are the prophets, named as a class, who stood apart and alone, and were not as a rule leaders of the people, but rather witnesses in sackcloth against their iniquities. Compare the series of kings, in point of conduct, with the series of judges. If we take the history from the Exodus to the Exile as a whole, the latter end was worse than the beginning, the cup of iniquity was full; it had been filled by a gradual process : and one of the marks of that process was a lowering of the method in which the chosen people were governed; it became more human and less divine.

Under these circumstances, does it not appear like a paradox, and even a rather wanton paradox, to refer the production of those sacred Mosaic books, which constituted the charter, and formed the character, of the Hebrews as a separate and peculiar people, to the epochs of a lowered and decaying spiritual life? These books, or the matter contained in them, surely formed the base on which the entire structure rested. It is hardly possible to separate the fabric from its foundation. Had they not been recorded and transmitted, it would have been reasonable, perhaps necessary, for us to presume their existence. They could only spring from a plant full of vigorous life, not from one comparatively sickly and exhausted.

Again, we are taught by the negative school that the entire portion of the Pentateuch, which specially describes the work of the Priest, and which they term the Priest-Code, is of late composition, probably the latest of all, and has been devised in the interest of the priestly order.

Now I think that there are ready means of applying the touchstone to this allegation. It seems the great aim of the assailants to bring down the date of the main contents of the legislative books to the Exile and the period which follows it. Now we have to remember that the schools of the prophets established a caste which was in professional rivalry with the priesthood, and which presented every likelihood of being its effec-

tive censor. We have the written and, I believe, unquestioned productions of this school of prophets,
reaching nearly into the ninth century (in the
Book of Amos), above two hundred years before
the Exile. The relation of the prophet to the
priest, somewhat accentuated, let us suppose, by
competing interests, was in certain respects one of
superiority; for, while the priest only administered
in a human way a system originally of divine ap-
pointment, the prophet believed himself to speak
under direct inspiration and command from the
Most High. The supposition pressed upon us is
that, during the period when the books of the
prophets were being produced, the priests foisted
upon the nation adulterated, nay, rather forged,
works, which they audaciously ascribed to Moses,
and which they shaped in the interests of the sacerdotal order. Is it not quite plain that, if this had
been true, nay, if it had been so much as an approach to the truth, the prophets would, in the
interests of righteousness even more than in their
own, have made use of the advantages of their po-

sition, and would have held up such a flagrant iniquity of the rival class to infamy or rebuke? Yet
they do nothing of the sort. And it is not even
open to us to refer this to some hidden cause,
as it would have been if we could have alleged
that, for some undeclared reason, it is their habit
to pass by the conduct of the priests in silence.
For, on the contrary, they do exercise the office of
reprimand most freely. They do reprove and denounce neglect of duty and abuse of power by the
priests; but they do this exactly in the same way
for the priestly order and for their own; and,
though they could not have been biassed against
their own schools, there is no sign that priests were
more faulty than prophets. By way of specimen
of their usual manner, I may quote the words of
the prophet Zephaniah, who in the following passage appears to administer justice impartially all
round :—

"Her princes within her are roaring lions; her judges are
evening wolves; they gnaw not the bones till the morrow.

"Her prophets are light and treacherous persons: her

priests have polluted the sanctuary, they have done violence
to the law " (Zeph. 3 : 3, 4).

All were human, all were alike. There is nowhere a tittle of evidence to show the gross and
very special offenses with which the priesthood are
now charged. In such a case the negative evidence carries positive force. It is evident, first,
that the prophets knew nothing of such delinquen-
cies : and secondly, that, if they were unknown to
the prophets through this long lapse of time, it was
because they were not committed.

We have, then, in the historic Moses, a great and
powerful genius, an organizing and constructing
mind. Degenerate ages cannot equip and furnish forth illustrious founders, only at the most
the counterfeits or shadows of them. Moses belongs to the great class of nation-makers ; to a
class of men, who have a place by themselves in
the history of politics, and who are among the
rarest and highest of the phenomena of our race.
And he stands in historic harmony with his work.
But we are now apparently asked to sever the

work from the worker, and to refer it to some doubtful and nameless person; whereas it is surely obvious or probable that the author of a work so wonderful and so far beyond example, so elaborate in its essential structure, and so designed for public use, could hardly fail to associate his name with it as if written upon a rock, and with a pen of iron. For, be it recollected, that name was the seal and stamp of the work itself. According to its own testimony he was the *apostolos* (Exod. 19 : 16-23, and *passim*), the messenger, who brought it from God, and gave it to the people. If the use of his name was a fiction, it was one of those fictions which cannot escape the brand of falsehood; for it altered essentially the character of the writings to which it was attached.

Supposing it to be granted that this or that portion of the legislative books may have been an addition in the way of development, of an appendage and supplement to a scheme already existing, how and why came it to be placed under the shelter of the great name of Moses, but because that name had already acquired and consolidated its authority, from its being inseparably attached to the original gift of the law?

Even so it was that, when the great and wonderful poems known as the Iliad and Odyssey had given to the name of Homer a surpassing celebrity, and other works of less exalted rank sought for fame by claiming him as their author, the simple fact that they so claimed him of itself supplied the proof that Homer was traditionally, and from immemorial time, taken to be the author of those greater works at the period when the lesser ones were imputed to him. If the title of Mosaic authorship was ever in any case attached to what Moses did not produce, the ascription was made in order to gain credit for the new supplemental matter, and of itself proved that, at the date when it was made, there was an older and immemorial belief in his being the author of the primary work, whereto the supplement was appended.

As we stand on historical ground in assuming that Moses was a great man, and a powerful agent

in the Hebrew history, so we stand on a like basis
in pointing to the fact that, from the Captivity onwards (I say nothing here of the prior period, as it
would beg the question), the Jewish nation paid
to the five books of the Pentateuch a special and
extraordinary regard, even beyond the rest of their
sacred books. These were known as the Torah;
and the fact of this special reverence is one so
generally acknowledged, that it may without discussion be safely assumed as a point of departure.

Before, then, any sort of acceptance or acquiescence is accorded to notions which virtually con-
sign to insignificance the most ancient of our sacred
books, let us well weigh the fact that the devout
regard of the Hebrews for the Torah took the form,
at or very soon after the Exile, of an extreme
vigilance on behalf of these particular books as
distinct from all others. This vigilance, which at
a later epoch reached its climax under the Massoretes, very naturally began, or greatly advanced,
at the time when the nation, or its leading classes,
having for the time lost their temple and their

visible home, clung more closely than ever to the
written word in their sacred books; to its body
either more, or not less, than to its spirit.

So early as in the days of Hezekiah, there is said
to have been a restorative process of some kind
performed upon the text of the law, as well as upon
the temple and its doors. [1] That clinging affection
to the Word, which the Captivity could not fail to
stimulate in pious minds, took effect, after the
Return, in the establishment of positive institutions
for its care; which, indeed, had become a necessity, in consequence of the change in the spoken
language, unless it were to be wholly lost to the
people. Hence we have the Jewish tradition of a
Great Synagogue, founded with this view. A guild
of scribes was appointed to copy, preserve, and
expound the divine Word,[2] and the Canon of the
Old Testament appears during the same period to
have assumed something of a regular form. Soon
grew up the Massorah, or body of traditions con-

[1] Paterson Smyth, " The Old Documents," p. 42.   2 Chron. 29 : 3.
[2] *Ibid.*, p. 66.

cerning the texts of the Torah, which is supposed to have become noticeable from about 300 B. C.[1] and which in after ages gave a name to the Massoretes, official students and guardians of the text.   This body is one without a parallel in the history of the world.[2]   Its existence not only afforded strong securities of a special nature for the faithful custody of the text from the date when its operations commenced, but it also bears witness to a profound and exacting veneration for the ancient books as such, which seems to pre-suppose as its root an unquestioning traditional belief in their antiquity and authenticity.

The Jews, perhaps exclusively among the early peoples, distinguished broadly between the matter and the corporeal form of a book, between its soul and its body.   They alone conceived the idea of using the material form of the words and letters as an instrument for ensuring the conservation of the contents.   Their conception was that, if they could secure the absolute identity of the manuscripts, and

[1] Paterson Smyth, "The Old Documents," p. 90.   [2] *Ibid.*, p. vii.

reckon up the actual numbers of the words they contain, and of the letters which compose the words, then they would have rendered change in them impossible, and conservation certain. Thus, for example, the words in the Book of Psalms were counted, and the middle word of the book was known. The letters in each word were also counted, and the middle letter was known. Rules for writing, placing, and arranging were laid down; readings were noted as *khetibh* and *keri;* as what was in the text, and as what ought to be in the text but, from a reverent unwillingness to alter, only took its place upon the margin. The Hebrews seem to have been the only people who built up by degrees a regular scientific method of handling the material forms, in which the substance of their sacred books was clothed; and this system had begun to grow from the time when a special reverence is known to have been concentrated upon the Torah.

I will not dwell upon the topic that this peculiarity of handling supplies of itself a certain amount

18

of presumption for peculiarity of origin. It may
have commenced before the Captivity. It may
have preceded, and may in that case probably have
been enhanced by, the division of the kingdoms.
It must have been in great force when, soon after
the Captivity, schools of scribes were entrusted
with the custody of the text of the law as a study
apart from that of its meaning. Now, in our time,
we are asked or tempted by the negative criticism
to believe that all this reverence for the books of
the Pentateuch, having primarily the sense for its
object, but so abounding and overflowing as to
embrace even the corporeal vehicle, was felt towards
a set of books not substantially genuine, but compounded and made up by operators, and these
recent operators, who may be mildly called editors,
but who were rather clandestine authors, such as
some might without ceremony call impostors. Is
this a probable or reasonable hypothesis? Is it
even possible that these books of recent concoction,
standing by the side of some among the prophetical
books possessing a much greater antiquity, should

nevertheless have attracted to themselves, and have permanently retained, an exceptional and superlative veneration, much exceeding that paid to the oldest among the books of the prophets, and such as surely presumes a belief in the remoteness of their date, the genuineness of their character, and their title to stand as the base, both doctrinal and historic, of the entire Hebrew system?

The result of this negative criticism ought to be viewed in its extreme form, and this for several reasons: such as, that, with the lapse of time, it continually adopts new negations; that the more conservative of the latest schools exhibit to us no principle, which separates them in the mass from the bolder disintegration; and that what is now the *ultima Thule* of the system may, a short time hence, appear only to have been a stage on the way to positions as yet undreamt of. So viewing the subject, do we not find that it comes to this: not merely that the Mosaic laws received secondary supplements or amendments from time to time, but that the entire fabric had grown up anonymously as well as recently, and that it rests upon no guarantee whatever, either of time, or of place, or of personal authority?

I have already endeavored to show the historic improbability that an upstart production could have leaped into an estimation such as belongs to a firm tradition and a general credit of antiquity. And now let us look for a moment at the rather crude and irregular form of the Mosaic books from Exodus to Deuteronomy. Taken as a whole, they have not that kind of consistency which belongs to consecutiveness of the parts, and which almost uniformly marks both historical and legal documents.[1] They mix narrative and legislation; they pass from one to the other without any obvious reason. They repeat themselves in a manner which seems to exclude the idea that they had undergone

[1] "As to this want of order (which seems to me to favor the idea of contemporaneity), a later codifier would have been more artificial in his arrangement" (Milman's " History of the Jews," 3d edition, 1863). Writing of the delivery of the law, the learned and very liberal-minded Dean Milman had before him the works of the critical school down to Bleek; and in the admirable note `I., 131) from which I have just

the careful and reflected processes of review, the comparison of part with part, which is generally bestowed upon works of great importance, completed with comparative leisure, and intended for the guidance not only of an individual but of a people. They are even accused of contradiction. They appear to omit adjustments, necessary in the light of the subsequent history: such, for instance, as we might desire to find between the sweeping proscription not only of image worship, but of images or shapen corporeal forms, in the Second Commandment, and the use actually made of them in the temple, and in the singular case of the serpent destroyed by Hezekiah (2 Kings 18 : 4). It seems not difficult to account for this roughness and crudeness of authorship in the case of Moses, under the circumstances of changeful nomad life,

quoted a few words, he expresses a firm and reasoned dissent from the negative conclusions as to the Pentateuch in its substance, while he strongly urges the likelihood of minor changes in the text with anachronism and inaccuracy here and there as the consequence. This note is in effect a succinct but highly pregnant treatise, and will well repay those who carefully peruse it.

and the constant pressure of anxious executive or judicial functions, combined with the effort of constructing a weighty legislative code, which required a totally different attitude of mind. The life of Moses, as it stands in the sacred text, must have been habitually a life of extraordinary, unintermitted strain, and one without remission of that strain even during its closing period. As some anomalies in the composition of the Koran may be referable to the circumstances of the life of Mahomet,[1] so we may apply a like idea to the configuration of the legislative books. It is not difficult to refer the anomalies of such authorship to the incidents of such a life, and to conceive that any

[1] See Rodwell's Preface to the Koran respecting the Suras. A critic in the Magazine and Book Review has cited against me the fourteenth chapter of Esdras 2, and the strange story it contains of the burning of the law and the rewriting of it by Ezra. This story dates at the earliest from the time of Cæsar, according to others from Domitian. Thus a tale, which first appears five centuries after the alleged fact, at once becomes authoritative, if it serves a purpose of negation. But even this story supports the argument in the text, for the law is continuously and miraculously reproduced by dictation to a body of five scribes.

changes, which have found their way into the text, may yet have been such as to leave unimpaired what may be called the originality, as well as the integrity, of its character. But how do these considerations hold, if we are to assume as our point of departure the hypothesis of the negative extremists? Under that supposition, the legislative books were principally not adjusted but composed, and this not only in a manner which totally falsifies their own solemn and often-repeated declarations, but which supposes something like hallucination on the part of a people that could have accepted such novelties, and almost worshipped them, as ancient. In addition to all this, they assumed their existing shape, so wanting as to series and method, in a settled state of things, in an old historic land, with an unbounded freedom of manipulation, at any rate with no restraint imposed by respect for original form, and with every condition in favor of the final editors, which could favor the production of a thoroughly systematic and orderly work. Does it not seem that if the preparation and presentation of the Hebrew code took place at the time and in the way imposed on us by the doctrine of the thorough disintegrationist, then we stand entirely at a loss to account for the somewhat loose and irregular form of the work before us? And conversely do not the peculiarities of that form constitute an objection to the negative hypothesis, which it is an absolute necessity for its promoters to get rid of as best they can?

Let me again illustrate the case by referring to the Iliad. Those who have referred that work to a variety of authors have been driven to very subtle and questionable arguments in order to exhibit some semblance of anomaly in the text, and have always been allowed to assume that the final editors under Pericles, or at whatever epoch, wrought with energy and purpose to weld the fragmentary material into a seemly whole. Is it conceivable that an operation, such as we are now required to believe in, could have been carried on without some sense of a similar necessity, or could so absolutely have failed in literary aim and effort?

I subjoin one further topic of the same class, as fit to be taken into view. The absence from the legislative books of all assertion of a future state, and of all motive derived from it with a view to conduct, has been already noticed. The probable reason of that absence from a code of laws framed by Moses under divine command or guidance is a subject alike of interest and obscurity. It has sometimes occurred to me as possible that the close connection of the doctrine with public religion in the Egyptian system might have supplied a reason for its disconnection from the Mosaic laws.[1] Even so I suppose we might, from other features of those laws, draw proof or strong presumption that, among the purposes of the legislator, there was included a determination to draw a broad and deep line, or even trench of demarcation, between the foreign religions in the neighborhood and the religious system of the Hebrews. The connection established by Moses between conduct

---

[1] I find this topic is touched by Bishop Alexander in his Bampton Lectures.

and earthly retribution or reward must of itself have tended to repress, if not the idea of a future state, yet the expression of that idea in public documents. Especially we should remember that the work of Moses was national rather than theological or personal.[1] His theology is a means of conserving the nationality, which was itself a forerunner and a means of preparation for the Advent. It is enough for my present purpose, that the absence of the doctrine of a future state from the work cannot be held to discredit the Mosaic authorship. But does not that absence help to discredit the idea of a post-Exilic authorship? Is it conceivable that Hebrews, proceeding to frame their legislative books, after the Captivity, and long after the Dispersion of the Ten Tribes, and with the aid of whatever light these events may have thrown upon the familiar ideas of a future life and an Underworld, as held both in the East and in Egypt, could have excluded all notice of it from their system of laws? We see something of this influence

[1] See Zincke, " Egypt of the Pharaohs and of the Khedive," p. 202.

in the noble passage on the dead, Wisdom 3 : 1-8, to which there is no parallel in any of the pre-Exilic books. If it was an influence impossible to exclude at the later date, then the fact of the exclusion becomes another difficulty in the way of our accepting any such date concerning the substance of the legislative books.[1]

It seems, then, that it is difficult to reconcile the results of the negative criticism on the Pentateuch with the known reverence of the Jews for their Torah, which appears absolutely to presuppose a tradition of undefined and probably immemorial age on its behalf, as a precondition of such universal and undoubting veneration. But if this be

[1] I desire to limit myself strictly to the argument as it stands in the text, and to leave untouched the question whether belief in a future state was more vigorous or more extended among the Jews after the Exile than before it. We cannot justly infer from the silence of the law, that the belief did not prevail among the people. It is in the prophetic and didactic books (as well as in the Psalms) that the future state is most clearly, or perhaps I should say most directly indicated. Quite apart from the evidence of the Psalms, I conceive that there is sufficient evidence from the Scripture text that the Hebrews of the Mosaic and regal periods believed in a future state.

necessary in the case of the Jew, how much more peremptorily is it required by the Samaritan contribution to the present argument, and what light does that contribution throw upon the general question?

It seems certain that in mediæval times, and until the seventeenth century, Christendom knew nothing of a Samaritan testimony to the authenticity of the Mosaic books, excepting from certain slight references in the works of the Fathers to "the ancient Hebrew according to the Samaritans." But, early in the seventeenth century, a traveller found, among the Samaritans of Damascus, a copy of the Pentateuch in the ancient Hebrew letters, and we are told that there are now about sixteen of these manuscripts in the various European libraries. The chief one in existence is guarded with sacred care at Nablous, the ancient Shechem, by a congregation still surviving of a few hundred Samaritans.[1] For questions of textual accuracy, this work is esteemed inferior to the Hebrew,

[1] See Paterson Smyth, p. 118.

though it is not wholly without a claim to more archaic forms.

The Samaritan Pentateuch is one of the most remarkable monuments of antiquity. Its testimony, of course, cannot be adduced to show that the books following the Pentateuch have been clothed from a very ancient date with the reverence due to the divine Word; indeed, it is even capable of being employed, in a limited measure, the other way. But as respects the Samaritan Pentateuch itself, how is it possible to conceive that it should have held as a divine work the supreme place in the regard of the Samaritans, if, about or near the year 500 B. C.,[1] or, still more, if at the time of Manasseh the seceder,[2] it had as matter of fact been a recent compilation of their enemies the Jews? or if it had been regarded as anything less than a record of a great revelation from God, historically known, or at the least universally believed, to have come down to them

[1] Paterson Smyth, p. 49.

[2] Placed by Wellhausen at about 375 B. C. "Hist. Israel" (Black), p. 498.

in the shape it then held from antiquity ? Be it remembered that this work itself, and an approximate date for its known existence, are not matters of mere speculation, but are accepted results of historical research. And it is in this as in other cases a matter for serious consideration, whether we can accept the ingenious conclusions of some critics before we know whether they are to be shattered and shivered when flung against the face of the strong rock of history.

I understand that, in cases where the Septuagint deviates from the Hebrew text, it very commonly agrees with the Samaritan. Now it is certain that the LXX. had access to manuscripts older than those which were at the command of those who finally fixed the Hebrew as it stands ; and it is to be assumed as matter of course that in executing their translation they followed the older copies in preference to the more modern. These circumstances of themselves go far to prove the great antiquity of the Torah of the Samaritans, and there seems absolutely nothing to allege on the other side. So that it is no wonder if among modern Hebraists there have been those who held this Pentateuch in higher estimation than the text as it was received by the Jews.[1]

The Samaritan Pentateuch, then, forms in itself a remarkable indication, nay, even a proof, that, at the date from which we know it to have been received, the Pentateuch was no novelty for the Hebrew race. But may we not state the argument in broader terms? Surely the reverence of the Samaritans for the Torah could not have begun at this period; nay, hardly could have had its first beginning at any period posterior to the schism. If these books grew by gradual accretion, still that must have been an accretion gathering round the work within a single channel. A double process could not have been carried on in harmony. Nor can we easily suppose that, when the Ten Tribes separated from the Two, they did not carry with them the law, on which their competing worship was to be founded. In effect, is there any

[1] See Kennicott, Dissertation I., p. 337 *seqq.*; II., p. 20 *seqq.*

rational supposition except that the kingdom of
Israel had possessed at the time of Rehoboam
some code corresponding in substance, in all except
pure detail, with that which was subsequently
written out in the famous manuscripts we now
possess?

I have not attempted in these essays to discuss
the general credit of the historic books; yet, in
connection with the Samaritans, I must here touch
briefly on a single point. The negative critics are
fairly challenged to explain to us how it is that
priestly fabricators, writing at a late date in the
interest of their order, have so notably abstained
from endeavors to glorify its virtues and honors,
or to conceal its lapses from right. The charge is
that fabrications were committed by priests in the
interests of their order: how then does it happen
that these fabrications contain nothing likely to
promote those interests? In a yet wider view we
may ask how it has come about that they have
entirely avoided attempts to magnify the religious
responsibilities of the schism which divided Israel.

It seems indeed strange that if these books were in substance framed after the Exile, and in times when a spirit of rigorous uniformity prevailed, a more emphatic and distinct censure should not have passed upon Jeroboam, on the simple ground of his having established a separate and rival worship.

The man of God, who came from Judah, did indeed testify against the altar in Bethel; but that altar was associated with the golden calf established and worshipped there (as well as in Dan) by Jeroboam; and the testimony of the prophet, or man of God, against this altar, embraced "all the houses of the high places which are in the cities of Samaria," and was therefore a testimony against idolatry, not against mere schism (1 Kings 12 : 28, 29, 32 ; 13 : 32). The special sin of Jeroboam, which caused his house to be cut off, was not that he divided Israel, but that he degraded his religion by making priests of the lowest of the people (1 Kings 13 : 33). Nay, the books present to us the two illustrious prophets, Elijah and Elisha as

19

having Israel for their field, and as working there not on behalf of the Levitical priesthood, but on behalf of righteousness as against sin, and of God as against Baal ; in complete conformity with the spirit of the prophetic books, which so largely concern the Ten Tribes. How is it conceivable that men wicked enough to forge should so carefully have eschewed gathering any fruits from their forgery ?

The references thus far made to the prophets have been purely incidental to the main argument. But it seems to me to deserve consideration, whether it is only by their predictive faculty that they supply us with a proof of divine revelation. Quite apart from their unfolding the veil that hid the future, does not their attitude and their office supply a reasonable proof that they were raised up and inspired by the Almighty ? This question does not refer to all the prophets. It does not refer to the false prophets who deceived Ahab (1 Kings 22 : 12), nor to the corrupt members of the order, who are so freely denounced in the prophetic books. It refers properly and principally to the authors of those books, and to the valiant witnesses for God and for righteousness whose deeds are otherwise recorded in the Scriptures.

Considered as champions of the right against the wrong, I do not suppose that anything approaching to a parallel with them is to be found elsewhere in history. It is true that we find among the early Greeks, in the poems of Homer, a *diasporè* or sprinkling of prophets: such as Tiresias, who foretells the future,[1] and such as Calchas who, when assured of protection by Achilles, denounces the outrage which had been committed by Agamemnon.[2] He does a good act, and a bold one; but the sin of Agamemnon consists entirely in the violation of a sacerdotal immunity. There is not to be found here, nor in the Homeric prophets elsewhere, nor in the heathen oracles, anything that can properly be called a stand for righteousness.

The prophets of the Old Testament, as an order, are alone in the world. They have been well called,

[1] Od., X. 537-540.   [2] Iliad, I. 92 *seqq.*

by a clerical writer of great ability, the conscience of the Jewish nation. It would not be easy to enumerate fully their claims on our admiration, I must add on our wonder. They are brave. They are honest. They are pure from every stain. They contend for right against wrong, never for wrong against right. They fear God, and have no respect of persons. They are the friends of the afflicted and the poor. Even upon their indignation, their justice is written broad and large. They are humble, for they refer all their lofty utterances to the Most High, and make no claim to the glorying wisdom of this world. They are impartial, for they were entirely emancipated from the spirit of class, and launched their withering censures both as freely and as frequently at the faulty members of their own orders, as at the kings, the priests, and the people. Nor were these censures due to pride or passion; for they yielded their hearts and faculties as freely to the gentle and touching influences of the Spirit in their commiseration of woe and in their prophecies of a suffering Messiah, as when He bade them sound the trumpet-notes of denunciation against outrageous wickedness.

Let us close this portion of the subject with a plea of a different order, one which, admitting probable imperfection in the text, deprecates, as opposed to the principles of sound criticism, any conclusion therefrom adverse to its general fidelity. It has caused me some surprise to notice (1) that some negative writers lay considerable stress upon what they deem to be numerical errors in the books of the Old Testament; and (2) that, so far as I have seen, they do not advert to the increased risks of mistake in the transmission of numbers as compared with other literary matter, whether it be by copying, or by word of mouth.

The increased risk, which accompanies all recording of numbers, extends likewise to enumerations, such as genealogical or other recitals of names in lists; subject, however, to the remark that, where metre is used, inasmuch as it supplies a framework for particular words which would not apply to other words, the danger is proportionably less; and also that, where the record is by writing and not by simple hearing, the eye has the opportunity of traversing again and again the names, as the mechanical process is carried on; and these names will in many cases stand in connection with, and so be seen to check, one another.

Bishop Colenso, for example, lays very great stress on the numbers assigned by the Old Testament to the children of Israel on their passage through the desert, and, observing on the practical difficulties which such a multitude must encounter on a march, treats the case as one which materially impugns the general credit of the history.[1]

I suppose that those who are practically conversant with the movement of men in large bodies may be much inclined to follow Colenso in questioning the statements of numbers, both at that point of their history, and in many other places of the narrative. It is quite another question whether, because errors may have crept into the numbers,

[1] See Colenso on the Pentateuch and Joshua, Part I., Chap. XII. *et alibi.*

the recitals of facts generally are therefore untrust-worthy.

There is a broad and clear difference, of which note ought to be taken. Both in copying and in original composition, as a general rule, the structure of the sentence, or what is called the context, is mentally carried onwards, and the general drift confines within narrow limits the possibility of error in the particular words. Mistake in the form would very commonly betray itself by inconsistency in the sense, and this inconsistency would not fail to be detected, because the relation between the parts of the sentence is ordinarily perceived as the process is carried on. But the relation between numerical amounts is not at once determined for the copyist by the context, and usually requires a distinct and careful examination by the arithmetical faculty to detect it.

I will give two practical illustrations of this statement, the one very old and the other very modern; the one touching oral, and the other written transmission.

The most elaborate invocation of the Muse, or
appeal for divine assistance, in the whole of the
poems of Homer, is the preface [1] to the catalogue
of the Greek troops and ships; and this, although
in no part of the poems could less of effort properly
poetic be required. But the catalogue consists
partly of numerical statements of the strength of the
contingents which made up the fleet, partly of
geographical detail, which sets forth the names of
towns and districts; and here we find the rationale
of the poet's call for special aid from heaven, and
for his care with a view to accuracy; this, too,
although he had metre to assist him.

I now turn to very modern practice. In the year
1853, it was my duty for the first time to submit to
Parliament one of the large and complex statements
of the public accounts for the year, which are
associated in our country with the familiar name of
the Budget. The speeches, in which these statements were contained, were habitually made known
to the country by reporting in the usual manner.

[1] Iliad, II. 484-493.

But the art of the highly skilled reporters could not be trusted to convey the figures with accuracy by the ear. A practice had consequently grown up of supplying them from the proper official source in carefully written statements for their guidance, which were sent to them during the delivery of the speech. It has now been found more convenient not to trust at all to the ear, and the Minister is understood to speak from printed figures; but this in no way weakens the illustration I have used.

My position amounts to but does not go beyond this, that the same care which ensures general fidelity of statement in ordinary recitals of fact does not suffice to secure numerical precision; and conversely that the want of such precision, which may sometimes be suspected in the Old Testament, does not raise presumptions adverse to general correctness.[1]

---

[1] I believe the experience of authors, who give themselves the trouble to make large use of numerical references, would support me in declaring that such references have a much higher average of printer's errors than the regular text.

The necessary limits of this essay do not permit of my entering on the contents of the Mosaic legislation. It is, I apprehend, both far more complex, and far deeper, than the other systems of ancient law known to us, as well as far higher in its moral aims. I humbly recommend that those who read it should fix their minds upon the skill with which it is addressed to the attainment of ends of such a nature as to render them, in their ordinary aspects, hardly reconcilable with one another. Severely proscriptive of the stranger, namely, of the nations whom it found in possession of Canaan, it is as singularly liberal and generous towards him when he has made his peace with Hebrewism. Again, the Pentateuchal code differs from (I believe) all others in the extraordinary amount of its sanitary legislation, and in investing rules of that class with a quasi-moral character. The first impression on a reader's mind is probably a sense of some strangeness in this respect. But it soon alters into a profound admiration of the sagacity, which includes in its far-reaching view provisions for giving an exceptionally high character even to the physical constitution of a people, that was meant to remain socially separate from the nations of the world. Again: while aiming much at equality, simplicity, and industry, as fountains of order and of strength, it embodies most peculiar regulations for the purpose of restraining within the narrowest limits both that growth of wealth, which is the natural fruit of such qualities; and also the spirit of enterprise, which would have burst prematurely the narrow bounds of Palestine, and destroyed the seclusion of the chosen people by untimely contact with the nations of the world. The design seemingly was to repress the latent powers of human nature, and to secure, until the appointed time should come, a conservative, even a stationary community, changeless as the truths of which it was the guardian. The completeness of the severance was not impaired by the Captivity and Dispersion of Israel, or by the Exile of the Jews in Babylon, or by the creation of Jewish factories abroad, or by the communication of their

sacred books to the world, or by the final destruction of the political independence of the country,
or by the invasion and supremacy of the Greek
language. The Jew, when our Lord came, was
still, and was even more than ever, the Jew; and
so, though it may have been in despite of himself,
the purpose of his great stewardship was accomplished.

Postscript to Chapter V.

Although the title of this volume does not pass
beyond the range of the sacred volume, there is a
crowning portion of the narrative which has its
scene laid in Palestine, which was an accomplished
fact before some of the books of the New Testament were written, and yet which does not appear
within its Canon. I refer to the fall of Jerusalem,
the destruction of the temple, and the dispersion
of the Jewish people.

Of the great and cardinal events, which had
marked the history, scarcely even the deliverance
from Egypt and establishment in Palestine are

more wonderful, than the final downfall of the
nation consummated through the destruction of
its capital. We have here presented to us a long
chain of the most astonishing facts. This nation,
which had often been a comparatively easy prey
in the times of its greatness, first to one neighbor
and then to another, offered to the overwhelming
power of Rome, after many generations of subjec-
tion, a resistance such as was experienced in no
other country of this world. Resistance to such a
power, when serious and protracted, has commonly
been the work of a united people. But, at the
time of this unexampled conflict, almost every
patriotic town in Palestine was to all appearance
hopelessly divided between a national and a roman-
izing party; and these parties subsisted in a state
of chronic civil war. Jerusalem itself was the
scene of incessant and bloody conflict among its
factions during the years which preceded the fatal
siege, and Vespasian actually postponed his march
to the southward in the hope that without his
active interference these factions might sufficiently

perform his work.   Again, the Roman policy as to the religion of subject races was essentially tolerant, and in intention mild.   It is unreasonable to suppose that corruption and oppression merely fiscal can have brought about results in that particular quarter so absolutely different from those which were exhibited in other portions of the Empire. And this supposition is also excluded by the fact that the men of rank and wealth, out of whom most treasure could be wrung, constituted everywhere the anti-national or Roman party in the local communities.   Animosity, dominating the mass (and this perhaps in other cities besides Jerusalem), carried the entire population into unexampled extremities of resistance.   Yet it seems evident that the Romans in these latter stages acted all along under a compulsion imposed by their adversaries, and in a manner alien to their own habits and standing conceptions.   Formidable indeed was the temple, in its very idea, as a focus of national feeling ; but Roman liberality had not even objected to the repetition in miniature of this most significant structure by the building of the temple of Onias at Alexandria. Once more; is it possible to conceive a more remarkable example of the tolerant, meaning thereby the neutral, spirit of the Roman policy in matters of religion, than is exhibited by the quiet allowance of the judicial proceedings taken against our Blessed Saviour, on the independent authority of the high priest and the Sanhedrim, in a city subjected to the exclusive control and dominion of a Roman governor? The difficulty is to conceive how, under such a system, so exceptional in all its circumstances, the fall of Jerusalem, with the almost equally remarkable catastrophes of several cities of the North, could be brought within the range of possibility. In such matters, the mainsprings of human action are religion and nationality. But nationality had, among the Jews, for many centuries been found compatible with subordination to foreign dominion. Religion, which had supplied so legitimate and so powerful a stimulus at the epoch of the Maccabees, when the temple had been profaned by Antiochus

Epiphanes, could furnish no cause, and hardly a pretext, for hostile activity under the imperial edict of Augustus.

It seems as if, at the three great crises of Jewish and Hebrew history, the Almighty Wisdom had determined to put a special stamp upon the events which happened, and to mark them as peculiarly its own. We recognize in Moses the most powerful man delineated in the Hebrew annals: one who both in thought and action was a mighty force available for the deliverance from Egypt. But how little had the people at that epoch to do with its own liberation! Again, at the time preceding the Babylonish Captivity, the Jews had not to encounter a wild and savage conqueror, such as the East has often seen, who shattered all he touched. The views of Nebuchadnezzar appear to have been politic and moderate. He had to encounter a determined partisanship of this people with his enemies in Egypt, accompanied with repeated breaches of faith. It was not at the first, but only at the second crisis, that he proceeded to extremities against the Jews; and, all through the period, the counsels of Jeremiah were deliberately adverse to the policy of resistance that was pursued. It was plain that Egypt was a broken reed.

This is not to be deemed one of the ordinary excesses of passion or errors in particular calculations, which mark the common page of history: it was an utter abnegation of all rational elements in the guidance of human conduct, both adopted and persisted in, such as we occasionally but rarely encounter, and such as when encountered we properly term infatuation. An exactly similar course, but attended with further exaggerations, marked the third of the great crises at the closing period of the national history. We have no sign that religion was hurt or endangered by the Roman supremacy. Many of the cities did not actively join in the revolt. The state, which had punished Verres, would surely not have permitted Florus to endanger the peace of the East by his rapacity.

The long delays of the Roman commander in laying siege to the city seem to find their most

20

rational interpretation in one supposition only. It is the supposition of his having believed that the majority of the population would see and feel that there was no cause for proceeding to extremities. The presence of Berenice, and her powerful influence over Titus, were of themselves a guaranty that no reasonable settlement would be refused. As in the time of Hezekiah with Isaiah, and in the time of Zechariah with Jeremiah, so here again the wisest and most trusted counsellor of the race was a firm opponent of the policy of resistance. Jochanan Ben Zakkai was the man who, after the destruction of the capital and dispersal of the nation, proved himself equal to the incredibly difficult task of establishing at Jamnia (or Jabuz)[1] what may be properly termed the new Judaism, the Judaism which had just been dislodged from a sanctuary held through fifteen centuries: the Judaism which no longer had a home, or a sacrifice, or a priest. Probably Jochanan saw that there was nothing in the supremacy of Rome to prevent the continued

[1] Graetz: "History of the Jews," Vol. II., Ch. XIII.

existence of such a Judaism as would be available for all the purposes of religion; a Judaism local, historical, and visible, shorn in fact of nothing except the political domination which it can hardly be said to have enjoyed in anything like fulness since the time of Solomon. Such was the man who stood before the people as the counsellor of peace before the fall of the city. But in spite of all this, the unhappy population of the capital rushed upon its ruin, even like that herd of swine which ran headlong down the steep place into the waters of Gennesaret, and perished.

In reviewing the detail of this astonishing case, we may well say there have been parallels, real though rare, scattered over the pages of history, to the indomitable courage of the Jews; there are none to their incurable fanaticism. A doom had been spoken, though spoken in sadness, by the Saviour of the world: and that doom behoved to be fulfilled, and fulfilled by the free, but incredibly misguided, agency of the sufferers. Without doubt, the power of nationality as an element of public and common life had been raised by all the incidents of the Maccabæan struggle to an extraordinary height. But that heroic history lay far in the distance of the past. A courtly, or Herodian, system had long been dominant. Two centuries and a half had passed away. For a large portion of this time they had lived under Roman dominion, which gave to the Jew unstintedly the advantages of a world-wide citizenship, and harbored him, sometimes even with favor, in the capital of the Empire. It seems impossible to account for the destruction of Jerusalem and the dispersion of the nation on the common principles of human action. After every effort to escape, we are driven to acknowledge the signal tribute which the excess of human error rendered to the efficacy of divine wisdom. If the second causes which brought about the destruction of the capital, and the dispersion of the race, were marked by the most singular and abnormal character, the prediction of our Lord was a prediction not founded on the likelihoods of ordinary policy, but on a most remarkable departure from them: and the catastrophe itself, in connection with that disclosure which his wonderful foreknowledge had imparted to the world, sums up the long chapter of rational evidences of a divine revelation which we derive from the history, so studded with vicissitude, of the children of Abraham.

Thus, the prophetic power of the Saviour, and the effectual action of divine Providence wrought out through the agency of causes altogether unusual, are alike exhibited with conclusive force in the fall of Jerusalem. But even this is not all. The destruction of the temple with the city, and the dispersion of the nation, belong essentially to the subject of this work. For through these events was fulfilled the original promise to Abraham, that in him should all the nations of the earth be blessed: and it is hard to see how without them that fulfilment could had been brought about.

It would be hardly too much to say that so long as the temple-worship lasted, and the obligations of the Mosaic system were acknowledged, the new scheme of the kingdom of God could not be developed, the Church could not become a city set upon a hill; and, as Christianity seemed to be in some sense a form of Judaism, the call to the nations to repent and be converted could hardly be made intelligible. The tendencies exhibited in St. Peter and St. Paul respectively, so menacing in themselves to the infant religion, would in all likelihood have continued to embarrass and to mar the promulgation of the Gospel by confusing the utterance of its preachers. And it is not to be forgotten that St. Paul himself, the champion of the larger system, did not exempt himself from the obligations of the law. It was plainly essential to the infant scheme that an effectual continuity should be established between the Apostles, who were a body of Hebrews, and those Gentiles who were to take up and carry forward their commission. Was it not equally necessary, or at least important in a degree to which we can hardly assign limits, that the original teachers themselves should receive their emancipation, at least in the persons of some among them, through the great catastrophe? That catastrophe effaced the outworn stamp, and left the title-page in the exclusive possession of the new covenant.[1]

---

[1] This book does not rise to the character of a history; and the narratives on which it may occasionally have touched are sufficiently familiar from the pages of the Bible. In the section, however, which here closes, the case is different. But I have not felt justified in entering upon the amount of detail which a regular statement of the facts would have required. It is probably enough to refer to any of the well-known works on the History of the Jews, such as that of Dean Milman (Murray), or the edition of Graetz, recently published in English by Mr. Nutt.

VI.

ON THE RECENT CORROBORATIONS OF SCRIPTURE FROM THE REGIONS OF HISTORY AND NATURAL SCIENCE.

I. PRELIMINARY; II. AS TO THE CREATION STORY; III. AS TO THE FLOOD STORY; IV. AS TO THE GREAT DISPERSION; V. AS TO THE SINAITIC JOURNEY.

It is to be observed that many of the favorite subjects of scientific or systematic thought in the present day are of a nature powerfully tending to reinforce or illustrate the arguments available for the proof of religion, and for the authority of Scripture. If it had been actually proved, as it is largely argued and seriously held, that the vast and diversified scheme of organic life throughout the world has been evolved from a few simple types or possibly from one, such a demonstration would both enlarge and confirm the great argument of design. For this argument, instead of being drawn from particular and separate constructions, would then be derived from the entire scheme of creation, and from the relation of all its parts to one another, inasmuch as every earlier portion of it would be an indication, and therefore a mute prediction, of all those which were to succeed; the seed of a long series of harvests to come. "Day unto day uttereth speech, and night unto night showeth knowledge" (Psa. 19 : 2).

Again, the formal treatment in recent years of the subject of heredity not only tends to link the generations of mankind in one, but, in proving that our nature undergoes incessant modification through the influence of progenitors, enlarges our conception of the width of its range, and the varieties of those forms which it is capable of assuming. It shows us, for example, how the nature, as well as the environment, of descendants, is deteriorated by the fault of ancestors, and how there may have been an education of the race from childhood to maturity, or (upon the same basis of reasoning) some converse process of decay. Thus the doctrine of birth-sin, as it is sometimes called, is simply the recognition of the hereditary disorder and degeneracy of our nature; and, of all men, the evolutionist would find it most difficult to establish a title to object to it in principle.

On these grounds, and on others more specific which it will be the aim of this chapter to set forth in given instances, we should dispel wholly from our minds those spectral notions of some broad antagonism between religion and science, which have been raised up by the action of prejudice on the one side, and perhaps by the occasional practice of bragging on the other. Of religion and of science, as of man and wife, let us boldly say, "What God hath joined, let not man put asunder." But I proceed to particular illustrations.

II.—AS TO THE CREATION STORY.

A double confirmation has, I conceive, in our time been supplied to the Creation Story of Genesis;

the first by natural, and the second by historic science.

Perhaps we have been too readily satisfied with assuming, in regard to this narrative, a defensive position; whereas it may be found to contain within its own brief compass, when rightly considered, the guarantee of a divine communication to man, strictly corresponding with what in familiar speech is termed revelation.

We have here in outline a primordial history of the planet which we inhabit, and of the celestial system to which it belongs. Of the planet, and of the first appearance and early developments of life upon it, anterior to the creation of man, in many of the principal stages which have been ascertained by geology. Of the celestial organization to which our earth belongs, whether in all its vastness or only within the limits of the solar system, we may be unable to say; but, at the least, a sketch of the formation of that system, or of our special portion of it, from a prior and unadjusted or chaotic state. Upon such a document a sharp issue is at once raised, at least as to the latter or strictly terrestrial part of it, the earth-history, for all those who hold it to be in its substance a true account. We accept from science, as demonstrated, a series of geological conclusions. We have found the geology of Genesis to stand in such a relation to these conclusions, as could not have been exhibited in a record framed by faculties merely human, at any date to which the origin of the Creation Story can now reasonably be referred. Starting from this premise, we have no means of avoiding or holding back from the conclusion that the materials of the story could not have been had without preterhuman aid; and such preterhuman aid is what we term divine revelation. And if the time shall ever come, when astronomers shall be in a condition to apply to the earlier portion of the chapter the demonstrative methods, which geology has found for the latter part, it may happen that we shall owe a debt of the same kind, and of as great amount, to astronomy, as we now owe to geologic science. My present purpose is to call particular attention to the exact nature and extraordinary amount of that debt.

There was nothing necessarily unreasonable in accepting as worthy of belief this portion of the Book of Genesis, along with the rest of the Book, and with other books of Holy Scripture, on general proofs of their inspiration, if sufficient, apart from any independent buttress furnished, either by science or by history, for the Creation Story. In a court of justice, the evidence of a witness is to be accepted on matters within his cognizance, when it is consistent with itself, and when neither his character nor his intelligence are questioned; or again, when the main part of a continuous narrative is sufficiently verified, it may sometimes be right to accept the rest without separate verification. If, however, a new witness comes into court, and pretends to give us fresh and scientific proof of the Creation Story, this may be true or may be false. If false, the story is not disproved; it stands where it stood before. Bad arguments are often made for a good cause. But if true, the event is one of vast importance.

Now the present position is as follows. Apart altogether from faith, and from the general evidences of revelation, a new witness has come into the court, in the shape of natural science. She builds up her system on the observation of facts, and upon inferences from them, which at length attain to a completeness and security such as, if not presenting us with a demonstration in the strictest sense, yet constrain us, as intelligent beings, and by the general laws of reasoning, to belief.

The Creation Story divides itself into the cosmological portion, occupying (mainly) the first nineteen verses of the chapter, and the geological portion, which is given in the last twelve. The former part has less, and the latter part has more, to do with the direct evidence of fact, and the stringency of the authority which the two may severally claim varies accordingly; but in both the narrative seems to demand, upon the evidence as it stands, rational assent. In regard to both, it is held on the affirmative side that the statements of Genesis have a certain relation both to the ascertained facts and to the best accepted reasonings ; and that this relation is of such a nature as to require us, in the character of rational investigators, to acknowledge in the written record the presence of elements such as must be referred to a superhuman origin. If this be so, then be it observed that natural science is now rendering a new and enormous service to the great cause of belief in the unseen ; and is under-pinning, so to speak, the structure of that divine revelation, which was contained in the Book of Genesis, by a new and solid pillar, built up, on a foundation of its own, from beneath.

It is, then, to be borne in mind that, as against those who by arbitrary or irrational interpretation, place Genesis and science at essential variance, our position is not one merely defensive. We are not mere reconcilers, as some call us, searching out ex-pedients to escape a difficulty, to repel an assault. We carry the war, or rather the argument, into the camp of the adversary. We seek to show, and we may claim to have shown, that the account re-corded in the Creation Story for the instruction of all ages has been framed on the principles which, for such an account, reason recommends ; and that, interpreted in this view, its entry into the argument is at this juncture like the arrival of a new auxiliary army in the field while the battle is in progress ; like the arrival, to choose a historical instance, of the Prussians at Waterloo.

Such is the confirmatory argument founded upon the contents. But now, yet another ally has come to join our ranks, under the title of archæologic and historic science. It has deciphered the cuneiform inscriptions, and has read among them a Creation Story inscribed on the tablets found at Nineveh. Here we have a new witness to the very early existence, among civilized or partly civilized men, of records of creation corresponding in very essential particulars with the Hebrew narrative. Such a witness plainly to some extent offers to it confirmation ; but also stands in competition with it. The competition is in those particulars where the accounts are not in harmony. As to these, standing on the character of its contents, the Hebrew

tradition lays claim to superior antiquity and authority. But in proving the vast antiquity of certain fundamental ideas, the two are concurrent, and
not competitive.

The Babylonian Creation Story is given by Mr.
Smith in his " Assyrian Discoveries,"[1] so far as its
multilated state permits. It runs as follows, and we
cannot, I think, but cherish the hope that it may
hereafter receive extension or elucidation. " When
the gods in their assembly made the universe, there
was confusion, and the gods sent out the spirit of
life. They then create the beast of the field, the
animal of the field, and the reptile or the creeping
thing of the field, and fix in them the spirit of life.
Next comes the creation of domestic animals, and
the creeping things of the city." Here we have, 1,
creation by the gods; 2, chaos; 3, life, and only by
inference, order; 4, wide extension of this life in
beasts and reptiles; 5, after this the domesticated
animals. Thus there is before us a real, though
rude and imperfect, structural resemblance to the

[1] Page 397.

21

Hebrew narrative, together with the lowering interpolation of polytheism.

From the works of Schrader[1] on the cuneiform inscriptions, some further particulars may be gathered. He observes that in Berosus, as in Genesis, we begin with water and darkness. On which I would only observe that Berosus, who wrote in Greek, may not improbably have known the Mosaic writings;[2] and, as I have already stated, that water, in the text of Genesis, may be equivalent to fluid. The marked points of correspondence appear to be these: that the heavenly bodies are created after the heavens, which last expression, I presume, may be meant to include the light. That the land population follows that of the water, and appears when vegetation has already begun. That the monuments name a Babylonian week, with the seventh day as a day of consecration, called also an evil day,[3] perhaps because evil for any work done on it. The inscription says—

[1] Schrader, " The Cuneiform Inscriptions and the Old Testament." Translated by Whitehouse.   Vol. I., p. 4 *seqq*.
[2] Smith, Biogr. Dict.   [3] Schrader, p. 19.

> " To redeem them, created mankind
>   The merciful one, in whom is the power
>   that summons to life "—

which is faintly comparable with the words of Genesis 2:7, and the Jehovistic account, "and breathed into his nostrils the breath of life." What seems to disappear from the Babylonian account is that evident intention of series and orderly development, or evolution, which is so wonderful a feature in the Mosaic narrative.

Dawson, in a recent work, observes that the polytheistic element is the distinctive feature of the Chaldean record; and that the originals of the tablets from Nineveh may have been very ancient, but that they are so mixed up with the history of the Chaldean hero, named Izdubar, as to suggest that there may have existed before it still older Creation legends. He compares this record with the corresponding account in Genesis, which is as broadly marked with the idea of the divine unity as the Chaldean legend is pervaded by the conception of polytheism. And he adds, " Is it not likely that the simpler belief is older than the more complex; that which required no priests, ritual, or temple, older than that with which all these things were necessarily associated?" He naturally assigns a marked superiority to the "Hebrew Genesis."[1] In truth, that superiority seems to be not great only, but immeasurable.

In one point only do the tablets carry us beyond the narrative of Genesis; they record the great struggle of Deity with rebellion, the war in heaven between Merodach and Tiamat. But, upon the whole, our Bible narrative is a regular structure; it is orderly, progressive, and rational; that of the tablets is dark and confused. This may, however, be referable in part to the imperfection of the tablets, the third of which, Mr. Sayce thinks, may probably have recounted the formation of the earth.[2] However this may be, the one account is charged in a marvellous way with instruction and moral purpose; from the other they have almost

[1] "Modern Science in Bible Lands," p. 32.

[2] "Hibbert Lectures," p. 394.

disappeared. The first has, as we believe, been receiving marked confirmation in the most vital particulars from cosmic and geologic science; on the second they can hardly be said to cast more than the faintest light. And yet this inferior document is itself of very great confirmatory value; for the Izdubar legends, says Mr. Smith,[1] appear to have been composed more than 2000 years B. C. There is no late date to which the Mosaic narrative can with a shadow of probability be referred. It could not have been formed without a miracle from the tablets as they stand. The two are evidently accounts proceeding from a common source, but derived through channels, partly or wholly independent. The one comes through a powerful and civilized empire, the other through an obscure nomad family. In the relative superiority of the Mosaic narrative, all the rules of merely human likelihoods are reversed; and the presumption of a divine illumination is proportionably augmented. But the unsuspected antiquity of the inferior legend attests by

[1] "Assyrian Discoveries," p. 166.

an independent witness, if not the truth, yet at least the presumable origin, of its transcendent rival.

So far as scientific opinion is concerned, another remarkable confirmation seems to have been given to the cosmical portion of the Creation Story in Genesis by the course which it has taken of late years. Writing in 1839, Dr. Whewell devoted a chapter of his "Bridgewater Treatise on Astronomy and Physics"[1] to the Nebular or, as it is often called, Rotatory Hypothesis. He described it in outline, as it had been conceived by Laplace. The idea of it was that the mass, which eventually centred in the sun, had revolved in a state of excessive heat; that, as it gradually cooled, the rapidity of the motion was increased; that, as the centrifugal force thus grew, the mass detached from itself exterior zones or rings of gas or vapor, which most commonly broke up into several minor masses, and so gradually formed the planetary system. Dr. Whewell's object in this early notice of a subject, which has since attracted, I believe, very general

[1] Chapter VII., p. 181.

attention in the world of astronomical science, was to sustain and illustrate his general argument, by showing how this theory did nothing whatever to explain the origin of the system, or to weaken the statement of Newton, that its admirable arrangement must be "the work of an intelligent and most powerful being." The origin of this rotation, said Dr. Whewell, remains unexplained, and still as powerfully as ever cries aloud for, and proclaims an Author. My purpose in here naming the subject is to point out that Dr. Whewell then found himself dealing with a theory which had not yet obtained any wide currency or authority, and he then "left to other persons and to future ages to decide upon the merits of the nebular hypothesis."[1] But, during the half-century which has elapsed since he produced his treatise, the hypothesis is understood to have gained very general, if not indeed unanimous, acceptance from astronomers. I refer to this result of the most modern studies as a new and remarkable establishment of accord between natural science on

[1] Page 190.

the one hand (so far as its reasonings have proceeded) and the Book of Genesis on the other.
Often has it been endeavored to place the Mosaic
geology in conflict with ascertained results, but
less, though even here something, of the same kind
has been attempted, so far as I know, by persons
of scientific authority, with regard to the cosmogony
which occupies the earlier portion of the chapter.
On the other hand, it has been shown, with what
seems to me conclusive clearness, that, without the
use of scientific language, that very process has
been described in slight outline, but in singular
correspondence with the hypothesis now so largely
accepted.   Such a hypothesis may not indeed
have reached the point of demonstration, and this
the subject-matter itself may be found not to permit; yet it has attained to so much of authority
from consent that Dr. Whewell, were he writing
now, would not have had simply to hand it over
to the future for consideration, but would more
probably have declared that it holds the field, and
seems little likely to be displaced from it.

With the creation of the world, or the solar system, the question of its termination is naturally associated. On this subject, however, I will not dwell at length, because the support here afforded by scientific opinion is given to the Scriptures of the New Testament, rather than the Old. To refer again to Dr. Whewell. In a passage of extraordinary grandeur, he delivered (I think it was in a sermon) his opinion that the world would end with a catastrophe, instead of dying what is termed a natural death. Such, as we know, is the emphatic declaration of the inspired Word. "The day of the Lord will come as a thief in the night: in the which the heavens shall pass away with a great noise, and the elements shall melt with fervent heat; the earth also, and the works that are therein, shall be burned up" (2 Peter 3: 10, 12). And again, "Looking for and hasting unto the coming of the day of God, wherein the heavens being on fire shall be dissolved, and the elements shall melt with fervent heat." Such was the judgment of Dr. Whewell nearly half a century ago. His words were delivered rather as by one uttering his own firm opinion, than as expressing the conviction of astronomers at large. Nevertheless, as I have been informed on high authority, it is now the established conclusion of astronomers, based upon reasoning from ascertained facts, that the Galilean fisherman knew, and wrote for our instruction, what all the genius and learning of the world for thousands of years failed to learn, and that—

> " The great globe itself,
> Yea, all which it inherit, shall dissolve." [1]

III.—AS TO THE FLOOD STORY.

I pass now to the Flood Legend, one form of which has come down through Berosus and Josephus, but which acquires much more certain antiquity, and greater grandeur, from the Assyrian inscriptions. Their account, says Schrader, whose bias cannot, I think, be considered as over-favorable to the Hebrew record, "brings the Biblical narra-

---

[1] Shakespeare, " Tempest," IV. 1.

tive into much closer relation with the Chaldean flood legend than could be assumed on the basis of the tradition in Berosus."[1] It forms part of the Izdubar legends discovered by Mr. George Smith, who published his account of them in 1872, and who assigns to them a date anterior to 2000 years B. C. under the early Babylonian empire.[2] The hero of the legends is believed by Mr. Smith to be the same as the Nimrod of Genesis. Like the Creation Story of Genesis,[3] that of the Flood derives corroboration from the Babylonian record, inasmuch as it is thus carried back by an independent testimony to a very great antiquity. That record, composed, as Mr. Smith thinks, not long after the time of Izdubar or Nimrod, gives us the tradition of a flood which was a divine punishment for the wickedness of the world, and of a holy man, who built an ark, and escaped the general destruction.[4] The particulars are set out in Mr. Smith's volume. They differ, in many respects, from those of Genesis, but

[1] Schrader, as above, p. 47.
[2] "Assyrian Discoveries," p. 166.
[3] *Ibid*. and 204.   [4] Pages 205, 206, *seqq.*

the essential features are in the highest degree marked, and, together with certain of the details, are singularly accordant.[1]   As in the case of the Creation Story, so here there is stamped upon them the note of a common source, and of channels of descent which separate at some later date.   In this case, however, the Babylonian narrative holds a higher position, relatively to the scriptural record, than in the case of the Creation.

The hero of the deluge is Hasisadra, a name which has been hellenized into Xisuthrus.   He, on the eleventh tablet, relates to Izdubar (the supposed Nimrod) the story of the deluge.   I shall only attempt an outline presenting the main points.[2]

In the ancient city of Surippah, where Anu and other chief gods were worshipped, Hasisadra was divinely warned by Hea, the great water-god, to construct a ship, of which the size is named; and to commit to it "the seed of life, all of it," as "the sinner and life" were about to be destroyed by a flood.   Food, furniture, wealth, servants, and ani-

[1] Page 184, *seqq.*   [2] Smith, pp. 184-194.

mals, were all to be embarked. The building and loading of the ship are then described, and the part taken by the several deities in bringing about the catastrophe. But "the gods" themselves feared the tempest, and "ascended to the heaven of Anu." This deluge lasted for six days: on the seventh all was quiet. There is sight of land from within the vessel. It is arrested by the mountain of Nizir. A dove is sent forth, and returns. A swallow is sent, and does the like. A raven goes, feeds on the corpses that are afloat, and returns not. Then comes landing from the vessel, sacrifice, the sending forth of animals. Next, Ninip and Hea remonstrate with Bel, and suggest other more usual means of chastising men, in which there seems to be some affinity to the promise of Genesis 8 : 21, 22, and 9 : 11-17, that there should never again be a flood upon the earth. And "then dwelt Hasisadra in a remote place, at the mouth of the rivers."

The resemblances between this narrative of the flood and that in Genesis are such as clearly to betoken a relationship at or near the source. The

most peculiar, and at the same time purely incidental, among all the details of the narrative,
appears to be the threefold experiment with birds
upon the decline of the waters; but this is found
alike in the three narratives of Chaldæa, the Bible,
and Berosus. No other nations have accounts so
full and precise as these.[1]

Mr. Smith has some judicious and impartial observations on the two accounts.[2] The Chaldean account indicates the nature of the country in which
the flood took place. Surippah is near the mouth
of the Euphrates, and there we learn that Hea was
worshipped as the god of the deluge. The Hebrew
account has no local corroborations of the story.
When Surippah was conquered, in the sixteenth
century B.C. or earlier, it is called in the record,
" the city of the ark." Hasisadra is, like Noah, a
devout man; and the Chaldean deluge is, like the
Hebrew, a punishment for gross and widespread
sin. Schrader argues with a view to attenuate this
statement, but, as it appears to me, in the spirit of

---

[1] Smith, p. 212.   [2] *Ibid.*

a partisan rather than a judge.[1] The dimensions
of the ark vary in the three accounts ; and on the
variations of numerals I have made remarks elsewhere. It may, however, be observed that the
Babylonian account, which presumably was written
down from a very early date, and in a durable form,
has in this respect a great advantage over oral
transmission, which is most of all dangerous for
numerical statements. The inscription describes a
regular vessel with boatmen, another incident of
local color. The accounts curiously coincide in
the minute point that, both inside and out, the ark
is coated with bitumen. The tablet tells us that
not eight only, but a comparatively large number
of persons, went on board. The Bible gives forty
days as the duration of the flood, meaning apparently when at the height. After 150 days the
waters all abated. The whole duration before dis-
appearance is a year and ten days (Gen. 7 : 11, 12,
13, 14, 17, 24). The tablet allows only seven days
for the fulness of the flood. On the seventh day

[1] Vol. I., p. 49.

all storm has ceased. Hasisadra then sends out the bird. The ship is stranded for seven days more on the mountains of Nizir, so that the total term mentioned is one of only fourteen days. Nizir lies away to the east, far from the site of Ararat mentioned in Genesis; on the other hand,[1] the present tradition of the country lands the ark at a site farther to the north, and nearer Ararat. Again as to the birds. In Genesis, Noah sends out a raven, which does not return; then a dove three times, at intervals of seven days; on the third occasion the dove does not return. The inscription sends, first, a dove, which returns, then a swallow, which returns, and then a raven, which does not return. Lastly, in the Bible, Noah lives after the flood for 350 years; the tablet and Berosus both assign to Hasisadra, associated (rather strangely) with his daughter and the helmsman,[2] that translation to heaven for his piety, which Genesis gives to Enoch. Before translation, he was visited by Izdubar, and the region was deemed a sacred region.

[1] Smith, p. 217.   [2] Schrader, I. 60.

On a general comparison of these two profoundly interesting records, the result appears to be that in what is circumstantial only there is much difference along with some curious resemblance; but in the outline of the fundamental facts, and in the moral considerations applicable, they are radically at one. The wickedness of the antediluvian world, the divine anger, the command to build, the use of this vehicle of escape, and the erection of an altar of thanksgiving, are recorded alike in each. We have no absolute right to assume that either of the accounts, as it stands, is exactly contemporary with the period of the flood. The points in which the Bible account may seem inferior are the absence of local coloring, and the probable relation of the numerical statements to actual fact. Yet this, so far from impairing its claim to our acceptance, appears on the contrary to accredit it, because it is a feature which, given the circumstances of the case, there was reason to expect. If, indeed, we ride the hobby of the negative criticism, the Bible account bristles everywhere with difficulty. It is inconceivable that the framers should have in that case departed so widely from the inscription on the tablets, in points so palpable to all the world, or should have let slip the local color, with which a fabricator, or late relator, would have been forward to dress up his narrative. But, if we take Abraham, with his ancestors and his posterity, as a nomad people, religious and of simple life such as the Bible represents them; at an earlier period hanging on the outskirts of the Babylonian power, at a later one migratory towards the West; it was natural for them to drop the local coloring of a region with which all their relations had come to an end, and also to fall somewhat behind in the exactitude of some among the particulars; and this is perhaps observable, as to the point of local color, not in the case of the flood only, but throughout the Abrahamic narrative down to the entry into the promised land.

The most significant difference of all between the two records is that the inscription is founded upon polytheism, while in the Bible, here as elsewhere, all is based upon the doctrine of one God. That is to say, the simpler form is the groundwork of the Bible narrative; and the simpler form, according to the generally recognized principle, is that nearest the source, most closely akin to the occurrence or the original record. The religion of Noah agrees with that of the common father, Adam; the religion of Hasisadra has departed from the primitive belief, and exhibits to us those multiplied and deteriorated images of the Deity, which human infirmity and sin had introduced or allowed.

While Schrader glances at the period when the Babylonian flood-legend reached the Hebrews as that of "the prophetic narrator of early Biblical history," he candidly adds, " I am led to the obvious conclusion that the Hebrews were acquainted with this legend at a much earlier period, and that it is far from impossible that they acquired a knowledge of these and the other primitive myths now under investigation as far back as in the time of their earlier settlements in Babylonia, and that they carried these stories with them from Ur of the Chaldees." For him they are all myths; the original invention is in Babylonia, and the Hebrews are early copyists. If this be a copy, and a copy made among an artless race, it seems not a little strange that the copy should in essentials so much excel the original. But for other observers, however, they are in the nature of primitive traditions, founded on histories; and the twin versions bear testimony by their concurrence, and even in some respects by their discrepancies, to their historical character. If there was remoulding, it may be the more detailed and circumstantial narration which is presumptively entitled to the credit of it; and the Bible story, more sparing in its details, but far broader and more direct in the terrible lesson it conveys, may reasonably be judged to have come down from the source with the smallest amount of variation in essentials from the original. It is here as elsewhere. " The wisdom of this world," the race favored with stable institutions, and with intellectual development, yet fails in the firmness of its hold, and the clearness of its view, where the appreciation of the tremendous moral lesson is concerned; while the race of wandering shepherds, who are but the "babes and sucklings" of intelligence, yet transmit that lesson in a type so fresh and clear that our Lord has only to quote and enlarge without correcting it, and so to launch it anew into the world as a solemn chapter of his gospel teaching.

It may be noticed that the translation to heaven of Hasisadra, the Noah of the tablets, is in curious accordance with that far larger development both of the Underworld and of the future state, which marks alike the Babylonian and the Egyptian systems in comparison with that of the Old Testament, and forms an interesting but separate subject of discussion.

The Hebrew story of the Deluge has long been supported by a diversity of traditions among the nations and races of the world, but never before with such particularity, or such corroboration in the sense and to the extent already described. But though we have now a new and important witness in court on our behalf, yet undoubtedly, if the narrative be provably untrue, the testimony of both, or of any number of traditional witnesses, must fall to the ground.

The voice of natural science has not been, and apparently is not at present, uniform on this subject. The negative has just been presented to the world, of course with great ability, and also in a sufficiently magisterial form, by Professor Huxley. He conceives that Christian theology must stand or fall with the historical trustworthiness of the Jewish Scriptures;[1] and, as these are not trustworthy, the consequence is that it must not stand, but fall. With this general proposition I have here nothing to do.

Mr. Huxley selects the flood-story for the capital article of his indictment. But he treats it as little worthy of serious notice. " It is difficult to persuade serious scientific inquirers to occupy themselves in any way with the Noachian deluge."[2] He finds, indeed, a sort of historic nucleus for a

---

[1] Nineteenth Century, July, 1890, p. 8.   [2] *Ibid.*, p. 12.

partial deluge in the occasional desolating floods
of the Euphrates and Tigris.[1]   But, be it a partial
or be it a general flood, he applies the negative
doctrine, in the same contemptuous form, to the
Deluge: perhaps most of all to what he terms a
particularly absurd attempt at reconciliation, which
places it "at the end of the glacial epoch."[2]   I am
far from intending to enter upon a controversy
which I have no capacity to handle.   Yet I may be
bold enough to mention, that, while Mr. Huxley is
speaking in the name of science at large, some
votaries of science hold an entirely different language.   Moreover, that the idea of a flood was not
thus summarily dismissed by the luminaries of the
scientific world anterior to the present day; and
that the grounds of this dismissal are not of recent
discovery, but were fully open to the geologists of
the last generation.   Quite recently, the doctrine
of a Deluge has been maintained by Sir J. Dawson,[3] by Mr. Howorth, and by the Duke of Argyll

---

[1] Nineteenth Century, July, 1890, p. 14.   [2] *Ibid.*, p. 13.
[3] " Modern Science in Bible Lands," p. 252.

(if I interpret him aright),[1] all of whom are, I suppose, to be considered as "serious scientific inquirers."

Mr. Howorth, in his learned and laborious work on "The Mammoth and the Flood," is certainly not bound by any superstitious reverence for the mere text of the Book of Genesis; for in his preface,[2] he seems to cast aside as null its traditions respecting all that preceded the creation of man. His treatise collects largely not only the diluvial traditions of so many races and countries, but an immense mass of palæontological evidence; and, having laid this wide ground for his induction, he declares that, in his judgment, the whole points unmistakably

" To a widespread calamity, involving a flood on a great scale. I do not see how the historian, the archæologist, and the palæontologist can avoid making this conclusion in future a prime factor in their discussions, and I venture to think that before long it will be accepted as unanswerable." [3]

[1] Good Words, January, 1884; and Scot. Geograph. Mag., April, 1890.   [2] Pages ix, x.   [3] Page 463.

Moreover, I am free to consider history no less a science, though a less determinate science, than geology or biology; and I quote in conclusion the following passage from Lenormant, which follows a copious collection of testimonies to the tradition of a Deluge in almost all lands:—

"La longue revue, à laquelle nous venons de nous livrer, nous permet d'affirmer que le récit du deluge est une tradition universelle dans tous les rameaux de l'humanité, à l'exception toutefois de la race noire. Mais un souvenir partout, aussi précis et aussi concordant, ne saurait être celui d'un mythe inventé à plaisir; aucun mythe religieux ou cosmogonique ne présente ce caractère d'universalité. C'est nécessairement le souvenir d'un événement réel et terrible, qui frappa assez puissamment l'imagination des ancêtres de notre espèce pour n'être jamais oublié de leurs descendants. Ce cataclysme se produit près du berceau primitif de l'humanité." [2]

[1] "Les Origines de l'Histoire," pp. 489, 490. Second edition, 1880. "The long review, to which we have just applied ourselves, warrants our affirming that the tale of the Deluge is a universal tradition among all the branches of the human family; excepting, however, the blacks. But a remembrance prevailing everywhere, so precise and so concordant, cannot belong to a myth arbitrarily invented. No

IV.—AS TO THE GREAT DISPERSION.

The contents of the tenth chapter of Genesis constitute a document of a character altogether extraordinary: for example, in the two following particulars. First, it is without parallel in the world. Nowhere else is there known to us a distinct and detailed endeavor to draw downwards from a single source the multiplication of men in the earth by families, and the distribution of them over the face of the earth. Secondly, this account, containing seventy-two names of men (to which more are added in connection with the descent of Abram when we reach chapter 12), is so particular, that the notion of its correct transmission by ordinary means may appear to present much difficulty. Abram, when he migrated westward, came from a

religious or cosmogonic myth presents such a character of universality. It must of necessity be a recollection of a great and terrible occurrence, which impressed the imagination of the ancestors of our race so powerfully as never to have been forgotten by their descendants. That cataclysm took place at a spot near the primeval cradle of humanity.

country, which we now know to have possessed in
his time means of durable record; but, as the head
of a nomad family, he could hardly have carried
with him written traditions: and a specific narrative
of this kind, like the Greek catalogue in the "Iliad,"
presented great difficulties in the way of oral transmission through several, perhaps many, generations, down to the time when we may reasonably
suppose the children of Israel to have acquired the
art of writing, namely, during their sojourn in
Egypt. The assisting providence of God may
suggest itself to the believing mind as having
supplied the needful measure of that aid, which
Homer[1] besought, in a kindred case, from the
Muses. But the document, if thus considered, lays
a certain weight upon our faculty of belief, and
even offers a tempting invitation to assault from
those who are adversely minded. This weight,
however, is converted at once into a prop, into a
buttress which well and stoutly supports the wall,
when we find that this singular and, so to speak,

[1] Iliad, II. 484.

exposed tradition has received in the most fundamental and vital points, from the researches of
philological and of historical science, striking and,
we may suppose, conclusive confirmation.

The foundation of the arrangement is the threefold division of the human race from a certain
period of its history. If such a division actually
took place, we might expect to find the traces of it
in a threefold division of language, which has an
unquestionable relation to race; and, conversely,
such a divarication in language proves an early
distribution of races or families, from which it took
its origin. Without entering into details, it may be
observed that the Book of Genesis, in its tenth and
eleventh chapters, associates the first distinctions
of language with the local dispersion of man; and
it is now known that, in days antecedent to the
permanent bond of literature, such an association
is agreeable not only to probability, but to the
ascertained laws of experience. And now we find
that comparative philology, dealing at large with
the languages of the world, has resolved them into

that very threefold division, which the distribution of man according to Genesis 10 into three great branches anticipates and requires. Here is again an important service, rendered by modern science to belief.

It is true that the Bible (Gen. 11 : 1) speaks of language as originally one, and that this proposition has not yet been generally affirmed by philology. Yet the way to it has been opened, and it need excite no surprise should the goal be soon attained. Professor Max Müller, I believe, says there is no proof that the Aryan, Semitic, and Turanian families of language had independent beginnings; that radicals existing in all the three can be traced to the common source, and that even the grammars may have been originally one. But this subject still awaits its scientific elucidation or decision.

The table of peoples presents on its surface some apparent anomalies; of which, however, a rational account can be given, and one which for the most part converts them into evidences in its favor. For instance, the Hamitic portion presents to us out of a total of thirty names no less than eighteen which are plural words, and which are therefore national or tribal, while only two of the same class are found in the rest of the account. But this seems upon consideration to illustrate what we know from history; namely, that the Hamitic races exhibited the most precocious development, and set up the earliest known civilizations of the world, those of Accadian Babylonia and of Egypt.

Again, the Cushite stock, after its regular order is arrested in verse 7 of the chapter, jumps as it were down to Nimrod in 8-10. But we must bear in mind the greatness assigned to his individual position. He is the only person in the table who is described as founding a kingdom, and the account of him has a great resemblance to that of Izdubar in the Assyrian tablets, with whom he is identified by Mr. George Smith.

Again, as Shem, Ham, and Japheth are four times mentioned together, and invariably in this order, it seems to follow naturally that this is the order of

their ages.[1]   In chapter 10, however, their descendants are set out in the inverse order, and Japheth
takes precedence.   But this also, upon reflection, we
may find to be quite intelligible.   Migration was
largely connected with considerations of space and
food.   It may be that the younger had to give place
to the elder, and that the children of Japheth had
on this account to be the first in moving from the
common centre.

Further, in the Japhetic line the genealogy wholly
stops with the next generation but one, whereas, it
is continued farther, not only in the Semitic line,
which had to be connected with Abram, but also in
the Hamitic, by the mention of Nimrod and of the
Philistines.   This, however, seems perfectly natural,
if the line of Japheth, as is probable, moved the
first, and, as is manifest, went the farthest, so as to
be out of sight of the narrator, while descendants
of Shem and Ham remained locally in contact with

[1] In a work of great research, not published, but printed for private
circulation, Lord Crawford expresses a confident opinion that Japheth
was the oldest of the three brothers.   (The Creed of Japheth: Letter
to Bishop Forbes, pp. xvi-xix).

each other.   Knobel[1] has observed, that in each of
the three branches the enumeration begins with
those who traveled to the greatest distance from
the common centre (which is taken by him to be
near Mount Ararat), and accordingly the Japhetites
are reckoned from the north-west, the Semites from
the south-east, and Hamites from the south-west.
Just as in the case of the Homeric catalogue,[2] this
methodical arrangement probably gave great assistance to the memory of the first recorder.

Knobel[3] has discussed with great minuteness and
care the particular names of the recital, and he
traces them to their historic seats.   Bishop Browne,
in the "Speaker's Commentary," has entered on the
same field.   Some examples may be given.   The Japhetites are those (Japhah=fair) of fair complexion.
They take to the isles or coast lands,[4] the seaward
countries of the north and west.   Here we meet

---

[1] "Völkertafel der Genesis."   Giessen.   1850.   Page 14.

[2] See "Juventus Mundi," p. 467.

[3] A similar process has been usefully set forth more briefly by the
Rev. A. K. Glover in his "Ethnographic Scope of the Tenth Chapter
of Genesis."   [4] See Revised Version. Gen. 10 : 5.

the name of Gomer reproduced in the Cimmerians, Cimbri, and Cwmry. Ashkenaz, the son of Gomer, is found in Scandinavia,[1] the Scangia of Jornandes, the chief seat of the German stock. Another route is marked in the same direction by Ascania,[2] in Asia Minor, a name found at various points of that region. Knobel thinks there is a trace of the Teutonic race in Teuthras, a name found on both sides in the war of the "Iliad."[3] He proceeds with the list of Japhetites as follows. Riphath, he thinks, is traced in the Carpathian country,[4] Togarma in Armenia, Magog in the Slavs, Madai in the Medes, Javan in the Iaones or Ionians, Elisa in Æolians, Tarshish in the Tursenoi, Kïttim in the Chitians of Cyprus, Dodanim in the Dardanians, Tubal in the Iberians, Meshech in the Meschi or Moschi, Tiras in the Thracians (Thrax or Thras).[5] Some among these particular interpretations—for instance, that given to Elisa—may be untenable. Bishop Browne[6]

---

[1] Knobel, *ibid.*, pp. 35-37.   [2] Page 39.
[3] Iliad, V. 705 and VI. 13.   [4] Knobel, *ibid.*, p. 44.
[5] Pages 53, 60, 71, 77, 81, 95, 117, 123.
[6] "Speaker's Commentary," Genesis, *in loc.*

sets out the various opinions that have been held, mostly without declaring a preference. It is not, however, the accuracy of each particular identification, nor even of every particular item of the text, but the principles of the general arrangement, and the large number of cases reasonably clear, which give importance to the argument.

The Semitic and Hamitic branches offer less difficulty to the investigator. No part of the tracking is more satisfactory than that which relates to the nations of Palestine, and to the names of Canaan, Sidon, and Heth, where every particular, known to us from independent history or tradition, supports, so far as I can judge, in a most remarkable manner, the trustworthiness of the record. Speaking generally, perhaps no one can go farther than Knobel in the work of identification. His treatise has become a considerable authority, and is of the greater value because he does not belong to the conservative school of criticism on the Old Testament.

V.—AS TO THE SINAITIC JOURNEY.

In his "Modern Science in Bible Lands," Sir J. Dawson has examined, with elaborate care, and with advantages beyond those of earlier inquirers,[1] first the dwelling-place of the Israelites in Egypt, and their probable route from it until they cross the Yam Suph; and then, still more particularly, the account of their journeyings beyond the Red Sea. His conclusion is that they crossed at a point,[2] now forming part of the Bitter Lakes of the Isthmus, but then a part of the Red Sea itself, which was fed in ancient times by a branch of the Nile flowing eastwards.[3] Yam Suph, or Sea of Weeds, is the name given to it in the Bible.[4]

Beyond the Red Sea, and onwards to the Sinaitic region, the country has now been surveyed by officers of the British Ordnance. All the instruments of modern science have been employed; the results

[1] For example, Brugsch, who, in his "Geschichte Ægyptens" (Leipzig, 1877), accepting the Mosaic narrative, assigns a different route to the march.

[2] Gesch. Ægypt., p. 389.   [3] Page 392.   [4] Page 404.

have been published on a large scale; and the effect, as reported by Sir J. Dawson, has been "entire agreement of the members of the party on essential points;"[1] and the ascertainment of such complete coincidence of the actual features of the country with the requirements of the Mosaic narrative, as to prove it to be a contemporary record of the events to which it relates.[2]

The route pursued by the Israelites down the coast of the Red Sea, and then to the eastward, is worthy of peculiar note, as it seems to have been dictated by a combination of strategical considerations with those which concerned the subsistence of the people, and especially the supply of water. The local indications are on this account all the more remarkable. It is not possible, without exceeding the limits proper for the present observations, to convey the full force of the evidence which shows how the stamp of Egypt was impressed both upon the Israelites themselves, and upon the narrative in Exodus of their escape; inasmuch as it

[1] Pages 371, 406.   [2] Page 407.

depends on the details of measurement, atmosphere, water-supply, and other physical circumstances, and upon their relation to the Mosaic narrative. The conclusions reached have only an indirect bearing upon the proofs of a divine revelation through the Scriptures, but they are of great historical importance in establishing the credit of the book, and its contemporaneous character as to the substance of its contents.

VII.

CONCLUSION.

In closing this series of papers, it is right to record the admission that they can lay no claim to anything more than touching, and that but slightly, certain parts of a great subject. They omit many things important, perhaps some things essential. The essay on the Creation Story, indeed, aims at bringing out, in lieu of simple apology, what seems to me a distinct and specific argument in proof of a divine revelation. Except in that instance, their main design is to draw out, so far as they go, the force of that cumulative evidence witnessing to such a revelation, which has been so wisely summed up by Bishop Butler;[1] and also to disembarrass relief in it from those difficulties which

---

[1] "Analogy," Part II., Chap. VII.

properly belong not to itself, but to exaggerations and excrescences against which it can carry no absolute guarantee. They form the testimony of an old man, in the closing period of his life. It is rendered with no special qualification but possibly this one. Few persons of our British race have lived through a longer period of incessant argumentative contention, or have had a more diversified experience in trying to ascertain, for purposes immediately practical, the difference between tenable and untenable propositions. Such experience is directly conversant with the nature of man, and with his varied relations; and I own my inclination to suppose that it is more germane to the treatment of subjects that lie directly between collective man and the Author of his being, more calculated to neutralize deficiencies, though not to impart capacity, than a familiarity with those material sciences which have supplied an arena for, perhaps, the most splendid triumphs of the century now far advanced in its decline. On this subject has been recorded the nobly candid admission of Mr. Darwin,[1] respecting the possible atrophy, through disuse, of the mental organs on which our higher tastes depend. Among those organs I cannot but include the organ of belief. On this subject, however, I am a biassed witness. It is for others to judge. I only offer a plea, not in proof of ability, but only in extenuation of defect.

There is in certain circles a very confident disposition to assert that, as regards belief in supernaturalism, the intellectual battle has been fought and won, and that victory is on the side of negation. It ought to be observed, before proceeding further, that supernaturalism is a term which includes the idea of God. A sense may be, indeed, loosely given to it, which confines it to the mode of his manifestations. But, essentially, if God be there, the supernatural is there; and the developments which proceed from that idea, even if they had been crushed and stamped out, might germinate again. It is not, then, a question of excrescences or of details; the life and essence of religion

[1] " Life and Letters," Vol. I., pp. 101, 102.

are at stake. It is the question of belief in what is not perhaps scientifically, but yet for practical purposes intelligibly, termed a personal God.

I shall presently enter on the moral causes which may have contributed, and even mainly contributed, to stimulate the negative tendencies of the day. I am now only endeavoring partially to test the justice of a pæan, and such a pæan as would not be warranted even by the established fact of a victory. For such a pæan of the victor is the epitaph of the vanquished: and the victory, which is to warrant it, must be a victory belonging to that class of victories, which end the war.

That such a song of triumph is raised there can be little doubt. It seems to have inspired the recent articles of that very distinguished and not less upright writer, Professor Huxley, in the Nineteenth Century. But I have never seen a better example of the plenary satisfaction which possesses the mind of many among the negative athletes than in the following passage, taken from a writer of ability:

"I set out from the standpoint that the mission of Free-thought is no longer to batter down old faiths. That has been long ago effectively accomplished; and I, for one, am ready to put a railing round the ruins, that they may be preserved from desecration, and serve as a landmark! Indeed, I confess to having yawned over a recent vigorous indictment of Christianity."[1]

This purports to be a description of a certain state of facts.[2]   Now, it is not the first time that we have heard description of the kind.   Such a description was supplied in an earlier time by no less a person than Bishop Butler, who, I apprehend, was not among those given to exaggeration.   His words both have been, and should be, quoted again and again.   They are these:[3]

"It is come, I know not how, to be taken for granted by many persons that Christianity is not so much as a subject

[1] Karl Pearson, "Ethics of Freethought," Preface, p. 5.   The dramatic character of this declaration is brought to its climax by the fact that the work is dedicated to the members of King's College, Cambridge.

[2] It is far from being isolated.   The same ideas are expressed with greater vehemence by Dr. Hardwicke, of Sheffield, in a preface to "Evolution," London, 1890.

[3] From the advertisement to the "Analogy."

of inquiry; but that it is now at length discovered to be fictitious. And, accordingly, they treat it as if, in the present age, this were an agreed point among all people of discernment, and nothing remained but to set it up as a principal subject of mirth and ridicule; as it were by way of reprisals, for its having so long interrupted the pleasures of the world."

It seems pretty plain that at the time when the Bishop published the "Analogy"[1] a wave of unbelief was passing over the land. The spiritual declension of the Hanoverian period had set in; and the general standard of life, and of the ideas current concerning life, was sinking almost from day to day. The negative movement of the period may have been quite as vigorous, as widespread, and as self-confident, as that of which we now sustain the pressure. Yet it dwindled, and almost disappeared; and we may even say that, at the time of Johnson's social predominance, it left hardly a trace behind.[2] Nor was this either the first or the

[1] In 1736.

[2] In 1797, when Wilberforce published his " Practical View," he spoke of " absolute unbelievers" as a class which he feared was an

last of the reverses which negation has suffered.
At the time of the great Renascence of ancient
learning in the fifteenth and sixteenth centuries,
the cultivated mind of Europe sank far back into
Paganism; but that ebb was succeeded by a flowing tide. Again, in my own earlier days, say in the
second quarter of the present century, there was a
great revival, both of the dogmatic sense and of the
religious life in England; and the temper of the
time, in the thinking world, was strongly adverse
alike to worldliness, to indifference, and to unbelief. No man, perhaps, was better qualified to
pass a judgment on this subject than the late Dr.
Whewell; and he, writing in November, 1853, and
referring to an opinion expressed by a contemporary
of smaller calibre than himself, says, "As to this
assertion that scepticism is increasing, it is con-

increasing one (Chap. VII. sect. 3). Perhaps the great war of the years
1793-1815 tended to debilitate the religious mind of the country by
drawing off mental force in another direction. I have, however, heard
from persons of high authority, who were old when I was young, that
the French Revolution generated a distinctly religious reaction on
this side of the Channel.

trary to all my knowledge of the cultivated classes."[1] But as the third quarter proceeded, the sceptical movement set in with a wide and subtle power. History, then, seems to prove that these negative movements are subject not only to a hazard, but even to a law, of mutation; and that every one of them, when it has done its work, may cease to be. Of one thing we may be assured: such a movement derives no real strength, no true promise of permanence, from an overweening self-assertion. The question is not what negation thinks of itself and of the opposing forces, but what is the intrinsic strength of the reasoning on which it rests.

I have said that, when it has done its work, it may cease to be. For doubtless it has a work to do. The wave that breaks and foams upon the rock exhibits to us not merely, as it might seem, a picture of violence and a source of danger, but a fraction of the vast oceanic movement, which is the indispensable condition of health and purity both

[1] " Life of Whewell," p. 431.

to the water and the air, and to the populations by
which they are respectively inhabited. If we believe in Providential government, we might rationally believe, even when we did not see, that those
boastful, and even powerful, agencies are not without their purposes, prefigured, and bounded too,
by the counsels of God. It seems, however, not
difficult to discern a portion of those purposes;
which may have been, first, to dispel the lethargy
and stimulate the zeal of believers; and, secondly,
to admonish their faith to keep terms with reason,
by testing it at all its points; lest fancy, or pride, or
indolence, or the intolerant spirit of sect or party,
should have imported into their beliefs merely
human elements that it may be both needful and
difficult to eject.

While leaving to the champions of negation their
title, whatever it may be, to insist on the utter blind-
ness of belief, this at least I urge upon them: they
ought to understand that it remains just as possible
now as it was in the early or middle ages to uphold
the cause of belief in perfect good faith and with

immovable conviction. In the advance of scientific knowledge, and of the critical art, I for one see much that corrects and chastens what was temporary or accidental, and at the same time erroneous, in our persuasions concerning the subjects of belief, but nothing that disintegrates or undermines the basis of belief itself: much, on the contrary, that confirms it.

It is sometimes taken for granted or alleged, that religion or its champions are reduced to the necessity of defending their cause only with arms which have been superseded, either by the introduction of forces previously unknown, or by new forms of construction better adapted to their ends. In a spirit which seems to fluctuate between pity and a good-natured contempt, Professor Huxley describes "the old-fashioned artillery of the Churches," on the one side, and "the weapons of precision," used by the advancing forces of science on the other.[1] Now let it be remembered that we have not here to do with the masses of mankind, to

[1] Nineteenth Century, July, 1890. p. 22.

whom historical and scientific arguments, whether
negative or affirmative, are, and probably must remain, inaccessible. We are speaking of that standing army, so to call it, of more or less instructed
persons, who, on the one side and the other, exe-
cute all the fighting on behalf of the community
at large. Writing, then, of those within the pali-
sades of the lists, and not appealing to mere numbers, I demur entirely to the statement of Professor
Huxley. I deny that the weapons of belief are an-
tiquated : I pause even before admitting that those
of scientific men are always, except in their own
particular sciences, weapons of precision. When
we decline the appeal to the established facts of
science, or to the conclusions upheld or reasonably
sustained by human experience through history, or
when we fall into the trap laid for us by Hume, and
treat the acceptance of our "holy religion" as a
matter in no way amenable to the view of reason ;
then we may be justly charged with the use of
weapons never worthy, and no longer serviceable.
But until then, we may quietly endeavor to proceed

as rational beings upon rational considerations. If these principles have not uniformly guided me in the composition of the essays I am now bringing to a close (on which it is not for me to judge), at least I can say that there has not been in any instance, even by a hair's-breadth, an intentional deviation from them.

The fact, however, of a strong and widespread negative movement among important and active sections of our countrymen during the latter portion of this century, is admitted; and now I propose to offer some remarks upon its alleged or probable causes.

I shall speak, first, of the detriment which religion is supposed by some to have suffered through the great and wonderful advance both of science and of rational speculation, mostly physical, but also critical, archæological, and historical.

Secondly, of the detriment it has really suffered through the exposure to the world of erroneous notions about religion, which are due to believers themselves: a detriment attending, in different man-

24

ners and degrees, either the retention, or even the abandonment of these opinions. Such detriment seems to me certain to ensue, when we uplift into the region of dogmatic truth (for example) such propositions as the following : 1. That the material volume of the Holy Scriptures, translated into our tongue, with every fact and sentiment it contains, must be received under the same (so to call it) materialized conception, as that under which Mahometans are supposed to receive the Koran, and held absolutely true; or 2, that there is no progression or distinction in the inspiration to which it is to be referred ; or 3, that the Adam portrayed in Scripture was the exclusive source of the race ; or 4, that he was furnished with large intellectual development and endowment.

Thirdly, I shall speak of the strength which the negative movement has in my opinion derived from causes greatly and subtly effective, yet wholly extrinsic to itself; causes, which I take to constitute its principal strength.

Of the first head I might dispose very briefly. I

have enumerated some of the great services which science has rendered, and is rendering, to religion. Of the damage it has inflicted I have heard much; but the allegations commonly appear to me upon examination to be found untrue: in some cases, like that of the first chapter of Genesis, to be not only untrue but the logical contradictory of the truth, inasmuch as science, when just principles of interpretation are called in, is found to have established what it has been charged with destroying.

The nearest semblance, that has attracted my notice, to palpable contradiction between modern science and Holy Writ is upon the statement that sin brought death into the world, whereas we now know that death was antecedent to the introduction of man, and therefore of sin. But in Scripture, beyond all dispute, the word " death " has many senses. For example, it means habitually, severance of spirit from body. It means separation from God, and domination of body over spirit (Luke 1 : 79; John 8 : 51; Eph. 2 : 1). It means reunion with God, and domination of spirit over body (Col. 2 :

20 ; 3 : 3 ; 2 Tim. 2 : 11). As it means the soul's disease, severance from God, so also it means the final consummation of that disease in the second death. These are various senses of the term, covering a very wide range, and dispersed about the Bible. How do we know that St. Paul used the words in the first of these and not in the second? And if he had used it in the first sense, and had intended to declare that there was no physical death before the sin of Adam, how much would this prove? Only that the apostle was ignorant of any pre-Adamite history of the planet, and that we should have to ask whether such ignorance, when proved, would destroy or impair the over-flowing proofs that he was commissioned of God to speak, and was taught of God how to speak, for the salvation of the world?

It remains, however, a vital portion of our duty, on the one hand, to estimate and to measure aright the differences between the divine revelation in it-self, and the subjective conceptions, whether affirm-ative or negative, which may be entertained and propagated concerning it; and, on the other hand, to inquire pretty strictly whether the professors of science are sometimes apt to push their legitimate authority beyond their own bounds into provinces where it becomes a usurpation, and whether the weapons which they hurl, are then always "weapons of precision."

On the first of these two points, I will give an illustration of my meaning from the latest writings of the Achilles of the opposing army. In a very recent article, which deals chiefly with the Deluge,[1] Mr. Huxley, in a succinct but decided way, administers capital punishment also to the Creation Story of Genesis. He does not enter much into particulars, but he says the Israelites were like all other men, curious to know their origin. Now, so far as the records of the past go, the cosmological curiosity of the ancients appears to have been comparatively small. The cosmologies of Babylon and Egypt hold an utterly insignificant place in their systems of knowledge. The Greeks, perhaps the

[1] Nineteenth Century, July, 1890, p. 21.

most inquisitive of men, cared little or nothing for
these things, through many centuries after they had
felt the passion of high poetry and of the legends
associated with it; and when their schools of philosophy arose, they dealt, and this only in outline,
with the origin of material things, rather than of
men. There was no nation, I believe, except the
Israelites, whose cosmology held a classical place
in their memory and in their devotions. But I am
perhaps wrong in arguing the question. What I
ought rather to point out is that while Professor
Huxley is fond, as he well may be, of claiming to
represent science, his *dictum* is entirely outside the
sciences he represents.

Again, in the same short space he proceeds to
lay it down that an opinion given by Dr. Riehm on
the subject of the seven Mosaic days (*i. e.*, that they
are natural days) should be final. We claim, however, to be, if not Freethinkers, yet free thinkers.
Why are we to renounce the faculty of discourse,
to square our minds to those of Dr. Riehm, to let
him do the thinking for us, and to accept his words

as " final "? Simply because Mr. Huxley has said
so. What right has Professor Huxley to close this
question ? For the question whether the Creation
Story of Genesis describes solar days or not is no
more a scientific question, than whether Parliament
should or should not meet in November, or whether
Shakespeare wrote or did not write the whole of
" Henry VIII." The assertion by a great scientist
that no one is entitled, now that " Dr. Riehm" has
spoken, further to discuss the question of the Mosaic
days, in the first place carries the claims of authority beyond the bounds of reason ; and, in the second
place, carries paradox almost to a point at which
it assumes a comic aspect.

But I have now to ask whether the weapons used
by this most distinguished scientist are always
" weapons of precision " ? On scientific grounds
he condemns, as we have seen, the narrative of the
Deluge, and pronounces it to be fabulous. One of
his reasons is this. The Mosaic account assigns a
period of one hundred and fifty days (the tablets
give only seven) for the subsidence of the waters.

Against this statement Mr. Huxley advances a *dictum*, of which the subject-matter is unquestionably scientific. He gives the length of the Mesopotamian plain[1] at three to four hundred miles, and the elevation of the higher end at five to six hundred feet. Had this plain been so covered with water, says Mr. Huxley, a "furious torrent" would have rushed downwards, and instead of a hundred and fifty days the plain generally (this word no doubt is meant to except particular hollows of the ground) would have been left bare in a very few hours.

Let us try this question a little more nearly. If the length of the plain be 350 miles, and the fall 525 feet, we have a descent of one foot and a half per mile; and this descent, says the Professor, would cause a furious torrent, such as would clear the plain in a very few hours. Let us assume twenty miles an hour as the rate of the "furious torrent;" on which assumption, the plain would be bare in seventeen and a half hours. I take these

[1] Nineteenth Century, July, 1890, p. 15.

rates and figures so as to translate approximately into definite quantities Mr. Huxley's more general expressions.

One foot and a half per mile represents a gradient of $\frac{1}{3420}$. I have sought information on this subject from an engineer, who is in charge of a portion of one of our British rivers. I understand from him that a fall of one in three thousand four hundred and twenty would probably produce a current of about two miles an hour. It may require all Professor Huxley's resources to show that a current of two miles an hour is a "furious torrent;" or that to represent as a furious torrent what is in truth an extremely slow stream is to use a "weapon of precision."

My informant, indeed, adds that each case has modifying circumstances of its own, and must be judged by itself; but he likewise tells me that if, instead of trying the matter by an ordinary English river, we remove the banks, and suppose the stream indefinitely widened, the fall remaining the same, the rate of the current would be not increased but slackened. Thus we seem to get farther and farther from the "weapons of precision." And it seems just possible that, after all, these weapons may, like our monster guns, sometimes damage those who handle them, or may fail to batter down so soon as is expected the undoubtedly ancient walls of the fortress of belief.[1]

The case, to which I have last referred, is one of elementary hydraulics. The obligation to be precise may be thought to rise with the elevation of the subject. If we may not ask from the scientific man that when he touches questions of the innermost feelings of believers, and of the highest destinies of man, he should be reverent, yet surely we are entitled to require of him that he should be circumspect; that he should take reasonable care to include in his survey of a case all elements which are obviously essential to a right judgment upon it.

[1] It is not without a minor interest to remark that, on the data before us, the time required for clearing the plain would be about 162 hours, or nearly seven days, the actual time mentioned in the Babylonian account.

In another recent article,[1] Mr. Huxley has
touched very lofty ground indeed. He selects
a crucial instance for the trial of the Gospels, to
which we owe our knowledge of the character of
our Lord, the miracle which happened in the country of the Gergesenes, or Gadarenes. It is nar-
rated, with certain variations, by three Evangelists;
the essential point being, that evil spirits, cast out
from the body of a demoniac, are permitted to
enter into a herd of swine, and that the animals so
possessed rush furiously into the sea. Mr. Huxley,
as a physiologist, disbelieves in demoniacal possession; and that is the point that has commonly
attracted the chief share of attention in connection
with this miracle. Such a physiological judgment
it is not for me to discuss. But he also very properly touches the question of the injury inflicted by
the destruction of the swine, which was due to our
Lord's permission. Mr. Huxley observes that the
Evangelist has no " inkling of the legal and moral
difficulties of the case," and adds, the devils entered

into the swine "to the great loss and damage of the innocent Gerasene or Gadarene pig-owners." Further, "everything that I know of law and justice convinces me that the wanton destruction of other people's property is a misdemeanor of evil example."

So then, after eighteen centuries of worship offered to our Lord by the most cultivated, the most developed, and the most progressive, portion of the human race, it has been reserved to a scientific inquirer to discover that three of the four writers, through whom his life has been recorded for us, formally assign to him acts which make him no better than a law-breaker and an evil-doer. If the feelings of Christians have been wounded by this assertion made, in order to establish a proposition of enormous importance which has been concealed for eighteen hundred years, it was right that they should suffer, and they ought to thank Professor Huxley as the great discoverer. But if there was no law-breaking and no evil-doing in the case as it stands recorded, what are we to say either of the Professor's tenderness in dealing with the inmost

hearts of his fellow-creatures, or, and more especially, of the temper and weight of his "weapons
of precision"?

Simple as it has been from this point of view,
the case (Matt. 8 : 30; Mark 5 : 2; Luke 8 : 31) is to
a reflective mind a very peculiar one. It offers
the only occasion on which our Lord exercised,
or co-operated in the exercise of, preternatural
power for the destruction of life.

It is observable that in certain instances, such as
that of the fig-tree, and of the ass with her colt, he
seems to assert himself as the universal owner. He
is the Lord to kill, as well as to make alive, according to his wisdom. But this consideration, to whatever conclusion it might lead, is of what may be
termed an esoteric nature, and is hardly suited to
an argument against the negative school, who are
plainly entitled to raise the question of the swine
as it affects the rights of property. Why, then,
does our Lord in this instance see cause to vary
from the philanthropic and beneficent tendencies,
which usually mark his miraculous agency? It

has been observed that the entrance into the swine may have been permitted, in order to certify the relieved man, or men, of the reality of the great and hardly credible deliverance vouchsafed in their persons to human suffering. And again, that the willing departure of the demons may have spared the victim or victims from the tortures, which it is natural to suppose would have attended their violent ejection. Yet something more seems to be desirable in order to meet the question that has just been raised. I find the answer to it in the reasonable, and (as it seems to me) almost necessary supposition, that the possession of the swine was unlawful, and, therefore, was justly punishable by the ensuing loss.

The scene is described by different Evangelists in different terms. It is the country of the Gergesenes, or the country of the Gadarenes. The distinction is immaterial to the present purpose. It was apparently part of the land of the Girgashites (Deut. 7 : 1), one of the seven Canaanitish nations, and was subject, therefore, as a matter of religious obligation, to the Mosaic law. Now that law contained a prohibition to use various meats, among which pork was included. But in the case of swine the law went farther than in other cases, and it was forbidden even to touch the carcass (Lev. 11 : 7, 8). Such a prohibition of course precluded all use whatever of the animals when dead; and it was only for use when dead that there could be any object in keeping them at all. Nor was this prohibition merely ceremonial. It was immediately related to the health of the people, as the use of pork (I am informed) is apt to produce, especially in hot climates, the disease called trichinosis, and I understand that the veto is down to this day regarded by well-informed Jews as of a more than ceremonial importance; while it is directly connected with a high sanitary condition.

It may be that the deeper counsels of Providence are more implicated in this prohibition, than even a less superficial reader of the Gospels than Professor Huxley might at first sight suppose. That calling of the Hebrew people, which is set before us in the Old Testament, demanded in them above and beyond all other qualities the quality of persistence. It may be that this purpose required the constitution of the race in body as well as in many points of character to be raised to a point unusually high. We know that man is a compound being, and we know that the Mosaic code took cognizance of bodily health to an extent quite unknown in other schemes of legislation. In the Book of Exodus (1 : 19), reference was made to the superior formation of the Hebrew women for the great office of a mother, and I am informed that the modern researches of anatomists, supporting the text, refer the fact to a physical cause. I have learned enough from some high medical authorities to be warranted in saying that the sanitary qualities of the Jewish race, even in our own time, and their superior longevity, appear in no small manner to be due to the strict observance of the Mosaic law. These remarks may be justifiable in connection with what I have said of the description of authority, which they attach to a particular prohibition. Yet, for the immediate purpose of the argument, it may suffice to have pointed out the illegality of keeping swine.

Mr. Huxley, exercising his rapid judgment on the text, does not appear to have encumbered himself with the labor of inquiring what anybody else had known or said about it. He has thus missed a point which might have been set up in support of his accusation against our Lord. Some commentators have alleged the authority of Josephus for stating that Gadara was a city of Greeks rather than of Jews, from whence it might be inferred that to keep swine was innocent and lawful. This is not quite the place for a critical examination of the matter; but I have examined it, and have satisfied myself that Josephus gives no reason whatever to suppose that the population of Gadara, still less (if less may be) the population of the neighborhood, and least of all the swine-herding or lower [1] portion of that population, were other

---

[1] It is clear that such people could not be the owners of 2000 swine. But (1) this is stated in St. Mark only; (2) it is stated in a parenthesis,

than Hebrews, bound by the Mosaic law. Now, this being the case, the punishment inflicted upon the owners of the swine by the permission of our Lord did not constitute a breach, but rather a vindication of the law; as a law would be vindicated if casks of smuggled spirits were caught and broken open after landing, and their contents wasted on the ground.[1]

Surely if these were only possibilities, instead of being, as they are, rather cogent likelihoods, they should have been examined and weighed before pronouncing sentence on a threefold record which is, in the eyes of Christendom, a very sacred record. Its authors could not but know how peculiar was this portion of their narrative, in which they ascribe to the Lamb of God an undoubted deviation from

whereas it would naturally appear in the direct narrative ; (3) so large a numeral suggests the error of a copyist or very possibly a marginal gloss, which afterwards crept into the text.

[1] For the further elucidation of this important case, I have added a note at the end. [Now altered and enlarged, in consequence of a defense of his position attempted by Professor Huxley in the Nineteenth Century for December, 1890.]

His usually beneficent and gentle methods. And, again, such hand-over-head reasoning is hard to reconcile either with the judicial temper, or with the claim, nay the exclusive claim, to the honor of using " weapons of precision."

There is yet another point of great importance, in regard to which I desire to challenge the methods pursued by some critics of the Holy Scriptures; and I cannot do better than again proceed on the recent article of Professor Huxley. He finds, on the one hand, a vast mass of diversified tradition, which agrees in reporting a Flood. He finds that, as we draw near to that central seat of civilization in Chaldæa, from which Abraham probably carried the Hebrew narrative, it unfolds itself largely into detail, and that the tradition, which thus travelled westwards, is supported in many very remarkable particulars by the history which has been recorded in the tablets. Detecting, however, in the Mosaic story, various statements, which he deems to be irreconcilable with natural laws, he protests, not against those particular statements, but against the entire relation; and he casts aside without more ado, not only the whole tale as it is given in Genesis, but the large mass of collateral testimony, from every quarter of the globe, which supports it. Is this a scientific, is it a philosophical, is it altogether a rational method of proceeding?

Errors, and even great errors, may creep into a true narration. This is a case where the tale had, according to all appearances, been carried onward orally for ages, perhaps for very many ages, before the race that have transmitted it to us had the means of giving it a written form. Was it not likely that some, perhaps even that much, variation of particulars would creep in? Could they be shut out except by miracle, and has the Christian Church ever taught us to believe in such a miracle? Is it not the fact that, as between the Chaldee and the Hebrew reports, the essence of the story remains in absolute integrity? A divine warning, a woful prevalence of sin, a terrible inundation or deluge as a punishment, the rescue of a small and righteous remnant; not only do these things remain,

but traditions supporting them in several or in all
points have descended to us independently through
a hundred channels; and we are now asked to
believe that, in each of these, imagination, and
imagination only, has been at work, and that in
each of them it has worked with an essentially
(though not circumstantially) identical result? May
not this be to substitute for a great physical a
greater moral miracle, and are we not even in some
danger of exchanging the unaccountable for the
absurd?

My conclusion, then, upon this part of the subject, be it worth much or little, is threefold. I am
grateful to science, both physical and historical, for
the noble services it has rendered to belief by the
establishment of truths, or by the rational acceptance of propositions, in its own domain. I feel that
science is not responsible for any errors of scientists,
either in the misconstruction of the Bible, or in
offenses which their share of human frailty may
have led them occasionally to commit against the
known laws of rational discussion. And, lastly,

I am grateful both to science and to scientists for having assisted, or for having compelled, those who believe, to correct errors which, in the wantonness of power, they may carelessly, or even insolently, have cherished, and to submit all their claims to free and critical investigation.

The retreat from an untenable to a tenable position is in itself an unmixed good. We feel that we have redressed a wrong which had been done to truth; and we breathe the more freely for the act. Still there is a retribution in store for error; and, given all the conditions of human feeling, thought, and action, this recession is an operation of invariable danger, and, for the time at least, of mixed result. Happy they who accurately know, and who exactly realize to themselves, in the practical part of their being, what it is that they ought to abandon and what to retain, nor only to retain, but to uphold with a determination enhanced in proportion to the difficulties of the day. But in the minds of many, perhaps of the greater part, the dominant sense, at least for a time, will be that they have passed from a ground old and familiar to one new and strange; that they have parted with something, they do not quite know how much; that if they have been wrong once, they may, perhaps, be wrong again. And then it is so much easier to believe in a volume, which the hand could grasp, than to hold fast the mental conception of a revelation conveyed in that volume. True, such a conception of God in the Bible, which may be, but ought not to have been, a new one, is strictly and solidly analogous to the familiar, and equally indispensable, conceptions of God in Nature, God in Providence, God in the Christian Church. But these we had from our cradles; they were thoroughly congenial through use. To apply the same rule to the Bible is really to integrate, rather than to disintegrate, the idea of our knowledge of God. But there is something like the discomfort of a new habiliment to be got over; and there are the ready, sometimes perhaps the too ready, taunts of the adversary to be endured.

I will not dwell at large upon other difficulties

springing from the errors or the incaution of believers; but they are grave in their nature. Whenever, under the idea of magnifying the grace or
favor of God, we derogate from his immutable
righteousness and justice; and whenever, in exalt-
ing the unspeakable mercy of his pardon, we un-
hinge its inseparable alliance with a profound and
penetrating moral work in the creature pardoned:
then we draw down dangers upon the Christian
system greater far than can ever be entailed upon
it by its enemies. But there may be worse still
than this. Worse there will be, if the believer in
Christ holds the doctrine without giving effect to it
in his life; and worst of all, if while he holds it he
not only is betrayed into the ordinary weaknesses
or excesses of human nature, but forgets also, and
derides or disregards, those primal sanctions of
natural morality, which even habitual vice is not
always hardened enough to discard. The constitution of the family, the ties between its members,
the nature of the woman and of the man, and the
relation of each one of them to himself, to that

SELF, which is entrusted by God to every one of us to study and to revere, as well as to cleanse, to cherish, and to sanctify; all these are regulated by laws the oldest, holiest, and most profound of all. Progress may be traced and tested by the regard it pays to these sacrosanct, though unwritten, ordinances. According as such regard is paid or is withheld, we shall know whether such progress be a reality or an imposture; and Christianity itself would lose all its titles were it capable of an attempt to disturb divine laws older than itself and forming the bed in which its foundation-stone was laid.

In the classes of difficulties thus roughly suggested there has subsisted, as I believe, not, indeed, a legitimate, but a powerfully operative, cause for the increase of scepticism.

But the gravest portion of the case remains. Negation is in part, and it professes and believes itself to be altogether, an affair of the intellect. It proclaims, for example, that the reason why unbelief has (at the moment) so much advanced, is that dogmas like those of the Trinity, the Incarnation, the Sacraments, and the future Judgment, have become insufferable to the cultivated human understanding. The conviction which possesses my mind, and which I may find it difficult to express in an unexceptionable manner, is that the main operative cause which has stimulated the growth of modern negation is not intellectual but moral; and is to be found in the increased and increasing dominion of the things seen over the things unseen.[1]

Such a proposition may at first sight appear to carry an odious meaning, pharisaical in the worst sense of the word; a meaning which would provoke, and might justify, an angry reply. It might be interpreted as implying that the elevation of moral character in individuals varied with and

---

[1] In a work of great ability just issued, and termed "Scientific Theology," Mr. Barber, a civil engineer, treats (Chap. III., p. 41) the question, "Why does not religion reach the masses?" His conclusion is stated thus: "The weak point is clearly the loss of spiritual motive, and increased strength of natural motives as springs of action and thought." Who will answer Mr. Barber?

according to the amount of their dogmatic belief;
a proposition which in my view is untrue, offensive,
and even absurd.   Had I ever been inclined to such
a conception, the experience, sometimes the very
sad experience, of my life, would long ago have
undeceived me.   My meaning is a very different
one.   I speak of that which touches not this or that
man only, but us all.   We have altered the standard
of wants; we have multiplied the demands of
appetite; we have established a new state of social
tradition, of that tradition which forms and guides
us, apart from and antecedently to thought or
choice of our own.   We have created a new atmosphere, which we breathe into ourselves, and by
breathing which our composition is modified unawares, according to the ingredients which that
atmosphere contains.   I do not say that we are the
creatures of what surrounds us, for we have power
to reflect upon and to control it.   Yet, reflection
and control are exercised but little, in comparison
with the need for them; and, in the absence of
such exercise, and of such exercise in a high degree,

it is the surrounding atmosphere, it is the ordinary standard, accepted, and to a great extent necessarily accepted, without examination, that both supplies the stock wherewith we individually begin the great adventure of the world, and that guides our life. I except the rare cases, where depravity on one side, or Christian heroism on the other, causes us to rise or fall to a separate standard for ourselves. Where both control and reflection range only within the zone marked out by fashionable opinion, it is sadly easy to point out men of high virtue with little creed, and men of low virtue with much creed, in the discipline and conduct of their personal lives respectively. And, in the region of opinion, it often seems as if liberty and justice among men fared quite as well with the heterodox, as with the orthodox.

A large part of these grave and even terrible anomalies is no doubt due to the fact, that to each of us personally our creed has come, not with the throes of struggle, sacrifice, and strong conviction, but rather, like most of what we hold—an easy

tenure !—by descent, through others, not from ourselves ; as matter of course, not of choice and
effort ; so that it sits upon us like an outward badge,
rather than pervades us as a principle and a power.

But, on the other hand, how true it will be found
that the sovereign tradition, which has filled the air,
is the Christian tradition. This it is, which has
made possible what without it would have been
wholly beyond reach. This it is, which carries
noiselessly into many minds and characters those
opinions on behalf of virtue, of self-denial, and of
philanthropy, together with the power of acting
upon them, which are often found so honorably to
distinguish creedless men. Just as many, who do
not reject Christianity, know not why or how they
came to hold it, so many, who have abjured Christianity, know not that, in the best of their thought,
their nature, and their practice, they are appropri-
ating its fruits. What is the modern word altruism?
As to its meaning, it is simply the second great
commandment of the Christian law, which was
" like unto the first." As to its form, it is merely

a disguise which has been put upon a borrowed idea, so that it often fails to be traced to its true original.   And this not by a conscious, but, if the phrase may be pardoned, by an unconscious fraud. We find ourselves in possession of the code of Christian ethics, which has gradually pervaded life, institutions, manners ; and which has become so blended with our ordinary life that the memory of its divine origin has faded away, as though it were like the title-deed of some inheritance which we hold by unquestioned use.   If we wish to know what the Christian tradition has done for us, we must examine the moral standard of nations who have differed from us mainly in not possessing it. For example, we must look to the Greeks of the fifth century before Christ, or the Romans at and after the period of the Advent, whose moral degradation was not less conspicuous than the intellectual splendor of the one, or the constructive political genius of the other.

My twofold proposition is that we have before us an increased power of things seen, and that this

increased power implies, as matters now seem to
stand, a diminishing hold upon us of things unseen.
The question is no new one. Throughout the history of mankind, the invisible, and the future which
is part of the invisible, have been in standing competition with what may be termed the things of this
world.

> " Two magnets, heaven and earth, allure to bliss;
> The larger loadstone that, the nearer this;
> The weak attraction of the greater fails,
> We nod awhile, but neighborhood prevails." [1]

There has never been a time in human history to
compare with the last half-century in two vital
respects: the multiplication of wealth, and the multiplication of the enjoyments which wealth pro-
cures: two things separate, yet concurrent, and
morally allied. To take a familiar example: men
(and the commodities they depend on) now travel
at (say) one-fourth of the former cost, just when
they have also an enlargement of their means to
bear the charge of travelling.

[1] Dryden, " Hind and Panther," Part III.

It is indeed true that the greater part of the human beings who constitute the community have not yet attained to a competent and secure satisfaction of the primary wants of life. But, in ascending from the lower to the higher conditions, we soon reach a level where comforts and enjoyments enter seriously into expenditure; and at length we attain a social plane, first where they compete with actual needs in the amount of attention given them, then where they predominate, and at last where they come to form the only serious object of habitual care. This is the region described in the Gospel as that of "the rich man." His relative condition varies with the circumstances of different periods. In the days of the patriarchs, the living of the rich man differed in but few and simple particulars from that of his dependants. But as life and the works of man developed, and moreover as individual rights have obtained fuller acknowledgment, the space, which separates classes in respect to wants and enjoyments, has been greatly widened. Sense, appetite, and taste, are solicited in a thousand forms previously unknown. We must not conceal it from ourselves that every such solicitation, though it be so frequent as to be almost continuous, is a new aggression of the things seen upon the province of the things unseen, and an alteration in the balance as it had previously been cast between them.

This deep-rooted and far-reaching change, of which as yet we perhaps see only the beginning, has gone, to an immense extent, towards the cure of actual want, and towards extending the sphere of that sufficiency, that modest and humble comfort, which do not at all come within the scope of the present argument. But it has also extended largely to the spheres of leisure and of comparative affluence; and in those spheres it is generally true that the apparatus of enjoyment has been immensely developed in small things and great, and that wants and appetites have grown along with it. It seems to me undeniable, if "the world was too much with us" when Wordsworth wrote his noble sonnet, it is more, much more, with us, and with a far larger number of us, now than it was even in

26

the early years of our own century. Obviously, almost mathematically, the increased powers of worldly attraction disturb the balance of our condition, unless and until they are countervailed by increased powers of unworldly attraction and elevation. Whence are such compensating powers to be had? I am afraid we can hardly say that, in the spheres now under view, there has been such a growth in unworldly motives and ideas, as to countervail the augmented strength of worldly attachment. And I apprehend that, if the unseen world and the ideas belonging to it operate upon us with a proportionately diminished force, it follows, almost as a matter of course, that creeds, which belong to that circle of unseen associations, will, so far, be more dimly and therefore more feebly appreciated. Materialism as a formulated system is probably not upon the increase. Those who think, as I am compelled to think, about the intellectual calibre and capabilities of such a system, will hardly include such a growth among the objects of their apprehension. But the power of a silent, unavowed, unconscious materialism, not philosophical but wholly practical, is a very different matter. I think Professor Max Müller has said that without language there cannot be thought. And this I suppose is true of all organized and conscious thought. But there are in human nature a multitude of undeveloped (so to speak) embryonic forces, of impressions received from without, and finding a congenial soil within, which never ripen to maturity, or make their way into articulate speech, or obtain a defined place in our consciousness; and yet these germs of thought may ripen, though not into propositions, yet into acts. Nay, they may have much, or even may have all, to do in the formation of our characters, and the government of our lives.

My belief is that at this moment these unspoken and untested movements, not so much of mind, as of appetite, or, to use a milder word, of propensity, pressing upon mind, these not thoughts, but rudiments of thoughts, are at work among us, and within us ; and that, were they translated or expanded into words, their sense would be no more

and no less than the old vulgar sense of those, who
in every age have held that after all this world is
the only world we securely know ; and that the
only labor that is worth laboring, the only care
worth caring, the only joy worth enjoying, are the
labor, the care, and joy that begin and end with it.
What can be more natural (in the lower sense of
nature) than that, among those on whom this world
really smiles, together with the increasing gravitation towards a terrestrial centre, too often a creeping palsy should silently come over the inward life?
And how easy it is to understand that, when such
a palsy has set in, a new and less ungenial color is
imparted to whatever undermines the written Word,
or the great Christian tradition, or in whatever other
way repels, or blinds and deadens, the sense of the
presence of God, and silences the reproaches of
the voice within. So that it is not either real or
pretended science, nor is it even the errors and
excesses of believers, illegitimately charged upon
belief, that form the root of the mischief. It is the
increased force within us of all which is sensuous

and worldly that furnishes every sceptical argument, good, bad, or indifferent, with an unseen ally,
and that recruits many and many a disciple of the
negative teaching. He indeed dreams that by the
free admission of doubt he is paying homage to
truth, when in reality he is only pampering the
inferior life ; for he allows fresh coadjutors, with
unexamined credentials, to enter and to reinforce
its already overweening power. Ideas in themselves weak are backed by propension, which is
ever strong. A latent conspiracy is established,
and two knights ride forth together to the war, to
the modern crusade which is against the Cross, one
of them fairly exhibiting his countenance, but the
other with his visor down.

And the chain of cause and consequence is
something like this. The Christian creed generates
a Christian tradition of idea and conduct. Of this
tradition men do not disown the precepts ; they
only deny the parentage. And then there appears
some great thinker, some really venerable man,
who has learned to cherish piety, while he discards

dogma. The next order of operators in the field carry the work a stage further, and cherish morality, while they discard piety. And the anti-moral, anti-spiritual force, that is strong even if it be hidden in us all, using what is substantive in the work as a cover for what is destructive, looks on with complacency, and swells the chorus of applause. The sceptical argument is in reality little more than a graft, set into, and deriving its life and energy mainly from, a tree stronger and more enduring than itself.

In thus stating my conviction, that it is the mighty world power within us and around us, which at the present time gives to scepticism the chief part of its breadth and its impetus, it will be seen that my remarks have little of special application to the officers (so to speak) of the thinking army; to those who really, and it may be laboriously, think out subjects admitted to be arduous for themselves. They apply more to the soldiers, and most to the camp-followers. These largely outnumber both, and their voices are not less good than others to swell an acclamation, as Falstaff's recruits were not less good than other men to fill a pit. The opinions of a man are due partly to himself, partly to his environment. In the thinking man they are due mainly to himself, though even he may be affected by latent influences never consciously present to his thoughts. But they are mainly, sometimes wholly, due to environment in those who do not industriously think; and environment, I need hardly say, includes the idols and the fancies, the shadows and the phantoms, of the passing day.

I must, however, in drawing these observations to a close, for a moment change my tone. In their nature apologetic, they themselves require an apology; and an apology, too, which is also in the nature of a protest. They are intended to meet, so far as they go, a state of things peculiar and perhaps without example, in which multitudes of men call into question the foundations of our religion and the prerogatives of our sacred books, without any reference to either their capacity or their opportunities for so grave an undertaking. In other matters, qualification must be known or shown; in religion, it is taken for granted, sometimes with the utmost levity.

We have to bring equally into view, on the one side and on the other, two great propositions. On the one hand, the Christian religion stands on the foundation of free and intelligent assent. On the other hand every man, whatever be his position, founds, and reasonably, nay, necessarily founds, the actions and experiences of his life principally upon trust. Upon trust, no doubt, which is both intelligent and free, but still upon *trust.* Upon trust, sometimes in particular individuals, sometimes upon traditions which are, in a narrower or wider sphere, the traditions of his race. Every one acting a special part in the world, be it great or small, and be it acted with or without consciousness of its character, is continually working for others as well as for himself; for others, either to their good or to their hurt. He is establishing and verifying on behalf of others, and in lieu of others, intellectual conclusions or material facts, which are needful for human life, but which the conditions of human life do not permit men in each case to establish and verify for themselves. To establish and verify for ourselves is undoubtedly best. Independent knowledge is to be preferred where, and as, it can be had. But the limiting law is found in capacity and in opportunity. Where we have not these, and it is often so, let us eschew the profession, that is, the pretense, of them : let us refuse to seek refuge in the falsehood of an affected or supposed examination.

But it seems to be beyond doubt that, more perhaps in these days than of old, numbers both of women and of men question the religion delivered to them from of old without, or in excess of, both capacity and opportunity. The turn and training of the mind, the nature of callings and pursuits, make it for some of us reasonable and necessary to put the great historic revelation on its trial as to its evidences of fact and doctrine, and its relation to the character and condition of man. This searching process is in itself thoroughly normal; and its application to the subject-matter, and the commonly affirmative results of such application, through so many ages and in minds so many and so great, have continually added force to the authority with which the gospel lays claim to our assent and our obedience.

As to the mass of mankind, however, reason teaches that the presumption is for each man in favor of that which he has received, until he has found solid cause to question it. This is the rule taught by common sense, and established in common life. It is doubt, and not belief, of the things received, which ought in all cases to be put upon its defense, and to show its credentials: credentials, not necessarily in terms of demonstration, but of rational likelihood. But untested doubt, which often makes a lodgment in our minds, is a tenant without a title, a dangerous and in the main an unlawful guest. It assumes unawares, and in default of examination, the attitude of demonstrated negation. It paralyses action; it casts into the

shade the sense of duty, and of the divine presence
encompassing us in all our ways; and it reduces
the pulse of our moral health. Doubt may eman-
cipate us. Or it may enslave us. But it must be
either a friend or an enemy: it cannot be a neutral.
And those doubts, which cannot be tested, ought
not to be entertained as having a title to affect
conduct or belief. And such inquiries as, from
being inadequate, are illusory, are but fresh forms
of temptation from the path of duty. Inquiry
should be undertaken as a solemn duty, when it
can be made the subject of effective prosecution.
But if we have not the means of effective prosecution, the so-called inquiry is a pretense and an
imposture, a falsehood and a forgery. Under its
name, we become the mere victims of assumptions
due to prejudice, to fashion, to propensity, to appetite, to the insidious pressure of the world-power,
to temptation in every one of its Protean shapes.
The universal vocation of man is for each to
regulate his own proper conduct in his own proper
sphere. A noble task for all. but even this an

arduous task; a task so arduous, that none can perform it in perfection. Duty does not require us to arrive at conclusions on

"Fixed fate, free-will, foreknowledge absolute,"

much less on the yet deeper and darker speculations which lie beyond, and which, so far as they are formidable, all run up into one single, one perhaps impenetrable problem, the presence and action of evil in the world. The Christian faith and the Holy Scriptures arm us with the means of neutralizing and repelling the assaults of evil in and from ourselves. That is a practical answer. Mist may rest upon the surrounding landscape, but our own path is visible from hour to hour, from day to day.

"I do not ask to see
The distant scene; one step enough for me."

Speculation, which is purposeless, becomes irreverent; and irreverent speculation on the doings and designs of God, by those who believe in him, is itself a sin. To leave the duty of governing conduct, to which every one of us is called, for other functions to which we are not called, unless the power of following them up reasonably guarantees our vocation for the work, is morally to pass from food to famine. It is as if one who possesses a piece or two of crockery full of cracks, should announce that he desires to give a sumptuous banquet to the neighborhood.

But besides acknowledging that the proper preconditions of legitimate inquiry are adequate capacity and adequate opportunity: and besides deploring the course of those who treat naked and unreasoned doubt as casting a burden of proof upon belief, we must bear in mind that religious inquiry, though it may raise conflicting issues, is not like a suit between parties who meet upon equal terms, or the conflict of emperors warring for a territory in dispute. Our Saviour astonished the people because, instead of being lost in the mazes of arbitrary and vicious excrescences that darkened the face of religion, he taught them " with authority, and not as the scribes." Taught them with authority; that is to say, with the title to command, and with the force of command. If God has given us a revelation of his will, whether in the laws of our nature, or in a kingdom of grace, that revelation not only illuminates, but binds. Like the credentials of an earthly ambassador, it is just and necessary that the credentials of that revelation should be tested. But if it be found genuine, if we have proofs of its being genuine equal to those of which, in the ordinary concerns of life, reason acknowledges the obligatory character, then we find ourselves to be not independent beings engaged in an optional inquiry, but the servants of a Master, the pupils of a Teacher, the children of a Father, and each of us already bound with the bonds which those relations imply. Then head and knee must bow before the Eternal, and the divine will must be embraced and followed by man with all his heart, with all his mind, with all his soul, and with all his strength.

I have yet one more closing word. I have desired to make this humble offering at the shrine of Christian belief in general, and have sought wholly to avoid the questions which concern this or that particular form of it. For there is a common cause, which warrants and requires common efforts. Far be from me the intention hereby to undervalue particular beliefs. I have not intentionally said a word to disparage any of them. It will in my view be an evil day, and a day of calamity, when men are tempted, even by the vision of a holy object, to abate, in any region or in the smallest fraction, the authority of conscience, or to forget that the supreme title and the supreme efficacy of truth lie in its integrity.

Note A.

In the Jewish Chronicle of September 12, 1890, I find a paragraph which appears to approve the general argument of my article on " The Mosaic Legislation," but impugns the statement that the Massoretes were a body without a parallel in history, and that the Hebrews were alone in building up a regularly scientific method of handling the material forms of their sacred oracles.   I have not the slightest pretension to speak with authority upon this subject, and I did no more than endeavor to report faithfully what I gathered from trustworthy sources.   But I have no reason to believe that my readers have been misled.   As regards the Hindus, I understand there is an opinion that they counted verses, words, syllables, and letters; but it does not appear that this statement is one historically authenticated.   Even if it were so, and if we add that the Samaritans imitated the proceedings of their Jewish brethren, and that similar enumeration was made by Syrians or others, yet the answer remains, that such a computation is a very small component part of the Massorah, and can no more be called an equivalent to it than a human limb can be called a human body. To the Massorah, so far as I can learn, there is nothing elsewhere that approaches an equivalent. As respects the Greeks, they had no sacred writings at all; and I am unaware of their having used, in any case, any such method as is here in question.

27

B.

Note on the Swine Miracle.

In the Nineteenth Century for December, 1890, Professor Huxley supported by argument and citation his assertion that the destruction of the swine was an act of immorality : justly corrected me for having said that he had charged this immorality on our Lord, and pointed out that his censure was on the narrative, not the person : and considered that such a narrative destroyed the authority of the Synoptic Gospels. This censure was founded on the threefold supposition that the event took place at Gadara ; that Gadara was as much a Gentile city as Ptolemais ; and that the herdsmen were presumably Gentiles, yet were, if we accept the narrative, lawlessly deprived of their property.

Some writers appear inclined to admit or pass without question, the contentions of fact, but point out that our Saviour was the organ of Omnipotence, and when he deemed it fit, was entitled thus to destroy, or share in the destruction of property at the expense of individuals, whether Jews or otherwise. I pass by this answer without examination ; but I observe that, if the case stands thus, the conduct of our Lord in this instance differed widely from the general lines of his ministry and miracles. It seems to me, then, richly worth our while to spend any amount of pains in ascertaining whether there is a basis of fact for the three assumptions.

Accordingly, with this persuasion, I made the most careful search I could into the evidence, and I found much matter in Josephus which had not even been noticed by Mr. Huxley, or by Schürer, a German author, undoubtedly of high reputation, who wrote with ability on the History of Palestine, but for whom the subject in question was no more than a by-point. Mr. Huxley appears to base his final reply[1] to me entirely on the assertion that Schürer's authority was of more weight than mine. Certainly. But in this case the original authority is Josephus, and the authority of Schürer cannot be high on passages which he appears not to have considered or perused.

I shall not reprint the lengthened examination, but I present a summary of the main propositions.

1. The testimony of Origen, though not contemporary, is express and weighty, and it informs us, with some verifying particulars, that the miracle took place not at Gadara, but at Gergesa, on the

[1] Nineteenth Century, March, 1891.

Lake of Tiberias. But I have also shown that, if it did happen at Gadara, that city was a great centre of Hebraism; that the Mosaic law was the civil law as well; that according to every likelihood the population round it, and especially those of the rank to which swineherds would belong, were of the Hebrew race.

2. Mr. Huxley argued that as the coinage of Gadara was Gentile, the people were also Gentile. But the coin in the hands of our Lord in Judæa was Roman, while the people were Jews.

3. The re-annexation of Gadara to the Syrian province by Pompey was popular, as it restored Roman authority. So Mr. Huxley; but Josephus[1] says it was popular because it restored local self-government. The centralizing influence of Jerusalem competed with the local influence in the provinces of Palestine.

According to Josephus, the revolted Jews burned some places in the district of Gadara,[2] and reduced others to submission. Jews, Mr. Huxley thinks, would not have destroyed Jews. But this is just what was done, and very frequently done, by one Jewish faction to another. Even in Jerusalem during the siege, says Milman, "when the insurgents had time to breathe from the assaults of the

---

[1] " Bell. Jud.," I. 7, 7.   [2] *Ibid.*, II. 18, 5.

Romans, they turned their swords against each other." [1]

I now come to the positive evidence respecting Gadara.

1. When Galinius became the administrator of Judæa, he divided Palestine into five districts of nearly equal size, each to have a Sanhedrim for the application of the Mosaic law. This was a great decentralizing measure, afterwards repealed. But the point material to the argument is that Gadara was the capital of one of these districts, and a Sanhedrim sat there. Such is the twice-stated assertion of Josephus.

It could not, then, be a town of Gentiles. True it is called *Hellenis polis*, a Grecian city, and it became such doubtless by its annexation to Syria; as Metz was a French town till 1871, and is a German one now. In another place Josephus calls it Syrian.

2. Gadara was a formidable seat of Jewish military power. When Vespasian was about to march upon Jerusalem, he went first to Gadara, the strong metropolis of Peraia, for, says Josephus, [2] it was necessary for him to leave nothing behind him which might prevent his prosecution of the siege. On the approach of his army, the war party fled;

---

[1] " Hist. Jews," II. 280-284.   [2] " Bell. Jud.," IV. 7, 3.

but in departing he both left a garrison, which was needless in any friendly town, and levelled the walls, evidently to prevent the war party, if it returned, from holding the city against the Romans. Mr. Huxley has not perceived that it was oftentimes not race or religion, but the question of war or peace, which determined opinion and action.

3. When Gadara was acquired by Alexander Jannæus for Judæa, it was placed, as matter of course, under the Mosaic law as the civil law of the country. The statement of Josephus[1] is indirect, but conclusive. We find Gadara in the list of the cities conquered by Jannæus; and it closes with Pella. But Pella, he adds, they destroyed, because the inhabitants would not submit to the Jewish law.

We have no evidence that the law thus established had been changed in our Saviour's time. It appears from Josephus to have required the sanction of Rome. Now we have an edict of Augustus,[2] which confirms to the Jews of all Asia, and as far as Cyrenais, the enjoyment of their own laws as they had stood under Hyrcanus. At the period of this remarkable edict, Gadara was part of Judæa.

4. Josephus is the classical authority on this

---

[1] " Bell. Jud.," II. 5, 3; " Antiq.," XVII. 11, 4.
[2] "Antiq.," XVI. 6, 1, 2.

subject. The knowledge of Strabo was defective, and his testimony is confused. Yet its effect is materially to support the view here stated.[1]

5. Josephus also informs us that Vespasian in commencing his campaign of A. D. 47, took Gadara by assault, and slaughtered the inhabitants of ﹍ili-tary age. He had two reasons, one of them being hatred of their race. This direct and conclusive statement is got rid of by altering the text from Gadara to Gabara. I have given[2] what seem to me ample reasons against such an alteration.

6. To all this is to be added the testimony of the four Evangelists, not merely with reference to the miracle recorded by three of them, but with respect to the localities of the ministry of our Lord. We must take into view his limited popular action in Judæa, his large connection with Galilee and especially with Eastern Galilee, and the inclusion of Decapolis, beyond Jordan, and the lake, within his missionary journeys. The Synoptic Gospels in particular presuppose for the whole region the predominance of a Hebrew nationality. To this we have to add the ancient law of the land. Neither of these vital incidents of the case is shaken either by an infusion of wealthy Greeks, who partook of

[1] Article on Swine Miracle in Nineteenth Century for February, 1891, sect. v.   [2] *Ibid.*, sect. vi.

the baths of Gadara, together with a few official representatives of the Roman power; nor by the supposition that there may have been in the population a strain of Syrian blood which in no way implies at this date an estrangement from the Hebrew law and worship.

I have thus summarily stated the case, without dwelling on a cluster of improbabilities which of themselves hopelessly envelop the notion entertained by Mr. Huxley. I refer to the pages of the Nineteenth Century for a more full exposition of the argument. In such a matter absolute demonstration is neither to be had nor sought for, but we have to follow in this as in other matters the rules established by good sense, experience, and the common consent of mankind. And I conceive it has been shown that to suppose the swineherds to have been punished by Christ for pursuing a calling which to them was an innocent one is to run counter to every law of reasonable historical interpretation.